The United States, 1865

The United States, 1865–1920: Reuniting a Nation explores how the U.S. attempted to heal Civil War-era divisions, as well as maintain and strengthen its unity as new rifts developed in the conflict's aftermath.

Taking a broadly thematic approach to the period, Adam Burns examines the development of the United States from political, social, and foreign relations perspectives. Concise and accessible, the volume uses a variety of primary source documents to help stimulate discussion and encourage the use of historical evidence as support for different interpretations of the era.

By exploring controversies over issues such as citizenship, ethnicity, regionalism, and economic disparity, all of which resonate strongly in the nation's political discourse today, the book will be an important staple for undergraduate students of American History and the period that followed the Civil War, as well as general enthusiasts.

Adam Burns is a senior lecturer in History at the University of Wolverhampton. He is the author of *American Imperialism* (2017) and *William Howard Taft and the Philippines: A Blueprint for Empire* (2020).

Series Introduction

History is the narrative constructed by historians from traces left by the past. Historical enquiry is often driven by contemporary issues and, in consequence, historical narratives are constantly reconsidered, reconstructed, and reshaped. The fact that different historians have different perspectives on issues means that there is often controversy and no universally agreed version of past events. *Seminar Studies* was designed to bridge the gap between current research and debate, and the broad, popular general surveys that often date rapidly.

The volumes in the series are written by historians who are not only familiar with the latest research and current debates concerning their topic, but who have themselves contributed to our understanding of the subject. The books are intended to provide the reader with a clear introduction to a major topic in history. They provide both a narrative of events and a critical analysis of contemporary interpretations. They include the kinds of tools generally omitted from specialist monographs: a chronology of events, a glossary of terms, and brief biographies of "who's who". They also include bibliographical essays in order to guide students to the literature on various aspects of the subject. Students and teachers alike will find that the selection of documents will stimulate discussion and offer insight into the raw materials used by historians in their attempt to understand the past.

Clive Emsley and Gordon Martel
Series Editors

The United States, 1865–1920

Reuniting a Nation

Adam Burns

Routledge
Taylor & Francis Group
LONDON AND NEW YORK

First published 2020
by Routledge
2 Park Square, Milton Park, Abingdon, Oxon OX14 4RN

and by Routledge
52 Vanderbilt Avenue, New York, NY 10017

Routledge is an imprint of the Taylor & Francis Group, an informa business

British Library Cataloguing-in-Publication Data
A catalogue record for this book is available from the British Library

Library of Congress Cataloging-in-Publication Data
Names: Burns, Adam D., author.
Title: The United States, 1865–1920 : reuniting a nation / Adam Burns.
Description: Abingdon, Oxon ; New York, NY : Routledge, 2020. |
Series: Seminar studies | Includes bibliographical references and index. |
Identifiers: LCCN 2020000007 (print) | LCCN 2020000008 (ebook) | ISBN 9781138482425 (paperback) | ISBN 9781138482418 (hardback) | ISBN 9781351057875 (ebook)
Subjects: LCSH: United States—History—1865-
Classification: LCC E661 .B96 2020 (print) | LCC E661 (ebook) | DDC 973.8—dc23
LC record available at https://lccn.loc.gov/2020000007
LC ebook record available at https://lccn.loc.gov/2020000008

ISBN: 978-1-138-48241-8 (hbk)
ISBN: 978-1-138-48242-5 (pbk)
ISBN: 978-1-351-05787-5 (ebk)

Typeset in Sabon
by Swales & Willis, Exeter, Devon, UK

Contents

Illustrations

Maps

Figures

Acknowledgements

This book draws extensively upon the scholarship of others and I would like to thank all of those whose work I have consulted in its preparation. To refine this book, I have also relied on the expertise of a number of scholars who have generously taken the time to read and critique earlier drafts of the chapters that follow. My thanks go to: Professor Frank Cogliano, Dr Howard Fuller, Dr George Gosling, Professor Susan-Mary Grant, Devin Grier, Dr Richard Hawkins, Professor Kevin Kenny, Professor Rhodri Jeffreys-Jones, Dr David Silkenat, Professor Gary Sheffield, and Professor Laura Ugolini.

Getting this book finished would not have been possible without the support and generosity of the Centre for Historical Research at the University of Wolverhampton, the production team at Routledge (particularly Kimberley Smith), and the Seminar Studies series editor Gordon Martel. I would also like to express my gratitude to the following libraries for allowing me to consult their excellent collections: the University of Bristol, the British Library, the University of Cambridge, and the University of Leicester. Finally, huge thanks go to Brian Greenwood and Julie Burns for their patience, invaluable feedback, and ongoing support with this project.

Chronology

1861	
12 April	The Battle of Fort Sumter begins. This attack by Confederate forces on a Union-held fort off the coast of Charleston, South Carolina, marked the start of hostilities in what became the U.S. Civil War.
1863	
1 January	Abraham Lincoln's Emancipation Proclamation is officially issued. The president's proclamation promised freedom to enslaved people in rebel Confederate states, but not in states that had remained loyal to the Union, nor in some Confederate territory already occupied by Union forces.
1865	
9 April	Confederate General Robert E. Lee surrenders to the Union forces of Ulysses Grant at Appomattox Court House in Virginia. This event marked the beginning of the end of the Civil War.
14–15 April	Abraham Lincoln is shot on the evening of the 14th whilst attending a play at Ford's Theater in the nation's capital—he died the following morning. Vice President Andrew Johnson was then sworn in as the seventeenth president of the United States.
6 December	The Thirteenth Amendment to the U.S. Constitution, although passed by Congress on 31 January, is finally ratified in December. The amendment formally abolishes slavery across the United States.
1867	
18 October	The former Russian territory of Alaska is formally transferred to the United States following the signing of the purchase treaty earlier that year.

1868	
9 July	The Fourteenth Amendment to the U.S. Constitution is ratified. The amendment grants citizenship rights to all persons born or naturalized in the United States, including those who were formally enslaved.
24 February	Andrew Johnson is the first U.S. president to be impeached by the House of Representatives. However, Johnson was formally acquitted that May, following his trial in the Senate.
1869	
10 May	The completion of the first transcontinental railroad to stretch across the United States is marked by the driving in of a golden spike at Promontory Summit in Utah.
1870	
3 February	The Fifteenth Amendment to the U.S. Constitution is ratified, extending the franchise by outlawing discrimination based on race, color, or previous condition of servitude.
1872	
1 March	President Ulysses Grant signs the legislation that establishes the first U.S. National Park at Yellowstone.
1873	
18 September	The failure of banking firm Jay Cooke and Co. helps catalyze the U.S. theater of the international economic "Panic of 1873" that preceded years of economic depression.
1876	
25 June	The Battle of the Little Bighorn (often referred to as "Custer's Last Stand") results in a rare victory for an alliance of Native American forces over U.S. forces.
1877	
2 March	A Congressional Commission finally agrees to award all disputed Electoral College votes from the presidential election of November 1876 to the Republican Rutherford B. Hayes. This results in Hayes winning in the Electoral College by a margin of 185:184, as part of what is often called the Compromise of 1877.
July	A series of railroad worker strikes develops into a major national situation, sometimes referred to as the Great Upheaval.

1881	
2 July	President James Garfield is shot in Washington D.C. by Charles Guiteau. Garfield died a few weeks later on 19 September.
1882	
6 May	President Chester Arthur signs the Chinese Exclusion Act, a law that severely restricted Chinese immigration to the United States. It was the first such act to target a particular ethnic group and lasted for ten years before being renewed by Congress in 1892.
1886	
4 May	The Haymarket bombing takes place during a labor demonstration in Chicago and leads to chaotic clashes between protesters and police. It led to a wave of increased anti-leftist feeling and xenophobia.
8 December	The American Federation of Labor is founded at a convention in Columbus, Ohio.
1887	
8 February	The Dawes Act (General Allotment Act) is passed by Congress, leading to the dismantling of many large Native American reservations into smaller, individual allotments.
1889	
18 September	Jane Addams and Ellen Gates Starr open Hull House in Chicago. It becomes an important template for settlement houses in the Progressive Era.
1890	
2 July	President Harrison signs the Sherman Antitrust Act into law. It is the first significant piece of antitrust legislation but was rarely enforced in its first decade.
29 December	U.S. troops open fire on a group of Native Americans in South Dakota after one person resists attempts to disarm him. The event, which resulted in the death of as many as 300 Native Americans, becomes known as the Wounded Knee Massacre.
1892	
6 July	Attempts to quell worker unrest at the Homestead Steelworks outside Pittsburgh leads to widespread violence and some fatalities.

1894	
11 May	The Pullman Strike of railroad car workers begins, leading to one of the most significant strikes in U.S. history over the following months.
1896	
18 May	The U.S. Supreme Court issue their ruling on *Plessy v. Ferguson*. It states that races can be "separate but equal". This ruling supported existing racial segregation legislation in many U.S. states.
1898	
25 April	The United States formally declares war on Spain, initiating the short Spanish–American War (sometimes called the War of 1898).
7 July	President McKinley signs the legislation providing for the formal annexation of the Hawaiian Islands.
1899	
4 February	Fighting in what would become the Philippine–American War begins, lasting in its main phase until 1902.
6 September	Secretary of State John Hay sends his first "Open Door" note to European powers, outlining the commitment of the United States to keeping China open to trade.
1901	
6 September	President William McKinley is shot by the assassin Leon Czolgosz at the Pan–American Exposition in Buffalo, New York. Theodore Roosevelt was sworn in as president upon McKinley's death on 14 September.
1904	
6 December	In his State of the Union address, President Roosevelt outlines the "Roosevelt Corollary" to the Monroe Doctrine of 1823. It projected a more active role for the United States in preventing European empires from interfering in the Western Hemisphere.
1906	
30 June	President Roosevelt signs the Pure Food and Drug Act, a piece of progressive legislation aimed at regulating the production and processing of food and medicines in the nation.

1907	
February	A "Gentlemen's Agreement" to severely limit Japanese migration to the United States is agreed after several exchanges between U.S. and Japanese officials.
20 February	President Roosevelt signs the 1907 Immigration Act, which created further restrictions on immigration to the United States. It also created the Dillingham Commission, established to explore the impacts of immigration in the country.
1909	
12 February	The National Association for the Advancement of Colored People (NAACP) is formed. The NAACP went on to become the leading civil rights organization for African Americans in the early twentieth century.
1912	
5 November	The presidential election sees the incumbent, William Howard Taft, come third, winning only eight electoral votes. The split of Republican votes between Taft and his rival Theodore Roosevelt, a former Republican president who ran for the Progressive Party in 1912, helps seal a landslide victory in the Electoral College for Democrat Woodrow Wilson.
1913	
3 February	The Sixteenth Amendment to the U.S. Constitution is ratified. This amendment allows for the federal government to levy a nationwide income tax.
8 April	The Seventeenth Amendment to the U.S. Constitution is ratified. This amendment provided for the direct election of U.S. senators. Prior to this they were elected by state legislatures.
1914	
28 June	Austrian Archduke Franz Ferdinand is assassinated in Sarajevo, Bosnia. His death precipitates the outbreak of the Great War (First World War) in Europe.
15 August	The Panama Canal opens, just over a decade after U.S. construction efforts began in 1904.
1915	
7 May	A German U-boat sinks the *RMS Lusitania*, resulting in the death of many passengers, including some U.S. citizens. The event became a rallying cry for those favoring U.S. entry to the Great War (First World War).

1917

6 April	The United States declares war on Germany. It declared war on Austria–Hungary the following day.

1918

16 May	President Wilson signs the Sedition Act into law. The act further restricted freedom of expression during the war, alongside other measures already in place.
11 November	An armistice is agreed to bring an end to fighting in the Great War (First World War).

1919

16 January	The Eighteenth Amendment to the U.S. Constitution is ratified. This amendment prohibited the manufacture, sale, and transportation of alcoholic beverages. It took effect one year afterwards.
January	The Paris Peace Conference begins, with the aim of formalizing the end of the Great War (First World War).
19 November	The U.S. Senate rejects the Treaty of Versailles.

1920

18 August	The Nineteenth Amendment to the U.S. Constitution is ratified. This amendment meant states could no longer discriminate against voters on the basis of sex, bringing about women's suffrage on a national scale.

Who's who

Addams, (Laura) Jane (1860–1935) Social reformer, progressive, and civil rights campaigner. Best known for establishing the settlement project, Hull House.

Arthur, Chester Alan (1829–1886) 21st U.S. President (1881–1885)—REPUBLICAN. Prior to becoming president, Arthur was Collector of the Port of New York (1871–1877) and U.S. Vice President (1881).

Blaine, James Gillespie (1830–1893) U.S. Secretary of State (1881 and 1889–1892)—REPUBLICAN. Prior to this Blaine was U.S. Representative for Maine's 3rd District (1863–1876) and U.S. Senator for Maine (1876–1881). He was also the Republican presidential candidate in 1884, when he lost to Grover Cleveland. Blaine was the leader of the "Half-breed" faction of the Republican Party.

Bryan, William Jennings (1860–1925) U.S. Secretary of State (1913–1915)—DEMOCRAT. Prior to this Bryan was U.S. Representative for Nebraska's 1st District (1891–1895). He was also the Democratic presidential candidate in 1896, 1900, and 1908, when he lost to William McKinley (twice) and William Howard Taft.

Carnegie, Andrew (1835–1919) Scottish-born steel magnate, anti-imperialist, and philanthropist.

Cleveland, (Stephen) Grover (1837–1908) 22nd and 24th U.S. President (1885–1889 and 1893–1897)—DEMOCRAT. Cleveland is thus far the only president to serve two non-consecutive terms, and was the losing Democratic presidential candidate in 1888, when he lost to Benjamin Harrison. Prior to becoming president, Cleveland was the Mayor of Buffalo (NY) (1882) and Governor of New York (1883–1885).

Conkling, Roscoe (1829–1888) U.S. Senator for New York (1867–1881)—REPUBLICAN. Conkling was the leader of the Stalwart faction of the Republican Party.

Debs, Eugene Victor (1855–1926) U.S. Presidential candidate for the Socialist Party in 1900, 1904, 1908, 1912, and 1920. Debs, originally a

Democrat, was a prominent trade unionist, leading the Pullman Strike in 1894, before becoming the public face of the Socialist Party. He was imprisoned after the Pullman Strike and again for seditious actions during the Great War. He ran his 1920 presidential campaign while still incarcerated.

Douglass, Frederick (c.1818–1895) Leading African American spokesperson and abolitionist. He wrote and spoke widely against slavery and—after the Civil War—for African American rights and civil rights more generally. His most famous work was the biographical volume, *Narrative of the Life of Frederick Douglass*, published in 1845.

Du Bois, William Edward Burghardt (1868–1963) Leading African American spokesperson, historian, and civil rights campaigner. Du Bois was the first African American to earn a PhD at Harvard University and was a leading voice in the establishment of the NAACP.

Garfield, James Abram (1831–1881) 20th U.S. President (1881)—REPUBLICAN. Prior to becoming president, Garfield was U.S. Representative for Ohio's 19th district (1863–1880). Garfield was shot by Charles Guiteau on 2 July 1881 and died several weeks later.

Gompers, Samuel (1850–1924) British-born U.S. trade unionist. Founder and first president of the American Federation of Labor (est. 1886).

Grant, (Hiram) Ulysses "S" (1822–1885) 18th U.S. President (1869–1877)—REPUBLICAN. Prior to becoming president, Grant had served for many years in the U.S. military before rising to become the Commanding General of the U.S. Army during the American Civil War.

Harrison, Benjamin (1833–1901) 23rd U.S. President (1889–1893)—REPUBLICAN. Prior to becoming president, Harrison was U.S. Senator for Indiana (1881–1887). He was the losing Republican presidential candidate in 1892, when he lost to Grover Cleveland.

Hayes, Rutherford Birchard (1822–1893) 19th U.S. President (1877–1881)—REPUBLICAN. Prior to becoming president, Hayes had twice been elected as Governor of Ohio (1868–1872 and 1876–1877).

Johnson, Andrew (1808–1875) 17th U.S. President (1865–1869)—DEMOCRAT (& NATIONAL UNION). Prior to becoming president, Johnson—who remained loyal to the Union unlike the majority of southern Democrats—served as Governor of Tennessee (1855–1857), Senator for Tennessee (1857–1862), Military Governor of Tennessee (1862–1864), and U.S. Vice President (1865).

Lincoln, Abraham (1809–1865) 16th U.S. President (1861–1865)—REPUBLICAN (& NATIONAL UNION). In 1860, Lincoln was the first Republican candidate to be elected to the presidency and led the Union through the majority of the Civil War before he was assassinated by John Wilkes Booth.

Lodge, Henry Cabot (1850–1924) U.S. Senator for Massachusetts (1893–1924)—REPUBLICAN. Lodge was a leading voice in the Republican Party, favored a "large policy" for the United States and later led a Republican faction in the Senate that had strong reservations about the 1919 Treaty of Versailles. He served as Chair of the influential Senate Foreign Relations Committee (1919–1924) and was Senate Majority Leader from 1918 until his death.

McKinley, William (1843–1901) 25th U.S. President (1897–1901)—REPUBLICAN. Prior to becoming president, McKinley had served as a U.S. Representative for various districts in Ohio (1877–1884, 1885–1891) and Governor of Ohio (1892–1896). McKinley was assassinated by Leon Czolgosz in 1901.

Pershing, John Joseph "Black Jack" (1860–1948) Pershing was the commander of the American Expeditionary Force in the Great War. Prior to this Pershing had risen through the ranks in the U.S. Army, taking part in wars against Native American nations, the Spanish–American and Philippine–American Wars, and the raids into Mexico against Pancho Villa.

Roosevelt, Theodore (1858–1919) 26th U.S. President (1901–1909)—REPUBLICAN. Prior to becoming president, Roosevelt had served as a Civil Service Commissioner, a Police Commissioner in New York City, Assistant Secretary of the Navy (1897–1898), Governor of New York (1899–1900), and U.S. Vice President (1901). Roosevelt left the Republican Party in 1912 and ran as the unsuccessful presidential candidate for the newly-formed Progressive Party.

Seward, William Henry (1801–1872) U.S. Secretary of State (1861–1869)—REPUBLICAN. Seward was a staunch advocate of U.S. territorial expansion and was the leading actor behind the purchase of Alaska from Russia in 1867. Prior to his appointment to the cabinet by President Lincoln, Seward was U.S. Senator for New York (1849–1861).

Sherman, William Tecumseh (1820–1891) Commanding General of the U.S. Army (1869–1883). Sherman rose rapidly through the U.S. Army's ranks during the Civil War and was promoted to its top rank when Ulysses Grant became U.S. President in 1869.

Sitting Bull (c.1831–1890) Teton Dakota Chief and leader of Sioux coalition against U.S. forces in the Battle of the Little Bighorn. Sitting Bull later worked in Buffalo Bill Cody's Wild West Show and was killed by U.S. forces in 1890.

Taft, William Howard (1857–1930) 27th U.S. President (1909–1913)—REPUBLICAN. Prior to becoming president, Taft had served as Civil Governor of the Philippines (1901–1903) and Secretary of War (1904–1908). He lost his presidential re-election campaign in 1912, and was later appointed as Chief Justice of the U.S. Supreme Court (1921–1930).

Tarbell, Ida Minerva (1857–1944) Muckraking journalist, whose most famous work was *The History of the Standard Oil Company* (1904).

Washington, Booker Taliaferro (1856–1915) Leading African American spokesperson, educator, and political advisor. Washington was born into enslavement but rose to become the leader of the Tuskegee Institute for African American education in Alabama. He was later a notable advisor on southern affairs to Presidents Theodore Roosevelt and William Howard Taft.

Wells, Ida Bell (Wells-Barnett) (1862–1931) Journalist and civil rights campaigner. Wells made her name through exposing the extent of, and reality behind, the southern lynching problem and was a founding member of the NAACP.

Wilson, (Thomas) Woodrow (1856–1924) 28th U.S. President (1913–1921)—DEMOCRAT. Prior to becoming president, Wilson had served as the President of Princeton University (1902–1910) and Governor of New Jersey (1911–1913).

Part I

Analysis and assessment

1 Introduction

The motto of the United States is *E Pluribus Unum*: out of many, one. This short phrase tells us a great deal about not only the origins of the nation but also about its subsequent history. The United States, as its very name declares, began as a union. It was a union of different colonies that had governed themselves in different ways and were made up of diverse peoples. Some settlements had been founded by religious dissidents seeking freedom to start societies according to their creed, while others were established with a more economic bent. In the southern states, enslaved Africans formed the foundations of a heavily rural economy, while in the North slavery was less viable and failed to take root. The thirteen colonies that declared independence from Great Britain in 1776 were far from a ready-made "nation in waiting".

After the War of Independence (1775–1783), the nation's Founding Fathers forged a new Constitution that would help hold together all thirteen new states. However, pooling sovereignty required a great deal of compromise. For example, though the Declaration of Independence had declared that 'all men are created equal', the new nation permitted the continued enslavement of African Americans. It also allowed states with small populations equal representation with far more populous ones in the newly created U.S. Senate. Compromise was needed to create the union and it remained necessary to maintain it. A succession of presidents held the states together for nearly a century with further compromises, and often the institution of slavery formed a part of these concessions. By 1860, however, the pressure along the fault lines between the states had grown too great. Beginning with South Carolina on 20 December 1860, a number of states gradually seceded from the Union. In February 1861, a rival Confederate States of America was declared and, within a few short weeks, the Union and the Confederacy were at war (see Map 1.1). The fate of a "United" States was in real doubt.

The American Civil War was the most damaging event in the nation's history. For the wartime president, **Abraham Lincoln**, the war was a test of whether a nation 'conceived in liberty, and dedicated to the proposition that all men are created equal ... can long endure' [*Doc. 1, p127*]. More Americans lost their lives in the conflict than in any other war before or

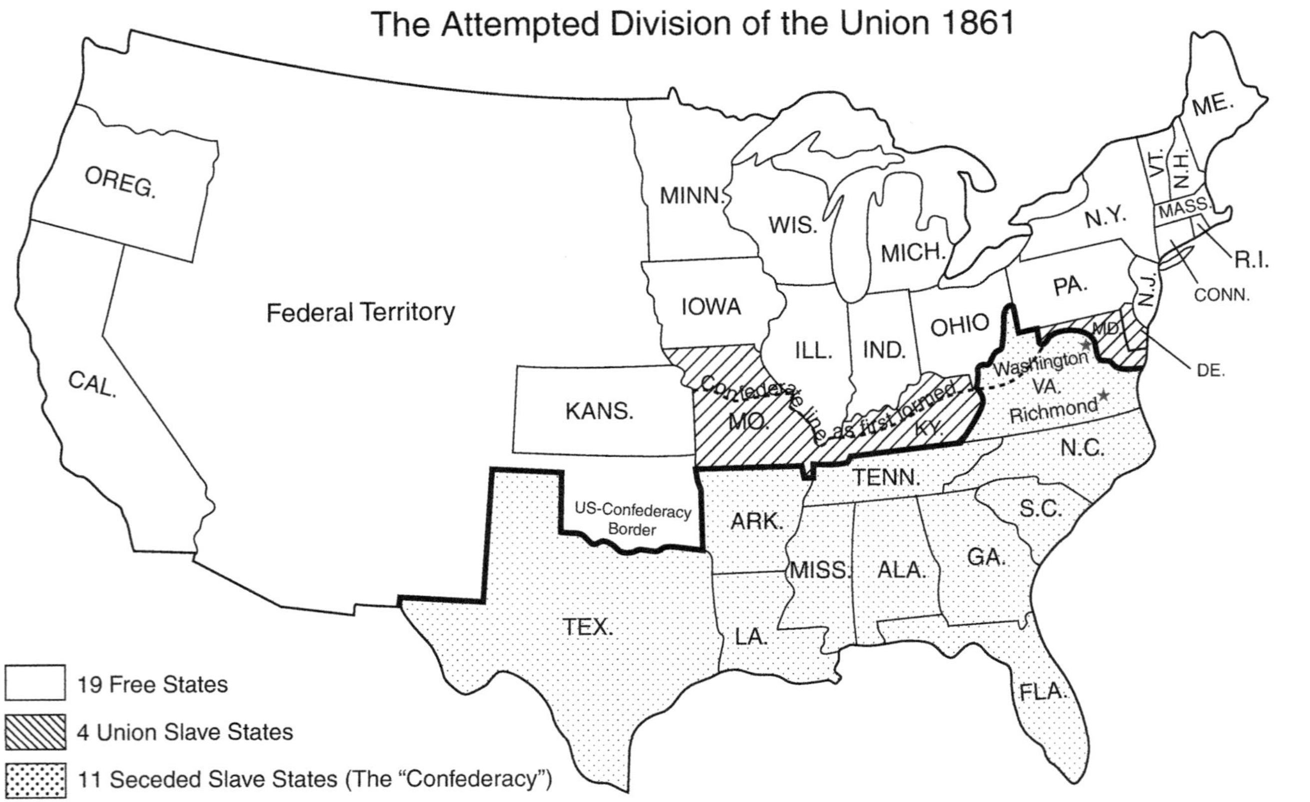

Map 1.1 The Union and Confederacy in 1861, after: ‘The Attempted Division of the Union, 1861 [within the entry “Civil War in America”]’ in: Frederick Converse Beach, ed., *The Encyclopedia Americana* (New York: The Americana Company, 1904), v. 7, n.p. [p.804], available from the Hathi Trust at: https://hdl.handle.net/2027/mdp.39015068387300 (accessed 14 December 2019)

since. However, the impact of the war was far more wide-ranging than even the great casualty lists can convey. The conflict touched upon every aspect of American life. It not only split the country physically in two, but exacerbated the tensions that had been growing across the previous decades: from views on individual rights and who should be entitled to them, to how the U.S. should (or should not) expand and interact with the wider world. It is fair to say that the United States is still recuperating from its aftereffects to this very day. Yet, despite being riven in two by the Civil War, the United States went on to become one of the great powers in global politics; the nation that most defined the course of world affairs after the Second World War. To help understand how the growth and expansion of the United States occurred, as well as the nature of the divisions that still exist in its society today, it is essential to look back to the half century or so after the Civil War. This was a time where restoring national unity was a political priority for successive governments, but also a time where the number of challenges to maintaining that unity evolved and grew along with the nation itself.

Shortly before the Civil War, in 1858, the then Republican presidential hopeful Abraham Lincoln had declared that the U.S. government could not endure 'half *slave* and half *free*'. He had gone on to suggest that the Union would not fail and that, when the slavery question was finally settled, the nation 'would cease to be divided' (Goodwin, 2005: 198). It turned out that he was only partially correct. Even in 1865, with the formal abolition of slavery—the burning issue that had seemed to overshadow all others in the decades before the war—the task of reuniting a nation was far from complete. Indeed, the end of slavery raised a host of new issues and allowed other grievances to rise again from the depths. Such concerns would combine to challenge the recuperating nation for years to come.

In April 1865, the same month in which Confederate General Robert E. Lee surrendered to Union General **Ulysses S. Grant** at Appomattox Court House, a formerly enslaved African American pointed to a "post-war" issue that to him was now a matter of urgency. **Frederick Douglass**, who by this point was an internationally-renowned abolitionist spokesperson, feared that an end to slavery might simply mean brutal oppression of African Americans in another form. To avoid this fate, Douglass argued that it was necessary to give black men the vote. He added, 'if we fail to do it now, if abolitionists fail to press it now, we may not see, for centuries to come, the same disposition that exists at this moment' [*Doc. 2, p127*]. African American enfranchisement was a key political issue in the post-war era and, even when black men won the vote, hardly a moment had passed before white supremacists were plotting to take it away again. Suffrage, be it for African Americans or women, was just one of the many issues that rose to the fore in the wake of the Civil War and continued to divide opinion in the recovering nation for years to come. Indeed, a century after Lincoln's wartime Gettysburg Address [*Doc. 1, p127*], the most famous African American orator of a different age, Dr Martin Luther King, gave a famous speech on the issue of suffrage. Standing in front of the Lincoln Memorial in Washington D.C., during a time when African Americans across the southern states were routinely segregated and disenfranchised, King stated that the U.S. had for too long defaulted on its promise to give its citizens their constitutional rights. Reuniting the nation, it appeared, was a long-term endeavor.

The chapters that follow here explore the long-term task of reunifying the nation through both regional and thematic lenses during a period in which the nation was run largely by those born before the Civil War. The early chapters begin with the Civil War era itself and trace the successes and failures of what became known as "**Reconstruction**" into the later nineteenth-century. They consider the reintegration of the southern states into the union and the fate of race relations in that region after the abolition of slavery. They also explore the rapid expansion of the nation into the West, bringing even greater diversity to the nation, and the role of the Republican and Democratic parties in overseeing these changes. The middle chapters consider the impact of industrial and economic growth on U.S. society, as well as the growing divides between rich and poor and urban and rural communities. In addition, these chapters investigate the impact of immigration, the growth of a U.S. overseas empire, and the effects that all of these changes had on relations with overseas powers. The final chapters focus upon the turn-of-the-century period, and the impacts of the Great War (First World War) on the United States. These final years saw the rise of new social and political movements, huge changes within the two main political parties, and the U.S. entering a "European war" about which many Americans were extremely dubious.

Regionalism, race, economics, immigration, foreign policy, and party politics—these were among the factors that posed the greatest challenges for those who sought to reunite the nation after the Civil War came to an end. It is true that the union was successfully preserved until a new generation was able to take over in 1920, with the election of the first president to be born after the Civil War. However, the fact that so many of the factors that divided the United States between 1865 and 1920 still divide its population today is an indication of just how difficult a task reuniting the nation in a broader sense really was. To understand the course of events in this critical period is to gain a far greater appreciation of the trials of the present.

2 Reconstructing a nation

In his first inaugural address on 4 March 1861, Abraham Lincoln spoke of the United States as being a 'perpetual' union:

> I hold that, in contemplation of universal law and of the Constitution, the Union of these States is perpetual. Perpetuity is implied, if not expressed, in the fundamental law of all national governments. It is safe to assert that no government proper ever had a provision in its organic law for its own termination. Continue to execute all the express provisions of our National Constitution, and the Union will endure forever—it being impossible to destroy it except by some action not provided for in the instrument itself.
>
> (Lincoln, 1861)

With the unity of the United States already being challenged by the secession of many southern states, Lincoln's stance remained that secession was unconstitutional and a radical departure from the union the Founding Fathers had envisaged. Many secessionists, however, saw Lincoln as the radical. With a president who came to office without southern votes, who had openly stated that the United States could not remain "half-slave" and "half-free," many southerners believed that secession was actually a conservative movement to retain the status quo (Collins, 2010: 40–41). Whatever side one took on this question, the outbreak of the Civil War proved that secession was far more than a debating issue.

As a Union victory began to look increasingly likely in the war's final phases, Lincoln indicated that some leniency toward the rebel states might be needed to "reconstruct" the nation after the fighting ended. Not everybody in his Republican Party agreed. However, before Lincoln got a chance to enact his version of "Reconstruction," his assassination brought a very different politician to the nation's highest office. **Andrew Johnson** was a Union Democrat who had joined Lincoln's presidential ticket in 1864 as a way of winning over more voters. Republicans in Congress had little faith in Johnson as an heir to Lincoln. The more radical members of the party felt Johnson (a southern Democrat) was even more likely than Lincoln to be too soft on the former Confederate states. Before long the president and Congress fell into a long running battle over who would control the nature of post-war Reconstruction.

The fight between Radical Republicans and Johnson eventually led to the first impeachment of a U.S. president, and Congress gradually took control of an increasingly hardline Reconstruction. In 1869, the incoming Republican president, Ulysses Grant, looked set to restore good relations with Congress and unite the nation on a path toward reunion. Though his time in office did see some success in uniting the federal government's direction, it failed to keep the nation united to the same ends. The federal government's punitive measures toward the South led the region to become increasingly estranged. By 1876, the nation's voters were once again deeply divided, especially along a north–south axis. The elections that November led to an exceptionally tight battle for the presidency. The following year, the Republican **Rutherford B. Hayes** was declared the winner, but this came at a cost for the hardline Reconstruction his party had promoted over the previous decade. In what is often called the "Compromise of 1877," Hayes secured the presidency, but in return he expedited the removal of federal troops who had enforced Republican policies in the South during the post-war era. The years between the end of the Civil War and 1877 were clearly a time of fierce and complex political battles. Indeed, sometimes post-war Reconstruction appeared to become a kind of "second civil war," just on a different sort of battlefield.

Reconstruction from Lincoln to Johnson

With the war between the Union and Confederacy still raging, on 8 December 1863 President Lincoln issued a Proclamation of Amnesty and Reconstruction in which he outlined a plan for national reunion. He proposed a full pardon and restoration of all rights to former Confederate "rebels" (excluding their rights over enslaved peoples), if they pledged allegiance and agreed to abolish slavery. This rather lenient plan became known as the "10 Percent Plan," as it required only ten percent of the 1860 electorate in a former Confederate state to agree to the terms in order to establish a new state government. Though seen as too soft by some of the more radical members of Lincoln's own party (the so-called "Radical Republicans"), it was a compromise that would nonetheless achieve the abolition of slavery in the South, which had become a key Republican policy since the Emancipation Proclamation that January. Historians remain divided over whether Lincoln's 10 Percent Plan was merely a stopgap measure aimed at bringing the war to a swift conclusion, or a more sincere long-term plan to reunite the nation (Foner, 1988/2002: 36; Harris, 1997: 2). Lincoln, of course, did not live long enough to make it clear which of these was the case.

On 11 April 1865, a diehard Confederate named John Wilkes Booth attended a speech given by Lincoln in which the president spoke about post-war Reconstruction. Booth was unwilling to accept that the war was over, yet alone any form of so-called Reconstruction that might follow. Three days later, Booth shot Lincoln while he attended a play at Ford's Theater in the nation's capital. The assassin's bullet altered the nation's political balance dramatically by bringing to power the relatively new vice president, Andrew Johnson. Johnson was born a southerner and had made a career in Tennessee as a Democrat—though unlike many in his party, he had remained solidly committed to the Union cause. In the election of 1864, Lincoln had opted to add Johnson to his ticket in order to add greater balance, with a view to keeping the door open to those outside of the traditional Republican fold. Lincoln and Johnson had run on a "National Union," rather than a "Republican" ticket. However, whatever the symbolic intentions of his selection, Johnson had a very different personality from his predecessor. Though the Republicans had unanimously agreed to add Johnson to the "National Union" ticket, when he became the nation's commander in chief, many had concerns about what his unanticipated leadership might mean for the course of post-war Reconstruction and the very future of the nation.

Johnson had built a successful career in his adopted home of Tennessee, but he failed to translate this success to the Executive Mansion. The new president was not, however, the pantomime villain that he eventually became in the popular imagination, and there was little evidence of popular opposition to the new president during his first few months in office (McKitrick, 1960/1988: 3–4). As his presidency progressed, though, some of Johnson's personality traits quickly soured those Republicans most suspicious of his leadership. Perhaps foremost among these traits was the president's racism. Johnson had grown up in a region of deeply entrenched racist views and had even "owned" enslaved African Americans. Although recent interpretations of Johnson's presidency have shown that there was more to Johnson than his belief in black inferiority, his deeply held sense that African Americans should remain a 'permanent underclass' in the South put him at odds with the prevailing views of Radical Republicans in Congress (Bergernon, 2011: 7). Furthermore, Johnson was a notoriously stubborn man. These traits combined to set him on a confrontational path with an equally immovable set of Radical Republicans that would lead to a political battle over what exactly Reconstruction should look like.

Though there are many ways in which Johnson differed from his predecessor, in the broadest sense they took a similar approach to Reconstruction. Like Lincoln, Johnson believed that the road to reunion should be a relatively quick and easy one for southern states to traverse. When the new president outlined his own policy of Reconstruction on 29 May 1865, he called for a general amnesty for former rebels, including the return of property seized by Union forces, though this did not include the return of enslaved peoples to their former masters. The amnesty was wide ranging, excluding only certain classes of southerners, particularly those of great wealth or significant seniority in the machinery of the former Confederacy. These individuals would need to appeal to the president directly for a pardon. To the cynical eye, Johnson's exclusions seemed to be guided by his dislike of the former slave-holding elites, or perhaps his ambition to build up a new electoral coalition, rather than by a mission to achieve Reconstruction as swiftly as possible. In this sense, Johnson's Reconstruction could even be regarded as more punitive than Lincoln's plans (Foner, 1988/2002: 183–184).

On the same day, Johnson also outlined a separate plan for the Reconstruction of the State of North Carolina. He authorized the appointment of a provisional governor and called for a state convention that would repeal its ordinance of secession, ratify the Thirteenth Amendment (abolishing slavery), and repudiate the state's war debt. Once these steps had been taken, North Carolina could then set about electing a new state government and send its representatives to the U.S. Congress. North Carolina's Reconstruction served as a model for Johnson's plan for full readmission of all the former Confederate states. Yet, despite seeming at least as tough as Lincoln's scheme, Johnson's plan proved far too soft for the Radical Republicans in Congress, who were most concerned with the safety and rights of the newly freed peoples of the South. Congress, however, was in recess until December, leaving the Radical Republicans to fume from the sidelines as a grateful South went about reassembling governments in line with Johnson's instructions.

Though Johnson had excluded many elite southerners from his general amnesty, he was extremely quick to use his powers of clemency to restore their rights. Such actions only fueled the frustrations of the Radical Republicans. These re-enfranchised southerners soon went about restoring much the same political leadership as they had during the war, with most southern states electing former Confederate politicians to take up their allocated seats in the U.S. Congress that December. Georgia went so far as to send former Confederate vice president, Alexander Stephens, to be one of its U.S. senators.

Despite these significant concessions to former Confederate leaders, there was one major step forward for congressional Republicans to take heart from by the end of 1865. The Thirteenth Amendment, which had been approved that January, was finally ratified in December. This measure brought a formal end to slavery throughout the United States, a significant step forward for the Republican agenda that had begun with Lincoln's Emancipation Proclamation in January 1863. With the ratification of the Thirteenth Amendment, President Johnson saw a final healing of the wounds caused by the Civil War:

> The adoption of the amendment reunites us beyond all power of disruption; it heals the wound that is still imperfectly closed: it removes slavery, the element which has so long perplexed and divided the country; it makes of us once more a united people, renewed and strengthened, bound more than ever to mutual affection and support.
>
> (Johnson, 1865)

To say that there was an element of wishful thinking in the president's sentiments is an understatement. There is no doubt that the Thirteenth Amendment was a significant step forward, but as civil rights campaigner Frederick Douglass noted, it was only the first step toward securing citizenship for African Americans [*Doc. 2, p127*]. As the year came to an end, Johnson declared that his brand of Reconstruction had been achieved, and that the restoration of the South into the Union was complete. Much of the nation, however, was far from convinced.

Congressional Reconstruction

When the Republican-dominated Congress reconvened on 4 December 1865, the day of Johnson's speech, it contained many who disagreed with the president's view that Reconstruction was over. Radical Republican leaders were incensed by the harsh restrictions already being placed on African Americans by white-dominated southern governments (see Chapter 3). They and many of their fellow Republican congressmen also balked at sitting alongside former Confederate leaders in the U.S. House and Senate and refused to seat the southern newcomers. Radical Republican leader Thaddeus Stevens called for a Joint Committee on Reconstruction (sometimes called the Joint Committee of Fifteen due to its size) to explore how best to deal with these newly restored southern governments and their representatives.

Although the Radicals were openly critical of Johnson's policies and the actions of the southern states, they did not control the Republican Party as a whole. Seated alongside these firebrands were a larger group of moderates, as well as a conservative faction that was broadly content with Johnson's Reconstruction. To have any chance of promoting a more thorough form of Reconstruction, with more protections for African American rights, the Radicals would need to win over some of their more centrist colleagues. In early 1866, two bills—the Freedmen's Bureau (Extension) Bill and the Civil Rights Bill—were introduced in Congress. Neither of these measures represented the full desires of the Radicals but they were important steps in the right direction which, more importantly, could carry along the moderates in the Republican Party.

Both of these 1866 Republican-backed bills were primarily concerned with defending African American rights and, as a result, would primarily affect the South. The first bill, as its name suggests, sought to prolong the existence of the Freedmen's Bureau, which had been established in March 1865 to provide support for newly emancipated African Americans (see Chapter 3). The second measure, the Civil Rights Bill of 1866, was far more significant. Acting as a precursor to the later Fourteenth Amendment, the Civil Rights Bill outlined for the first time the rights of formerly enslaved peoples, regardless of their race. Yet, despite Congress passing both measures without too much difficulty, Johnson used his presidential veto to stop them becoming law. The president argued that he had serious constitutional objections to the provisions of the bills, while somewhat unconvincingly pledging his broader support for their basic aims. Johnson suggested that Congress was attempting to overstep its authority with these bills: that they represented overreaching federal power and discrimination against the rights of the southern states. The president called upon Congress to allow the former Confederate states their due representation in the House and Senate, in line with the Christian virtue of forgiveness and their shared aim of reunifying the nation (McKitrick, 1960/1988: 291–293). However, though the president was able to stop the bills for the meantime, his actions had another important effect. By defying the will of Congress, Johnson began to push moderate Republicans toward their radical colleagues.

On 6 April 1866, Congress began to stand up more forcefully to Johnson. By the margin of a single vote in the Senate, Congress overrode the president's veto of the Civil Rights Bill. This shift in momentum against the president soon gathered pace. At the end of April the Joint Committee introduced the first draft of what would become the Fourteenth Amendment [*Doc. 3, p128*]. It would secure similar rights to those outlined in the Civil Rights Act but, as part of the Constitution, would be much harder to retract if the Republicans lost power in the future. The Fourteenth Amendment also included measures that directly attacked parts of Johnson's lenient Reconstruction. It not only excluded former Confederate officeholders from Congress, it even threatened to reduce the representation of states that did not permit all of their entitled citizens the right to vote. Though the amendment was passed by the Senate and House in June, it would be another two years before it received the backing of enough states to be ratified. Meanwhile, in May, Congress had passed a new version of the Freedmen's Bureau Bill and in July it overrode another veto. This turning of the tide against President Johnson is widely regarded by historians as the end of "Presidential Reconstruction" and the beginning of a new phase, a more radical "Congressional Reconstruction". For the former Confederate states, Johnson's declaration that Reconstruction had been achieved the previous December was starting to look exceedingly premature.

That summer, Congress started to take the lead when it came to the Reconstruction agenda. In July, Congressmen allowed representatives from Tennessee back into Congress, setting the bar for other states to reach. Tennessee had been torn apart by divided loyalties during the Civil War and was the only one of the eleven secessionist states to have ratified the Fourteenth Amendment. This illustrated the sort of commitment to African Americans' rights that Congressional Republicans expected from the rebel states in order to take their seats once again. For a fleeting moment, it looked like Congressional Reconstruction might prove to be quicker and more effective than Johnson had predicted (Franklin, 1961: 62). However, serious race riots soon broke out that summer in Memphis, Tennessee, and New Orleans, Louisiana. Where Johnson's Reconstruction had frustrated northern Republicans and African Americans, Congressional Reconstruction had also failed to bring about national harmony.

President Johnson was not willing to become sidelined for the rest of his time in office. Indeed, with the Republican-dominated Congress taking charge, Johnson looked to the midterm elections that fall as the staging post for a comeback. Johnson was not up for election himself, but he did seek to help likeminded Democrats and conservative Republicans who might then help him get Reconstruction back on its original course. Starting in August, the president toured the country in what was labeled his "Swing around the Circle". He made a series of sharply critical speeches about the Radical Republicans and their allies, accusing them of perpetuating disunity. Johnson and his opponents soon turned the 1866 midterms into a sort of referendum on the type of Reconstruction the country wanted. When the anti-Johnson Republicans won a decisive victory that November, the question seemed to be answered (Downs, 2015: 163–164; McKitrick, 1960/1988: 467–470). The South, however, had little voice in these elections, and soon enough it was clear they had little interest in how a "northern" Congress thought they should act.

The ten "suspended" southern states made their rejection of Congressional Reconstruction known through "masterly inactivity"—they refused to ratify the all-important Fourteenth Amendment. In response, an emboldened Congress decided to increase the pressure on the recalcitrant states to comply with their demands. As 1867 dawned, Congress drew up the terms of what became known as "Military Reconstruction". The Reconstruction Act of 2 March 1867, the first of four acts that would set out the rules for the nature of readmission of southern states, has been regarded as perhaps 'the most ambitious and far-reaching piece of domestic legislation in the history of the United States' (Perman, 1973: 270). The truculent ten states were divided into five military districts under the command of a federally-mandated general. They were also barred from sending former Confederate politicians to Washington, required to rewrite their state constitutions to enfranchise male (though not female) African Americans, and ratify the Fourteenth Amendment. To nobody's great surprise President Johnson once more vetoed the legislation, claiming that what Congress sought to achieve through this measure was 'absolute despotism' [*Doc. 4, p130*]. Once more, however, Congress overrode the president's veto. The Reconstruction Act placed the military in a position to secure Congressional Reconstruction, but with one major shortcoming: the president was still the commander in chief.

To stop any further interference from the president in achieving their brand of Reconstruction, Congress passed two further pieces of legislation in early 1867, overriding two more presidential vetoes in the process. The first of these measures was the Command of the Army Act (attached to the Army Appropriations Act), which required the president to conduct all communications with the Army (and the military governors of the South) through General of the Army, Ulysses Grant. Grant was to stay in Washington, near Congress, and could not be removed from office without consent of the Senate. This final point was echoed in the second piece of legislation. Although the Senate already approved presidential nominations to the cabinet, the Tenure of Office Act made it so that he would now need their approval to remove cabinet members as well. The aim of both acts was to limit the president's ability to frustrate Congressional Reconstruction. The president had already accused Congress of expanding its power at the expense of states' rights, now it appeared it was doing so at the expense of his own authority.

With legislation passed to restrict the president's actions, the ball returned to Johnson's court: would he act against insubordinate cabinet members who now felt emboldened to openly defy him? Secretary of War Edwin Stanton was one of the more vocal critics of the president's approach to Reconstruction still in the cabinet. In the normal course of things, it would be entirely reasonable for Johnson to replace him. Instead, the president "suspended" Stanton while Congress was in recess and replaced him with General Grant. When Congress reconvened Johnson explained that he could no longer work with Stanton, but Congress demanded he be reinstated. Grant, thinking ahead to the following year's presidential election, stood down from his temporary cabinet assignment and resumed his role as General of the Army (Stewart, 2010: 117–120). Johnson, also thinking of a potential run in 1868 (as a Democrat) and badly needing to reassert himself, decided to fight. First, he moved to replace various military commanders without first consulting the General of the Army, Grant (in defiance of the Command of the Army Act). Then, on 21 February, the president dismissed Stanton, which was counter to the terms of the Tenure of Office Act. The president had directly defied two acts of Congress that had been designed to keep him from reimposing his vision of Reconstruction. The battle to control how the nation was to be reunified was testing the structure of the federal government to breaking point.

By defying Congress in such an obvious manner, Johnson set himself up to be the first U.S. president to be impeached. In February 1868, the House of Representatives made this certain. Removing the president from office, however, would require a two-thirds conviction by the Senate which was not a foregone conclusion. The Republican-controlled Senate was divided over several issues. Some feared the replacement of Johnson with the very "Radical" president pro tempore of the Senate, Ben Wade. Others were concerned about the damage Johnson's removal would do to the doctrine of the separation of powers (Foner, 1988/2002: 335–336). In the end, seven Republicans voted in the president's favor, leaving the Republicans one vote short of the two-thirds majority required to remove him from office. Johnson's authority was seriously wounded but, unsurprisingly, he did not quietly see out his remaining days in office. Instead, he proceeded to offer amnesty to every former rebel (including former Confederate President Jefferson Davis), nominate his favored candidates to high office, and continued to veto Congressional legislation that displeased him (Stewart, 2010: 300–301). Congress had won the battle for control of Reconstruction, but the war to make it happen was far from over.

The 1868 election looked likely to be yet another referendum on Reconstruction. Johnson felt he had a good chance of winning the Democratic nomination, but the party eventually opted for a compromise candidate in the form of Horatio Seymour of New York. In contrast, the Republicans were unanimous from the outset in their support for the war hero, and relative moderate, Ulysses Grant. Grant's campaign slogan in 1868 was "Let Us Have Peace," a slogan that chimed with his belief that both the Civil War and Reconstruction were part of the same struggle for unity, the abolition of slavery, and a 'durable peace' (Simpson, 1991: xiv). Despite other factors influencing voters, the clearest dividing line between the parties was on the issue of black civil rights in the South. The Democrats ran as the party of white supremacy and the Republicans in favor of African American rights, a pattern set to be repeated for many decades to follow. By the time of the election, seven more southern states were readmitted to the U.S. Congress, giving the Democrats a far greater chance than they had stood in the 1866 midterms. Only Mississippi, Texas, and Virginia were yet to be fully reintegrated. Nevertheless, Grant's Republicans were also set to benefit from southern reintegration. The Republicans could now count on the votes of many newly enfranchised African Americans and the continued disenfranchisement of some high-ranking former Confederates who would have voted Democrat. In November, only two of the reintegrated southern states—Georgia and Louisiana—cast their electoral votes for Seymour. Across the rest of the nation, in the **Electoral College** at least, Grant won an easy victory. The lame duck President Johnson accused the victorious Republican Party of perpetuating national disunity and racial disharmony. It was now up to Grant, former head of the Union Army, and briefly acting secretary of war, to make good on his campaign slogan, "Let Us Have Peace".

Grant's Reconstruction

By the time Grant took office, post-war America had already witnessed the ratification of two new constitutional amendments: the Thirteenth Amendment in December 1865 and the Fourteenth Amendment in July 1868. But as 1869 dawned, the reinvigorated Congressional Republicans pushed for the adoption of yet another. Although the 1867 Reconstruction Act had forced southern states to allow black men the right to vote, Republicans in Congress felt that a constitutional amendment would safeguard this achievement from future Congressional backpedaling. In February, the House and Senate passed what would later become the Fifteenth Amendment, which would forbid voter discrimination based on race, color, or previous condition of servitude. Ratification was also made a precondition for the readmission of the three southern states that had not returned to Congress by the

1868 election (and for Georgia, which had been resuspended). The Fifteenth Amendment was finally ratified in March 1870, and by the end of that year all former Confederate states had been fully readmitted to Congress. The end of 1870 could, with only these facts in mind, be seen as a symbolic end to Reconstruction: African American rights looked to be secured within the Constitution and the rebel southern states had been brought back fully into the union. However, for civil rights activist and historian **W. E. B. Du Bois** (1935/1998: 378), 1870 was the beginning of the nation's gradual desertion of African Americans now that 'their selfish interests were safe'.

The abandonment of the African American cause by the Republican Party and many northerners certainly did not happen overnight. Indeed, during Grant's first term, further measures were enacted that bolstered the provisions of the Fourteenth and Fifteenth Amendments. These measures became collectively known as the Enforcement Acts. The first Enforcement Act (1870) underlined the duty of the federal government to enforce the constitutional rights of citizens, and Grant acted swiftly to prove that this was not just empty rhetoric. Federal troops were sent to North Carolina, where hundreds were charged, and punitive measures were soon taken elsewhere in the South. In 1871, a second Enforcement Act added further stipulations to allow for federal supervision of elections. That same year, a third and more wide-ranging enforcement bill was proposed, commonly called the Ku Klux Klan Bill. It provided further guidance on how the federal government needed to intervene to prevent civil rights violations where the states themselves had failed. However, opinion in the North had now started to shift, with many tired of the ongoing Reconstruction efforts. Others worried about the continuing enlargement of federal power through the Enforcement Acts, which appeared to come at the expense of states' rights. Indeed, only with the full public backing of Grant himself did Congress reluctantly pass the Ku Klux Klan Act (Smith, 2001: 545–547). The Enforcement Acts were both the high point of interventionist Congressional Reconstruction and the beginning of its rapid and terminal decline.

As Grant entered the election year of 1872, he was the leader of a severely divided party. In line with the views of an increasing part of the northern electorate, an emergent "liberal" wing of the Republican Party called for an end to federal intervention in the South and, with it, the acceptance that Reconstruction was complete (McPherson, 1975: 24–25). Despite the other apparent failings of Grant's administration (see Chapter 5), a larger section of his party supported his renomination and the continuation of intervention in the South, particularly to support the rights of African Americans. In order to unite voters opposed to an interventionist Reconstruction, the "Liberal–Republicans" joined with the Democrats to support a joint ticket of Horace Greeley (a northern newspaper editor) and Benjamin Brown (a southern Republican). The result that November saw Grant reelected with ease, even winning in several southern states. It appeared to be a clear mandate for continued government activism.

Despite Grant's reelection victory, interventionist Reconstruction efforts did not continue with anything like the same force in his second term. In 1873, the U.S. Supreme Court issued their verdict on an ongoing dispute known as the *Slaughterhouse Cases*. The case was initially concerned with the granting of a monopoly by the State of Louisiana over the slaughter-houses of New Orleans. The court's decision, however, had much wider ramifications. The justices ruled that Louisiana had the right to grant this monopoly and that those opposed to the monopoly had not been denied their rights under the Fourteenth Amendment, which was primarily there to safeguard the rights of African Americans. The wider implication was that the Fourteenth Amendment could not be used as a blank check to allow for increased federal interference in state matters. Though this was certainly a setback for interventionist Republicans, far more worrying was the economic crisis that arose that year: the Panic of 1873. The deep depression that hit the United States in the fall saw both public and government attention drawn away from Reconstruction and focused instead on sorting out the nation's economic problems. With an economic crisis underway, and the Supreme Court ruling in support of states' rights, things were poised for the end of Republican Reconstruction.

The 1874 midterm elections spelled yet another setback for Reconstruction. Presiding over an economic crisis, and with the party linked to a series of scandals (see Chapter 5), the Republicans would have expected some bad news. The result meant that, in 1875, the Democrats would take control of the House of Representatives—the first time the party would control a chamber of Congress since the Civil War. However, during their final weeks in control of Congress, the more Radical Republicans decided to make the most of their time-limited power. They resurrected a bill calling for an end to racial discrimination in public accommodations and on public transport. Though this sounds like a significant measure, the weakened Republican Party did little to enforce the resulting Civil Rights Act of 1875 (and in 1883 the Supreme Court declared the act unconstitutional). The 1875 Force Bill, a further effort to bolster interventionist Reconstruction by broadening presidential powers, failed to even make it out of the Senate (McPherson, 1975: 50). By the end of 1875, Republican Reconstruction, which three years earlier had seemed full of life, appeared to have lost all momentum.

With another election looming in 1876, the Republican Party sensed the political winds had moved firmly against continued federal intervention in the South and neither party made Reconstruction policy the centerpiece of their campaigns (see Chapter 5). Instead, both parties chose reform candidates—Rutherford B. Hayes (Rep.) and Samuel Tilden (Dem.)—who focused instead upon cleaning up national politics (Nester, 2013: 286). The presidential election result was tight and fiercely contested. Some felt that the nation was once again on the brink of a civil war. As a result, Congress created a commission to decide the election result in the three most hotly disputed states. The Republicans, however, held the majority of seats on the commission and awarded Hayes all three states' votes. In the end, Hayes won in the Electoral College by 185 votes to 184. The Republicans would retain control of the executive branch, but it was hardly a mandate for Republican Reconstruction policy. Indeed, for many onlookers, it was no mandate at all.

Fortunately, Hayes' victory did not lead to widespread civil unrest, or another sectional war. At least part of this was because a deal had been struck between the Republicans and Democrats—the so-called "Compromise of 1877". Democrats would grudgingly accept Hayes as president, in return for a commitment from the Republicans to end federal interventions in the South. Shortly after taking office, Hayes removed federal troops from Louisiana and South Carolina allowing two contested gubernatorial seats to be filled by Democrats. For historian C. Vann Woodward (1951/1991: 3), it was 1877 that saw the abandonment of principles and of force, and a return to the traditional ways of 'expediency and concession'. Compromise had been the watchword of federal politics in the decades before the Civil War, and it was what finally brought an end to Republican Reconstruction in the years that followed.

More than a decade after the Civil War had come to an end, it might well be argued that the war's political warriors only really ceased their fire in 1877. Yet, though the "political war" was finally over on a national level, the same could not necessarily be said of Reconstruction itself—especially in the South. Eric Foner's still unsurpassed volume on Reconstruction refers to the project as America's "unfinished revolution" (Foner, 1988/2002). In line with this idea, many historians have argued that we should look beyond 1877 to a longer era of Reconstruction. For them, Reconstruction could be said to have continued until as late as 1901, when the last African American congressman of the period left the U.S. House of Representatives (Gates, 2019: 8). The next chapter here explores the impacts of Reconstruction in the South in more detail and traces its story through into this later period. The nation in 1877 might have been physically reunited, in that the former Confederacy was restored within the union once more but, in many other senses, the nation became even more divided in the years that followed.

3 The road to redemption

Reconstruction was a period that succeeded in bringing the former Confederate states back into the union. It was also a period characterized by a great deal of federal legislation aimed at directing the way the South was governed. From the perspective of newly emancipated southern African Americans, this attention was broadly positive, while it lasted. However, from the viewpoint of most white southerners, the attention was most unwelcome. For the white South, this federal "interference" represented the imposed will of the North and, in particular, the hated Republican Party. It appeared that the victors not only dictated the peace, but also how southerners would live for years afterwards.

From 1863 to 1875, the Republicans shepherded through measure after measure aimed at supporting, enfranchising, and protecting the rights of African Americans. These moves began during the war itself, with the establishment of the Freedmen's Bureau and Lincoln's Emancipation Proclamation. They were followed by more concrete changes, such as new laws and three constitutional amendments abolishing slavery, giving African Americans full citizenship, and finally giving all male citizens—regardless of color—the vote. Momentum appeared to be fully behind African American rights and this was supported, where necessary, by the use of federal force.

This impetus, however, was not to last. By the time of the Compromise of 1877, ongoing resistance from white southerners had gained sufficient traction to shift momentum back toward their white supremacist agenda. Slowly but surely white southerners, and their favored Democratic Party, were able to regain control of the southern states. They then began unpicking Reconstruction-era reforms that had enabled African American participation in southern life along more equal terms. The North, and the Republican Party, effectively abandoned black southerners. By 1901, the final African American congressman had left the House of Representatives and the vast majority of black southerners lived in segregated areas, used segregated facilities, and were systematically denied their right to vote. White southerners called this period "**Redemption**," yet for African Americans it was anything but. The union might have been knitted back together but, in the South, the notion of "race" kept the region as divided as ever.

African American rights secured?

Slavery was central to both the origins and progress of the Civil War, whatever some may argue. From 1863 onwards, abolition became the clarion call of the Union and its Republican leader Abraham Lincoln. However, as abolition had not always been the Republicans' stated goal, one might ask whether Lincoln's Emancipation Proclamation was primarily a pragmatic measure aimed at boosting Union manpower and morale. Figure 3.1, certainly supports this viewpoint. Added to this, the Proclamation was definitely a limited measure as it offered liberty only to enslaved people in lands under Confederate control or in certain Union-occupied regions of the Confederacy. Lincoln did not offer emancipation to enslaved people in the states that had remained loyal to the Union. Indeed, the president knew that abolishing slavery was something the white South would never willingly accept and he remained unsure it was even constitutional. However, after 1863 it would prove nearly impossible to reverse course. From this point onward, reuniting the nation after the conflict's end was bound to the idea that African Americans could no longer be enslaved: something finally settled in 1865 by the Thirteenth Amendment. What status and rights African Americans might then lay claim to remained a matter of national debate.

Figure 3.1 "Abe Lincoln's Last Card; Or, Rouge-et-Noir," by John Tenniel (1862)
Album/Alamy Stock Photo

One key question surrounding abolition was how formerly enslaved African Americans would be able to provide for themselves. A potential answer to this arose during the war itself. In 1865, General **William Tecumseh Sherman** issued Special Field Orders No. 15, setting aside 400,000 acres of coastal lands in South Carolina and Georgia for black settlement. It would be allotted at a ratio of forty acres per family—a promise that would become widely known as "forty acres and a mule". Though well-sounding, Sherman's actions were even more pragmatic than Lincoln's, aiming to unburden Union forces of newly liberated African American refugees who were deemed an encumbrance to military advances (Freehling, 2001: 205; Rubin, 2014: 89–91). However, wartime contingencies did not always transform into post-war progress and Sherman's land grants, along with similar moves elsewhere, were soon halted and reversed.

One wartime contingency measure that managed to outlast the war, if not for long, was the creation of the Freedmen's Bureau in March 1865. Initially, the Bureau was charged with supporting black refugees with vital medical supplies and rations, allotting them sections of abandoned land (like those distributed by Sherman), and helping them to find gainful employment. The Bureau also set up numerous schools across the region in the late 1860s, many of which far outlived the Bureau itself (Vaughn, 1974: 11–17). However, it was economic impulses that often dominated Bureau efforts, which frequently focused more on restoring an effective workforce than on its humanitarian mandate (Silkenat, 2016: 185). Though the Bureau was far from perfect, its fate was ultimately dictated more by the growing rift between Congress and President Johnson than its shortcomings. For Johnson, the Bureau stood in the way of the full reunion of the nation and he therefore vetoed the Bureau's renewal in February 1866. He argued that it had expanded its power at the expense of the southern states and had ignored the needs of white southerners. Congress failed to override the president's first veto but, when a similar bill to prolong the Bureau was introduced in May 1866, it did override his second veto. Despite this reprieve, Congress finally abandoned the Bureau in 1872 following continued objections from the white South and increased frustrations in the North concerning the length of federal intervention.

With the rejection of Sherman's land redistribution scheme and the gradual erosion of the Freedmen's Bureau, many freedmen and women were soon drawn back into an economic system not all that far removed from that which existed before the war. Thousands of African Americans still worked the southern plantations in supervised gangs that, on the face of it, differed little from former arrangements. Many others went on to become tenant farmers, or "sharecroppers". Under this system, tenants paid landowners rent *and* for equipment purchased on credit, with either their profits or a share of their own crop (Aiken, 1998: 17–19). Though the tenant system might have seemed to offer greater autonomy, much of this was illusory due to what is often termed "debt peonage". Many tenants soon became so indebted to landowners that they had to remain where they were and work simply to pay off their debts. Both gang laborers and sharecroppers technically had far more independence than before the war, in that they chose their work and could—in theory—move elsewhere. In reality, however, many found they were almost as tied to the plantations and the will of the landowners as they had been before the war.

Though the Thirteenth Amendment had ended slavery in 1865, political equality for African Americans was an altogether more complex and prolonged battle. In the years that followed, the federal government initiated a series of measures that sought to define the new political status of African Americans. The Civil Rights Act of 1866, and the Fourteenth and Fifteenth Amendments to the U.S. Constitution, all outlined the rights of formerly enslaved Americans (see Chapter 2). In the years that followed the act, biracial southern state conventions rewrote their own constitutions to confirm this new *status quo*. In theory, these measures secured African Americans full citizenship and protection under the law, as well as the right of black men to vote. For a time, this led to black participation in southern politics alongside whites. However, while white supremacists acknowledged the end of slavery they proved determined to stop any further concessions toward African American equality.

Although not all white southerners opposed black participation in politics, those who did made themselves known from the very start. In 1865, those seeking to restrict black rights in South Carolina and Mississippi drew up so-called "Black Codes". These were a series of laws aimed at restricting any emerging black freedoms before they were able to take root. The Mississippi codes, for example, forbade interracial marriage and required freed people to carry documentary evidence of their employment contracts [*Doc. 5, p131*]. These draconian measures sparked a vocal reaction in the North, as well as protests from blacks in the South (Foner, 1988/2002: 200–201). Such codes were enacted across much of the South by 1866, though many were soon watered down or repealed entirely by biracial Reconstruction state governments. Nevertheless, precedents for future white resistance were clear. If African American rights were to be safeguarded, biracial southern state governments were going to prove crucial.

African American participation in government was one of the greatest changes to both state and federal politics in the period after the war. It was an important sign that voting was not the only way black people could help affect the nation's politics. Those who led the way at a federal level were the Methodist minister Hiram Revels, elected to a short Senate term representing Mississippi in 1870, and Joseph H. Rainey and Jefferson Long, who were elected to the House of Representatives from districts in South Carolina and Georgia respectively. However, despite these early changes, only sixteen African Americans sat in the U.S. Congress during Reconstruction. Black southerners were also very poorly represented in high-level positions at a state level (Foner, 1988/2002: 352–353). Though African Americans *could* hold office, they faced many more obstacles in getting elected than their white southern counterparts.

White supremacists who fiercely resented black participation in politics, and particularly their election to state and federal office, did all they could to portray black politicians in the worst possible light. Since white supremacists controlled the vast majority of political offices in the region, as well as many of the leading newspapers, their continued propaganda against African Americans was hard to avoid. Black politicians were routinely presented as unfit to hold office due to their assumed lack of qualifications and experience, as well as their supposed racial inferiority. Since the Democratic Party in the South was openly racist, and the federal Republican Party was the driving force behind black rights, there was also a party political angle to the propaganda. White critics presented black politicians as puppets of the northern Republicans, who owed their election not to popularity among southerners but to the heirs of the widely reviled Abraham Lincoln.

Alongside the continued criticism from Democrats in the South, black politicians also faced opposition from some in the southern Republican Party. Some white southern Republicans feared that the election of black Republicans—coupled with the party's reliance on black votes—meant they were becoming a "black man's party" which would become unelectable in the South. Many of them simply left and joined the Democrats (Perman, 1984: 50–51). However, although the Republican Party relied heavily on southern black voters, it was a white Republican minority who tended to dominate most top political roles and offices in the region.

White Republicans in the South came in for almost as much scorn from white supremacists as their black colleagues. The Dunning School of historians—active in the early twentieth century—presented Reconstruction as an unjust northern imposition and helped legitimize the caricatures of white Republicans common during Reconstruction. First, there were the "scalawags," native white southerners willing to support the Republicans for patronage from the federal government. Second were the "carpetbaggers"—northerners who ventured south, also seeking to become Republican spoilsmen. White Republican southerners were, of course, motivated by a far more complex combination of factors. Some were committed Unionists, some were indeed cynical opportunists, while others were genuinely motivated by a desire to reform the South (Baggett, 2004: 14). Regardless of their motivation and actions, the Democrats quite successfully presented the biracial Republican Party as representing an era of misrule in the South.

Whatever one thought of the quality of southern Republicans, their time in power was very short indeed. One of the great southern historians of the twentieth century, C. Vann Woodward, called Republican rule in the South an 'ephemeral experiment'. With the exceptions of South Carolina, Louisiana, and Florida, the average period of control for Republican Reconstruction governments in the South was less than three and a half years (Woodward, 1971: 22). In contrast, the era of Democratic domination that followed lasted for decades. For African Americans in the South, the demise of Republican rule in the region ushered in an altogether different period. White supremacists would come to refer to it as a time of southern "Redemption". The changing fortunes of African Americans and their role in the politics of the South did not end with the Compromise of 1877. This might have been when the federal government ceased to intervene but, for the South, the story continued. As a result, more recent historians talk of a "long Reconstruction" that lasted well beyond 1876 and into the 1890s or beyond (Downs, 2011: 13). "Redemption" and white resistance form part of the "long Reconstruction" and, just like the Republican-led Reconstruction, its roots lie in the Civil War era.

White resistance

White supremacists' use of violence to resist Republican-led Reconstruction can be dated back—symbolically at least—to John Wilkes Booth's assassination of Abraham Lincoln. Well before the retreat of federal troops in the late 1870s, campaigns of terror and violence, euphemistically referred to as "riots," had been perpetrated across the South. Such violence sought to deter African Americans from their attempts to challenge and subvert antebellum social and political norms. In May 1866, Memphis, Tennessee saw the first large-scale riot against African Americans. Other towns and cities soon followed suit. New Orleans saw dozens killed and many more wounded in violent clashes across the city. However, one of the most notorious riots occurred in 1873 during the latter stages of Republican-led Reconstruction in Colfax, Louisiana. In what is now widely termed the Colfax Massacre, approximately 150 African Americans were murdered when white southerners violently resisted black involvement in politics (Keith, 2008: xi–xii). Such displays of violence served to create a psychological climate of fear while physically preventing blacks from exercising their democratic rights. Violence would prove a vital weapon in the arsenal of white supremacists keen to reassert their authority over the South.

Vigilante groups were one of the most effective forms of physical and psychological violence aimed at restoring white rule in the South (see Figure 3.2). One of the earliest, and most well-known of these groups was the **Ku Klux Klan (KKK)**. Organized in Tennessee in 1866 by a group of Confederate veterans, the KKK became known for its distinctive clothing, rites, and rituals. Its mission was to re-establish good order in the South and stop the sort of misrule and criminality allegedly created by biracial Republican rule. As Republican Reconstruction governments spread out across the South, so too did the activities of the KKK. Where in some places they resorted to mere hostile newspaper advertisements, in others they roamed as bands of "nightriders," terrorizing African Americans and their supporters. Similar vigilante groups arose in states where the Klan was less well-established, such as Louisiana, where the grandly named Knights of the White Camellia were formed in 1867 (Rable, 1984/2017: 69–72). So dire did the scale of

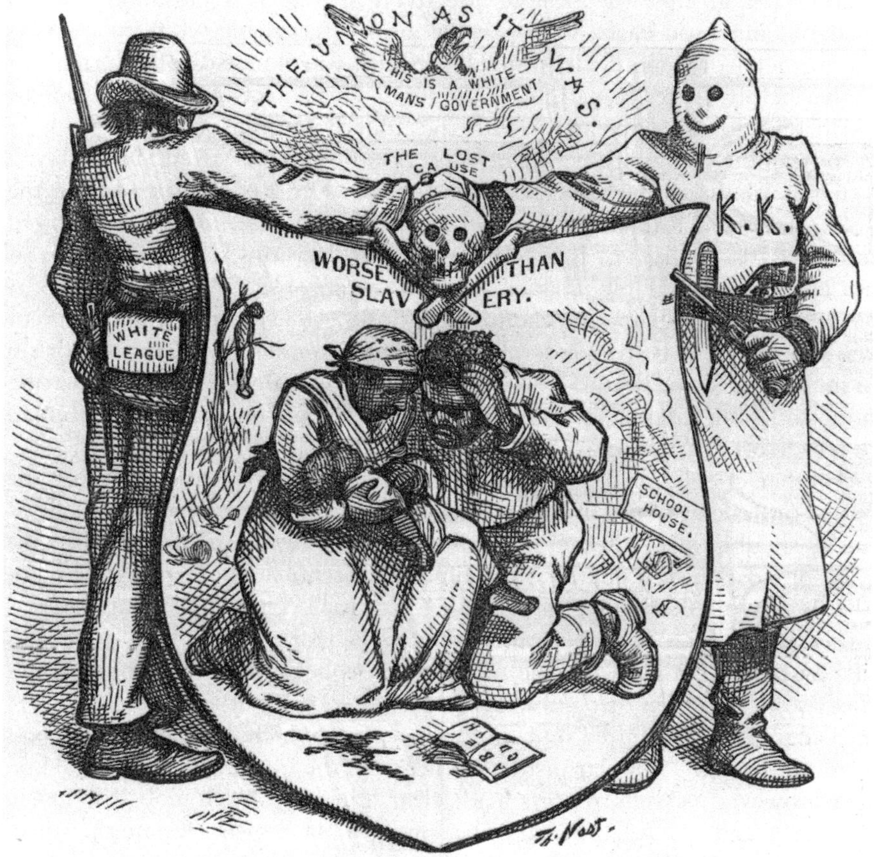

Figure 3.2 "The Union as it Was. The Lost Cause, Worse than Slavery," by Thomas Nast (1874)

Everett Collection Inc/Alamy Stock Photo

vigilantism become during Reconstruction, the federal government resorted to further legislation to protect black rights and lives. This came in the form of the Enforcement Acts (see Chapter 2). The Third Enforcement Act (1871)—more commonly known as the Ku Klux Klan Act—expressly aimed to boost state militias with federal force and allowed for the arrest of hundreds of Klansmen. The Enforcement Acts were largely successful in curbing the actions of the Klan, but where one head of the white supremacy hydra was chopped off, several more soon rose to take its place.

Only three years after the Ku Klux Klan Act, Louisiana gave birth to the White League, which organized mass meetings to enflame crowds against black suffrage and paid special attention to intimidating white Republicans.

Like earlier groups, the League effectively served as a paramilitary arm of the Democratic Party, with parallel aims of restoring white rule across the former Confederacy. In states like South Carolina, so-called "rifle" or "saber" clubs were formed, ostensibly to help protect whites from potential black violence, but again with the underlying aim of intimidating or even lynching Republicans. Meanwhile, South Carolina's Red Shirts played a major role in intimidating both black and white Republicans during the 1876 elections (Rable, 1984/2017: 173). As vigilante groups re-emerged in the 1870s, a series of U.S. Supreme Court decisions served to enable, if not encourage, their renaissance. *The Slaughterhouse Cases* (1873), *U.S. v. Cruikshank* (1876), and the *Civil Rights Cases* (1883) combined in different ways to gradually restrict federal government intervention against terrorism in the South (Kato, 2016: 119–121). As with so many aspects of Reconstruction, over time federal activism against white terrorism in the South seemed to recede ever further into the distance.

Another closely-related phenomenon that grew exponentially during the period of Redemption was the prevalence of "lynch-law" in the South. Lynching by small groups, often in front of large and enthusiastic crowds, became widespread in the last quarter of the nineteenth century. For historian Christopher Waldrep (2009: xxv), the year 1877 was the beginning of what he terms an 'age of lynching' in the region. Thanks to the work of civil rights advocates like journalist **Ida B. Wells**, the northern press began to carry stories about this rise in southern atrocities. Typically, the victims of a lynch mob were alleged to have committed some notorious crime, which the mob felt was best avenged through "popular justice" rather than the time-consuming legal system. However, as Wells' reports made clear, almost all lynch mobs' victims in the 1880s and 1890s happened to be southern black men. Despite rhetorical outrage from the North, the all-white juries and justice systems in southern states rarely challenged lynch mobs, often conveniently recording the verdict that lynching victims had died at the hands of "persons unknown". Later efforts to make lynching a federal—rather than state—crime failed, and at the dawn of the twentieth century lynch-law was still firmly entrenched in many southern states (Burns, 2010). Lynching, "rioting," and organized terrorist groups combined across the latter stages of the nineteenth century to create a climate of fear that discouraged most southerners from voting Republican and caused African Americans to think twice before voting at all.

Although terrorism and violence played a major role in white supremacist Redemption, it fell to the Democratic Party to bring about the official restoration of white rule in the region. It would be a mistake to assume that with the Compromise of 1877, and the removal of federal troops, the politics of the South transformed overnight. After all, African American participation in southern politics continued on into the period of Redemption, though in an ever-decreasing number of states and localities. Yet, by 1877 the Democrats had—with the help of controversial successes in Louisiana and Florida—regained control of all state legislatures across the former Confederacy. This put them well on course to begin undoing the work of Republican Reconstruction. However, just as the Republican Party divided into stark factions in the aftermath of the Civil War (see Chapter 5), so too did the southern Democrats.

During Republican-led Reconstruction, the future of the southern Democratic Party had appeared to be in the balance. Fearing obsolescence, a faction known as the "Conservative–Democrats" considered dropping their opposition to black civil rights and some Republican reforms. This was labeled the "New Departure". This faction was opposed by the so-called **Bourbon Democrats**, who stuck firmly to the antebellum party line in the South: committed to states' rights, a minor role for the federal government, and white supremacy. The faction's detractors gave them the moniker "Bourbon," in reference to the French royal dynasty of that name. As such, the nickname "Bourbon" not only characterized an aristocratic and self-entitled faction, but also a group that wanted to undo a series of radical reforms and revert to an antebellum society. Following President Grant's re-election in 1872, it was the Bourbons that seized control of the southern wing of the party, running successfully in elections as the great "Redeemers" of the region. Between 1873 and 1876, Bourbon Democrats began winning seats across the southern states, and soon began to appoint their own officials and strengthen their grip on power (Perman, 1984: 178).

In the 1870s a number of southern states drew up new white "Redeemer constitutions" to replace those that had been drafted by the biracial conventions in the 1860s. These new constitutions restored small governments along states' rights lines. Though, perhaps the most significant impact of the new Bourbon governments' policies was to be felt in their economic reforms. The Democrats dramatically cut government spending, which in turn allowed for significant tax cuts. Though very popular with the rich and influential, the biggest impact of these reforms was on the poor (especially small farmers and sharecroppers) who scarcely noticed the tax cuts, but certainly felt the cuts to state education and infrastructure spending (Perman, 1984: 211–212). By following such economic policies, one might expect that the Bourbons would have alienated the majority of the southern population. However, a combination of white supremacist ideology, force, fraud, and an appeal to traditional conservative values allowed the Bourbons to keep the substantial black and white underclasses from uniting to usurp them (Feldman, 2013: 27). Nevertheless, it was not long before the Democrats looked to an even more fruitful route to securing power in the South: removing the black vote entirely.

Rebuilding a white South

In the Deep South, moves to restrict black suffrage were made almost as soon as federal troops left in 1877. This was despite the provisions of the Fifteenth Amendment. Some electoral districts achieved this by stuffing ballot boxes and gerrymandering electoral districts in order to disperse black votes into insignificance. Other places adopted poll taxes requiring people to pay in order to vote, a move aimed squarely at the poorest, who also happened to be primarily African American. Michael Perman (2001: 22) contends that widespread moves towards black disfranchisement did not really gain pace across the South as a whole until 1890, a year he sees as the end of the period of "Redemption" and the beginning of a period of "Restoration". However, even with so many obstacles erected against black voters, it was not until 1901 that the final southern black congressman left office: North Carolina's George White. Though these increasing moves towards disenfranchisement were clearly racially motivated, they were also—almost exclusively—aimed at African Americans. In southern states with large Latino populations, such as Texas, the Democrats were more eager to win over Latino voters than to deprive them of the vote. Indeed, the Texan Redeemer government of 1873 actually made it easier for recent immigrants from Latin America to obtain the vote in the hope of boosting their electoral prospects going forward (Williams, 2007: 7–8).

Of course, it was not only the black vote that white supremacists resented, but any semblance of social equality between the races at all. After the weakening of the Black Codes during the period of Republican ascendancy, African Americans had achieved a good deal of integration in many areas of the South. They increasingly rode in the same railroad carriages and ate in the same diners as whites. Yet, after a decade of Democratic rule had passed, southern states began to pass laws to reintroduce racial segregation. These so-called "Jim Crow" laws sought to strip African Americans of a sense of equality, without technically denying them their constitutional rights. The first Jim Crow laws were enacted in Florida in 1887, followed by Mississippi in 1888, Texas in 1889, and most other southern states by 1891 (Woodward, 1971: 211–212). Jim Crow society saw rigid racial lines drawn up to divide a whole host of public services and facilities, leading to an apartheid society that survived largely intact until the mid-twentieth century. Jim Crow affected everything: from churches and restaurants, to playgrounds and prisons. They even went so far as to segregate cemeteries (Woodward, 1955/2002: 7). With disenfranchisement and Jim Crow in full effect by the early 1890s and the ever-present threat of vigilante justice hanging like the sword of Damocles, the age of "Restoration" had truly arrived.

Although the Republican Party was retreating into obsolescence in most parts of the South by the 1890s, there was one final significant challenge to Democratic domination in the South during this period that needs to be accounted for. This came in the form of the farmers' and populist movements. The most politically significant of these movements was the Populist (or People's) Party of the early 1890s. With southern states reconfiguring their economies at the expense of the poorest farmers, some electoral reaction further down the road was not unexpected. This was especially the case when an economic depression hit. Like the main parties, the Populist Party was not a uniform entity across the southern states and its success and composition depended heavily on local social structures—particularly along lines of class and race.

In 1892, the influential Populist leader Tom Watson of Georgia, called for all southerners, black and white, to join together for social justice. He stated: 'It will be to the interest of both that each should have justice' [*Doc. 6, p132*]. In some areas of the South, **Populism** did indeed become a biracial movement. In North Carolina the Populists formed a coalition of sorts with the Republican Party. However, in many other states the Populists remained a white-led movement, and ultimately ended up merging into the Democratic Party (see Chapter 9). Like the earlier Republican threat to their supremacy, the Democrats marshalled all the forces at their disposal to counter the threat of Populism in the South—both legal and "extralegal". Ultimately, the collapse of this new party proved far more rapid and long lasting than that of the southern Republicans (Beeby, 2012: x–xi). By the end of the century the Democrats had a firm hold over the region, which became known as the "**Solid South**".

A New South?

Though the South as envisioned by Democratic politicians might have increased pressure on small farmers in the 1880s and 1890s, there was more to the economic shifts in this period than simply the rich becoming richer. There arose a "New South Movement," calling for industrialization and an overhaul of agriculture, as well as a renewed friendship with the North (Davis, 1990: 13). The editor of the Atlanta *Constitution*, Henry Grady, spoke to an enchanted audience in New England of this "New South"—one of 'new conditions, new adjustments, and, if you please, new ideas and aspirations' (*Sierra Country Advocate*, 1887: 1). New towns arose with increasing frequency, and industrialization belatedly took hold across the South. The Bourbons sought to encourage growth through low taxation not just on the rich, but on railroads and land. Encouraging the growth of rail certainly succeeded and, by 1890, ninety percent of southerners lived in a railroad county. Furthermore, in the 1880s the rate of urban growth in the South was nearly twice the national average. With better communication and increased transport links, southerners began to slowly feel more connected, not only to the rest of their home states, but to the nation as a whole (Ayres, 1992/2007: 7–9). However, these positive figures somewhat distort the overall picture. The South still lagged some way behind the rest of the nation when it came to industrialization. The vast majority of the southern population and its jobs were based in the countryside and within the agricultural sector. The idea of an economic miracle in the New South was far from being all style over substance, but its self-propaganda should not be taken without a few pinches of salt either (Woodward, 1971: 138–141).

Another area in which the South lagged somewhat behind other regions of the nation was in advancing women's rights. The issue of women's suffrage had arisen in the South alongside debates over black suffrage, and again when southern state constitutions were revised during the period of Redemption. However, though women did engage in these debates, few formal organizations arose, and those that did were often short-lived. Indeed, unlike other parts of the country, the South did not see a significant women's suffrage movement form until the late 1890s. Historian Elna Green suggests that one of the reasons for this was the lack of southern involvement in early to mid-century reform movements, especially the abolitionist movement. This meant that women in the South had had fewer opportunities to organize political action groups and engage in debates about human rights. It is not surprising, therefore, that women played a smaller role in the politics of the South during the nineteenth century than women across the rest of the country (Green, 1997: 6–8). Most southern white women adhered to the ideals of "Victorian womanhood," where a woman's place was as a mother and within the home. Indeed, many actively supported this notion. As the years progressed, increasing numbers did start to form women's clubs and reform organizations, and many more sought actively to secure their economic independence (Ayres, 1992/2007: 29). Nonetheless, by the end of the century, the South was almost exclusively run by white, male Democrats.

By the early 1890s, the South had undergone three decades of radical shifts in power. However, it was the region's African American population that had been through the most tumultuous time of all. Though African Americans gained all the rights of U.S. citizenship and had, for a period, enjoyed the rights to vote and hold political office, after the mid-1870s these changes had slowly been reversed. In 1890, Republican congressman Henry Cabot Lodge's "Force Bill," which sought to revive the role of the federal government in supervising elections in the South, was filibustered in the U.S. Senate. In many respects the Lodge Bill represented the last concerted effort by the federal government to stop the "Restoration" of white supremacist rule in the South. By the mid-1890s not only were African Americans being systematically denied the right to vote, but the Jim Crow social order had become firmly entrenched. In 1895, the leading African American spokesperson of the era, **Booker T. Washington**, delivered his famous "Atlanta Compromise" address—where he uttered the memorable line: 'In all things that are purely social we can be as separate as the fingers, yet one as the hand in all things essential to mutual progress' [*Doc. 7, p133*]. Although Washington is often unfairly characterized as being too concessionary when it came to civil rights, he had ultimately chosen to work within—rather than against—the southern system in order to achieve progress for other black Americans. Washington was best known for espousing black technical education, through institutions such as his own in Tuskegee, Alabama, but—at least in public—argued that seeking social equality was asking too much, too soon.

The year after Washington's address, the U.S. Supreme Court echoed his public sentiments in their infamous decision, *Plessy v. Ferguson* (1896).

The majority decision of the court stated: 'We consider the underlying fallacy of the plaintiff's argument to consist in the assumption that the enforced separation of the two races stamps the colored race with a badge of inferiority'. The Supreme Court felt that black and white citizens could be both "separate" and "equal"—that so long as constitutional rights were not undermined, segregation was an acceptable state of affairs. In his dissenting opinion, Justice John Marshall Harlan called southern segregation statutes 'sinister legislation' that sought to relegate blacks to 'a condition of legal inferiority'. Harlan's view, however, was not to be recognized until a far later Supreme Court decision in 1954, when *Brown v. Board of Education* finally started to overturn the doctrine of "separate but equal".

The "long Reconstruction" period in the South saw many of the rhetorical battles of the Civil War refought: issues such as states' rights and African American rights arose time and again. For African American activists, like historian W. E. B. Du Bois, the reality of the "New South" by the 1890s was that of a renewed slave society in all but name. For many white southerners, this was exactly what had been intended. Many of them adhered to what became known as the "Lost Cause": a halfway house between accepting the new order of abolition and reunion, and holding onto the antebellum ideals of states' rights, white supremacy, and the sense that their grievances in 1861 were fair (Foster, 1987: 5).

Just as the Bourbon monarchy had re-established a watered-down form of their *ancien régime* in France after the fall of Napoleon, so the Bourbon Democrats had re-established their diminished form of an antebellum slave society in the 1890s. These words from a Union soldier to a group of freedmen and women in South Carolina in the aftermath of the Civil War might well have seemed even more pertinent in 1896 than they did when delivered in the 1860s:

> You are free but you must know that the only difference you can feel yet, between slavery and freedom, is that neither you nor your children can be bought or sold. You may have a harder time ... than ever before; it will be the price you pay for your freedom.
>
> (Aiken, 1998: 17)

Though the New South was far more stable than the fractious Reconstruction regime that had preceded it, regional stability and increasingly cordial relations with the rest of the nation had ultimately been achieved through sacrificing African American civil rights altogether. Perhaps no event better represented the culmination of this than the Wilmington race riot of 1898: a campaign of violence led by white southerners bent on gaining control of a majority-black city in North Carolina. It resulted in several deaths and a victory for white supremacy (Tyson and Cecelski, 1998). Far from bringing unity to the region, Redemption and Restoration had firmly enshrined the doctrine of racial "separation" across the South for decades to come.

4 The course of westward expansion

At the start of the Civil War the United States was not just torn apart along a north–south axis; there was also a great division between its east and west. The fast-growing nation laid claim to lands spanning from Atlantic-bound Maine in the Northeast, to the relatively new state of California on the Pacific border with Mexico. However, between the established states in the East and West lay vast expanses of land largely unsettled by U.S. citizens: the "frontier" of American civilization. Although migrants from the East had started to settle, and many Hispanic settlers and Native Americans already called this region their home, these populations were still very sparse. As Map 4.1 shows, U.S. territory had grown rapidly in the early nineteenth century, but settlement of these new regions had only just started to gather pace before the Civil War.

Many Native Americans who lived in the West had been forced there during earlier decades when the U.S. had expanded into some of the more easterly regions Native peoples had previously inhabited. However, it was not just Native Americans who felt pressured into settling in the West before the war. Thousands of Mormons moved west to escape persecution further east, largely settling in Utah territory by the 1830s and 1840s. Hundreds of others trekked overland via routes to the Pacific Coast, such as the Oregon and Santa Fe trails, in order to seek greater freedom, a new start, or greater economic possibilities. These early settlers, however, were just a precursor to the far greater interest in U.S. expansion to the region that followed.

In the 1840s, fervor in the U.S. grew for the country to formally expand into the West. By 1845, journalist John O'Sullivan had coined the phrase "**Manifest Destiny**" to describe the belief that the United States had a divine right to expand across North America from the Atlantic to the Pacific. Soon enough this concept became a rallying cry for expansionists. The years that followed saw the United States stretch its borders all the way to the Pacific, following war with Mexico and negotiations with Great Britain. With all of this new territory, including Texas (a "slave state") and California (a "free state"), the onus then fell upon the government to connect the West to the rest of the nation. However, the great issue of slavery loomed heavily over this task, just as it did over almost every aspect of policymaking before the

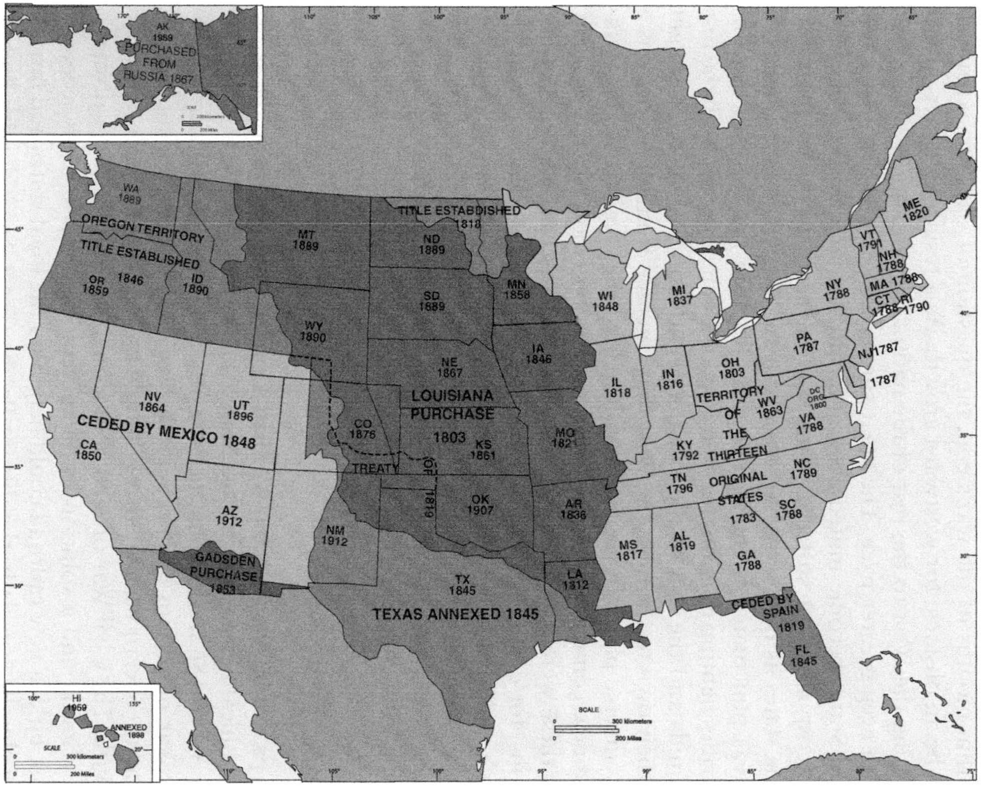

Map 4.1 U.S. Expansion and Admission of New States, after: "Admission of States and Territorial Acquisition," U.S. Bureau of the Census, available from Perry–Castañeda Library at the University of Texas at Austin at: https://legacy.lib.utexas.edu/maps/united_states/territory.jpg (accessed 14 December 2019)

war. Debates over the extension of slavery into the rest of the western territories complicated expansion. The South in particular feared that countless new states in the West might threaten the delicate pro-slavery/anti-slavery balance in the U.S. Senate. As a result, westward expansion became a key issue in driving the nation toward civil war.

During the war, the Union government had set the groundwork for enlargement, partly to connect the loyal Union states and partly because southern opposition to expansion had been temporarily removed. Furthermore, within months of the war's end, the question of slavery's expansion ceased to be an obstacle for westward growth. As a result, the great project of connecting the West to the rest of the nation, by rail and by settlement, began with even greater pace. The great surge of westward expansion saw the United States become united geographically. Of course, this expansion came at a cost; and none suffered so much at the hands of the great unification of the states as the Native Americans of the West. The late nineteenth century was punctuated by numerous wars between the U.S. and various western tribes fighting to maintain their way of life; fending off both the loss of their lands and the loss of their distinctive identities as the U.S. sought to unify their own territories. The West that emerged from all of this was a markedly diverse place. In common with many other regions of the country where new communities arose, differences soon emerged, and in many instances these were imported with the settlers themselves. Minority ethnic populations, for example, faced a great deal of discrimination, particularly in securing and maintaining jobs. The quest to unify the West succeeded in the broadest sense, via rail and settlement, but during this process new divisions arose—divisions not all that dissimilar from those apparent in other parts of the country.

Connecting the West

Two acts passed during the Civil War had a long-lasting impact on the growing geographical unity of the United States. The first of these was the Pacific Railroad Act of 1862. Although the idea of a transcontinental railroad predated the war, politicians had been divided over where exactly it should run. Of particular concern was whether it should pass mainly through the North or the South. The Civil War offered both a further stimulus for a railway to unite the country and a solution to the difficulties of passing the necessary legislation. First, a new railroad could help bind the loyal states and territories more closely, especially the distant Pacific Coast. Second, with "rebel" southern politicians absent from the U.S. Congress, the arguments against a northern route for the railroad swiftly evaporated. In order to encourage the success of this new venture, the government gave generous grants of federal land to railroad companies, and a second act (in 1864) offered further financial incentives (Billings, 2012: 705–708). This new railroad would not only physically connect the distant reaches of the nation, but provide a vital artery for moving people, goods, and equipment far more rapidly. When completed in May 1869, one Iowa newspaper stated:

> It is a matter of pride to know that the rail is now laid that binds the East and West together. On Monday last, the last spike was driven in the last rail that completes the Pacific Railroad, at Promontory Summit [Utah], among the mountains. Chicago rejoiceth greatly thereat, and so, too, does the whole country. Now, at last, we have a railroad completed from ocean to ocean.
>
> (*Tama County Republican*, 1869: 2)

Although the railroads now helped to connect the growing nation's disparate parts, the next move to develop greater unity was to settle the areas that divided them. Just as the route of a transcontinental railroad had divided the nation before the war, so had the issue of settling the West. Southern politicians had insisted that slavery should be allowed to take root in the West, whereas the North increasingly rejected this idea. The Civil War removed this obstacle. The Homestead Act of 1862 was a piece of legislation that had been vetoed before the war by President Buchanan but was passed without issue in the midst of war. Its primary purpose was to draw settlers into the West by offering them 160 acres of land, which homesteaders would need to cultivate and settle for five years before they could finally call it their own. Within three years 25,000 settlers had claimed around three million acres of land (Nester, 2013: 166). In the decades that followed, Congress passed further legislation to encourage settlement of the more difficult terrain of the West; The Timber Culture Act (1873), the Desert Land Act (1877), and the Timber and Stone Act (1878). These various government measures drew thousands more settlers into the territories that lay between the existing states. Like the growth of railroads, the Homestead Act and other legislative incentives helped to bring the nation together in a more physical sense.

While the government clearly did its best to incentivize westward settlement, it was important that those considering such a move saw the frontier as an attractive prospect. For some, this inducement came in the form of the cattle industry, which had grown up feeding the mining and railroad towns of earlier periods of migration. With increased railroad connections and improvements in refrigeration, cattle could now be moved to the far larger markets of the East Coast with ease. The cattle trails established in the mid-1860s by early "cattle barons" like Charles Goodnight were used by hundreds of cowboys in the years that followed. In the two decades after the Civil War, cattlemen introduced over five million animals, primarily Texan Longhorns, during a veritable cattle boom (Knowlton, 2017: 6–7). Entrepreneurs like Joseph G. McCoy sought to exploit this situation. McCoy built the small settlement of Abilene, Kansas, into the first real "cow town"; it sat at the end of certain cattle drives and so the steers could be loaded directly onto trains travelling east. As rail links grew ever easier, and selective breeding created cows with a greater meat yield than the Longhorns, the early success of pioneers like McCoy led to a vast industry spanning the entire West (Billington & Ridge, 2001: 323–324). James Brisbin's 1881 best seller, *The Beef Bonanza, or How to Get Rich on the Plains*, described a mythical frontier where 'the buffalo still roams and the wild savage dwells', but where fortunes could also be made from the cattle industry. Accounts such as Brisbin's influenced migrants from the East Coast and from Europe, who were drawn to the potential of the West as a place to get rich quick (Brown, 1995: 291–292). The potential to make money was vital in drawing settlers west and helping increase the population of the western territories.

The cattle bonanza in the West was, however, not without its negative consequences. The popularity of the cattle trade led to overstocking and overgrazing of the land. Ever-larger herds were increasingly susceptible to predators, wildfires, and diseases. These latter problems were further exacerbated by the division of land by fences and barbed wire—itself an American innovation of this period, patented in 1874 by Joseph Glidden—that kept herds from the free-ranging of earlier years and literally penned them in. Diverting water supplies for farmlands and cattle also resulted in the depletion of groundwater, another environmental error that would only grow more problematic with time. As early as the 1880s, these problems were clear enough to make cattle barons think again about their practices, and many started to move towards a system of cattle ranging mixed with farming (Donahue, 1999: 127–128; Elofson, 2000: 144–155). However, life on the plains after the 1880s never yielded the great returns of the earlier era, and by the end of the century the consequences of earlier exploitation still hit hard.

Beyond cattle, the natural resources below the ground also continued to lure settlers long after the great gold rushes in California (from 1849) and Colorado (from 1859). During the Civil War, petitions to organize formal territories in the West were driven by many interest groups, but perhaps none more vocal than the various mining groups. Even as Congress was debating the status of Idaho Territory in the 1860s, mining interests were moving to the region seeking to beat other potential fortune seekers. In the mid-1870s, following rumors of gold in the Dakota badlands, there was a rush to the Black Hills. Soon after, Colorado became the silver hub of the West following discoveries in Leadville and Aspen, and by 1887 the city of Butte in Montana had become the world's leading copper producer (Rohrbough, 2004: 119–120). The rushes for gold and other such valuable resources led to the formation of numerous boom towns across the West, such as Custer City and Deadwood. Although the potential for fortunes to be made in the West encouraged settlement, it was not always permanent and often had negative long term effects on the region's environment. The legacy of many of these boom towns and mining communities often being the abandoned waste and polluted rivers that were left behind, along with the ghost towns, where the once burgeoning populations disappeared after the area's resources were exhausted (Billington & Ridge, 2001: 273–278).

One common frustration for those seeking to tame the West and join the nation together was the bison or "American buffalo". Tens of millions of bison roamed across lands the cattle industry wished to clear and exploit, and rail and telegraph companies remained concerned by the damage these creatures could do to their lines when stampeding in their thousands. The result was a war of extermination waged against the bison of the plains. Though pioneers had hunted bison long before the Civil War; after the conflict even soldiers were made to take up the job. Tourists traveling on the new railroads were encouraged to hunt for pleasure, while professional hunters capitalized on the growing market for bison hides at home and abroad. While the decimation of the bison population smoothed the way for the unification of the nation by communication and settlement, it had a huge impact on those who had called the plains home for far longer. Native Americans of the region, who relied on the bison as a source of food, shelter, fuel, and clothing, were robbed of a vital part of their ecosystem (Knowlton, 2017: 5–14). It remains impossible to say whether the Native American reliance on bison was environmentally sustainable in the long term, but the additional impact of U.S. settlers and hunters after the Civil War saw the bison population collapse within a staggering fifteen years (Flores, 1991: 484–485). The fact that the war against bison had such a negative impact on Native Americans was viewed by some U.S. settlers as a positive thing. After all, when it came to "clearing" the West for U.S. settlement, Native Americans were also on the list of unwanted inconveniences from the point of view of policymakers.

Native Americans

Native Americans were the primary settlers of the Great Plains of the West prior to the Civil War, often having been driven from homes elsewhere during earlier eras of expansion by European powers and the United States. When it came to reuniting the nation after the Civil War, the U.S. approach to Native Americans took on a number of forms. The most basic of these was violent confrontation leading to either the removal or "extermination" of Native Americans by the increasing numbers of U.S. troops moved to the plains after the war. An early example of such action came in 1864, when Colonel John M. Chivington felt removing Native Americans might serve his growing political ambitions in Colorado. In late November, after half-hearted efforts at diplomacy had broken down, his drunken men massacred a Cheyenne village. While the men were out hunting, over 100 women and children were slaughtered. In response to force, and fearing future U.S. expansion, some Native Americans took the initiative in trying to turn the tide. In December 1866, Native Americans in Wyoming struck a mighty blow against U.S. troops at Fort Philip Kearny in what became known as the "Fetterman Massacre" (after the captain in charge of the U.S. forces) (White, 1991: 96–97). The settling of the West saw many such violent encounters, and wars with Native Americans continued to punctuate U.S. expansion into this region in the decades after the Civil War's end.

A second method the United States had long used to move Native Americans from land they desired was diplomacy (often combined with the threat of violence). The U.S. had signed numerous treaties with different Native American peoples, treating them as separate "nations" within their own growing country. By 1867, when numerous Native American tribes and U.S. troops had tired of continual fighting, they came together to agree the Treaty of Medicine Lodge. Like many earlier agreements, the treaty aimed to move the plains tribes. In this case, the immediate aim was to settle Native Americans on reservations within Indian Territory (later Oklahoma), with a future goal of making them U.S. citizens and bringing them fully under U.S. control (Calloway, 2013: 182). The U.S. thus managed to control the movement and settlement of Native Americans, with a view to imposing further controls in the future.

Throughout the history of U.S. treaty making with Native American peoples, a deal was no sooner sealed than calls for its retraction were being made. A good example of this was the 1868 Fort Laramie Treaty with the Sioux people, assigning the sacred Black Hills of Dakota to their reservation. As was so often the case, the U.S. ceded land it considered valueless only for value to be found later. By 1874, rumors of gold in the Black Hills saw miners trespassing onto Native American land and meeting staunch resistance from the Sioux. These repeated clashes soon led to calls for U.S. military support. In a bid to avoid military involvement, the Native Americans met with U.S. representatives but their aims were entirely at odds, and the U.S. commissioners returned to Washington with a recommendation that Congress force a land sale upon the Sioux (Brown, 1970/1991: 279–284). The result was the U.S. engineering yet another conflict by demanding submission of Native Americans willing to take up arms to defend their land. This particular conflict was to prove the most oft-described and ill-fated of them all from a U.S. point of view. The famed "last stand" of General George Custer at the Battle of the Little Bighorn in 1876 was an impressive Native American rout of U.S. forces. Yet, though it represented the highpoint of Native American resistance in the post-war period, it also turned out to be the spark for its rapid and terminal decline. The death of Custer saw him rise to become a popular martyr (see Figure 4.1) and his name became a rallying cry for a nation already set upon realizing its "Manifest Destiny". Following the Battle of the Little Bighorn, the U.S. redoubled its efforts to thwart Native American defiance and moved even more troops to the plains (Utley & Washburn, 1977/1987: 246–247). By the following year, the Sioux were defeated and the U.S. government seized the lands they had refused to part with.

If the Battle of the Little Bighorn marked a turning point for U.S.–Native American relations, another event represented the final stand of Native American resistance in the West. For those unwilling to surrender to continued

Figure 4.1 "General Custer's Death Struggle: The Battle of the Little Big Horn" (1878)

Niday Picture Library/Alamy Stock Photo

U.S. encroachment on their lands and annulment of their treaties, the end came at Wounded Knee Creek in 1890. In December 1890, the U.S. military took 350 suspected Native American "ghost dancers" prisoner at Wounded Knee (230 of whom were women and children). The "Ghost Dance" was a religious movement that believed white settlers would soon be swept from North America and Native Americans' ancestors would return to reclaim the continent; a destiny that could be hastened by ritualistic dancing. When troops went to disarm their prisoners, the resistance of one led to an indiscriminate massacre by U.S. soldiers using Hotchkiss machine guns. One estimate suggested that nearly 300 of the original 350 Native Americans were killed, as well as 25 U.S. soldiers (many of the latter being struck by their own fire). The Massacre of Wounded Knee became an enduring symbol of the end of Native American resistance and the final conquest of the West by the United States military (Brown, 1970/1991: 439–445).

In the years coinciding with intermittent diplomacy and more frequent violent suppression of Native tribes, there was a third method the United States used to neutralize Native American resistance: incorporating them into the nation and making them "American". This method became all the more pressing as the amount of "empty" land to move Native peoples onto was rapidly disappearing. The primary government agency for dealing with

Native peoples in this era was the Office of Indian Affairs (OIA), which dated back to 1824. By 1869 the OIA had approximately 500 field staff and was headed by its first Native American commissioner, Ely S. Parker. Parker advocated a formal change in the relationship between the federal government and Native tribes, from the status of sovereign "nations" to "wards" of the U.S. government. For anthropologist Valerie Lambert (2016: 345), Parker's Civil War-influenced ideals led him to believe that this was a route toward greater national unity. Just as the Confederacy had been forced to cede sovereignty for the greater good of the nation, the same could be the case with Native Americans. From this point of view, the ongoing fighting against Native Americans after the Civil War was an extension of the war's unifying mission. Only when all of those who lived between the East and West Coasts of the United States were pacified *and* integrated, could the Union continue its rebuilding mission in earnest.

For assimilation to be successful, however, even greater changes would need to be brought about for Native American societies than those of the defeated southern states. Native Americans were far more culturally distinct and many in the U.S. regarded them—like African Americans—as racially inferior and in need of uplift. One solution was the establishment of Native American boarding schools. The U.S. federal government oversaw a system whereby Native American children were taken from their communities to spend several years being taught Anglo–American culture, so that ultimately this would turn them into "true" Americans (Gram, 2016: 252–253). By 1879 there were around 500 teachers in 64 boarding schools, as well as almost 300 day schools, educating over 13,000 Native American students. Though the goals of such education might have seemed progressive, the alternative to accepting "civilization" along U.S. lines was, in the view of Carl Schurz (President Hayes' Secretary of the Interior), extermination (Reyhner & Eder, 2004: 72–80). In order to encourage the next generation to embrace American citizenship, Native Americans were, over time, to be stripped of the characteristics the United States considered as uncivilized and un-American. Assimilation and "Americanization" would be key to bringing the West fully into the Union.

Once assimilation or extermination had become the choice presented by the U.S. government to most Native American peoples, the final step was to end their separate land rights and erode the large reservations they had previously been moved onto. In 1871, President Grant signed into law an act that formally ended treaty making with Native American tribes. No longer would the United States recognize these peoples as sovereign political entities (Prucha, 1994: 310). Agreements and land cessions would continue apace but, from this point onward, the U.S. openly acknowledged a lowering in status of the agreements being made. In the years that followed, white settlement on lands reserved for Native Americans increased rapidly. By 1890, the non-Native American population even of Indian Territory was around seventy percent. The U.S government tacitly encouraged white settlement onto lands that were technically out-of-bounds, as it helped bolster their aim to assimilate the Native peoples (Marks, 1998: 155–156).

The continuing erosion of Native Americans' land rights was noted at length by Sioux leader, **Sitting Bull**, a veteran of the Little Bighorn. In his testimony before a Senate Committee, set up to investigate the condition of the Sioux Indians upon their reservation, he noted:

> Our reservation is not as large as we want it to be, and I suppose the Great Father [U.S. president] owes us money now for land he has taken from us in the past … I sit here and look around me now, and I see my people starving.
>
> [*Doc. 8, p134*]

Despite such entreaties, U.S. moves to dispossess Native Americans continued unimpeded. In 1887, the most decisive move toward breaking up Native American lands came with the passage of the Dawes Act. This measure attempted to introduce American values such as "individualism" to the Native American communities, while having the useful side effect of dividing up reservations into small plots and allowing other U.S. citizens to buy any "surplus" land (Reyhner & Eder, 2004: 81–82). By the dawn of the twentieth century, the entire West had been organized and rearranged as either U.S. territories or new states of the union. The final three states of the forty-eight contiguous states: Oklahoma (1907) and New Mexico and Arizona (1912) were organized in areas with large Native American populations. With the recognition of these new states, the concept of Manifest Destiny—which had dominated the mid-nineteenth century—was effectively realized. However, the West that was created was not quite as harmoniously "integrated" as some had hoped it would be.

Life in the West

As Native Americans were increasingly moved to ever-shrinking reservations, the various attractions and government incentives noted earlier led thousands to settle in areas of the West that had previously seen little if any settlement by migrants. However, despite the tales of prosperity that came out of the region, the lifestyle that faced many new settlers was challenging. Although railroads connected the region in parts and fear of Native Americans gradually subsided, vast areas were still remote and relatively hostile environments. Large tracts of land lacked adequate fuel or building materials for new arrivals. In these areas, settlers were forced to use dry bison dung for fuel and build "sod" houses from the very earth itself. Though some moved in groups and formed new communities in the West, many rural settlers remained relatively isolated. The idea that the country felt more united seemed more real on a map than in day-to-day life. Meanwhile, the boom towns that grew rapidly around cattle stations and mineral resources were so hastily constructed that little held them together beyond the local saloon. These towns lacked a clear sense of community or cohesiveness. The West, it seemed, was growing to be quite a varied patchwork of a place.

The communities that settled on the western frontier were often as diverse as those across the rest of the nation. In fact, by 1900 the foreign-born population of North Dakota stood at 35.4 percent—the highest in the country, and well above the national average of 13.6 percent (Luebke, 1998: x–xvi). Though the majority of these foreign-born migrants were from Europe (see Chapter 8 for more on these groups), and particularly nations that fit with many white, Anglo-Saxon, protestant (WASP) credentials, there were many "non-white" settlers that made the West more ethnically diverse than some might think. As ideas of racial and ethnic diversity caused divisions and controversy across the rest of the country, the West proved to be no exception.

Aside from the many remaining Native Americans, the other primary "non-white" settlers in the West can be divided roughly into three groups: Hispanics, Asians, and African Americans. Hispanic settlers had long cultural roots in the region, particularly the rural parts of the West that had once been part of Mexico. However, as the century progressed, many Hispanic Americans and newer Hispanic migrants moved to the growing towns and cities where there was great demand for unskilled manual work (White, 1991: 322–324). Asian migrants were also drawn to the region by the growing demand for labor, and economic potential was also a factor for many African Americans moving west. For some, such as the African American "Exodusters" who moved to Kansas in the 1870s, the West also offered the potential of a fresh start away from the more oppressive social order being re-established in other states. The West offered white and "non-white" immigrants alike the potential of a new beginning, but the communities they created were not always more progressive or unified than those they had left behind.

The American West of the nineteenth century is frequently portrayed, both in historical texts and popular culture, as the "Wild West". Even during the time the West was being settled, dime novels and travelling shows (such as those of "Buffalo Bill" Cody), spread a sense of the West as being a place of conflict and violence. Although a good part of this image tended to focus on clashes between Native Americans and U.S. citizens, it also applied to disputes within the western communities themselves. Violence on the frontier manifested itself in a variety of different ways and, as most settlements had little in the way of formal legal infrastructure, violence often went unpunished by law enforcement officials. Many of the minority ethnic groups that lived in the West suffered at the hands of a harsh form of "frontier justice," which was not all that far removed from the racially-motivated lynchings that prevailed across the South in the late nineteenth century. California, for example, saw a number of malicious attacks directed toward its Chinese and Hispanic populations. Many white workers disliked the additional competition from "non-white" workers for low-paid and unskilled jobs. White workers often assumed that non-white laborers would work for less money than they would, and this would either lead to lower wages for them or their replacement. Although the bulk of anti-Chinese violence was found in California, where most Chinese immigrants had settled, in time it spread to far more remote settlements. For example, in 1885, white miners in Rock Springs, Wyoming viciously attacked their Chinese workmates, killing and injuring several of them in the process. The West might have brought people together in a new place, but it did not always bring them together as a cohesive society.

As well as the high levels of racially motivated violence in the West, there was also a good deal of lawlessness that went beyond race. Roger McGrath's (1984) study of the towns of Aurora and Bodie in Nevada shows that such lawlessness was far from uncommon, even if it did not characterize the West to quite the extent that many novels and movies have suggested. So infamous did the lawlessness in towns such as Dodge City, Kansas, become that their leaders hired lawmen to try and curb their citizens' propensity for 'killing a man for breakfast every morning' (Brown, 1995: 280). Gunfights, such as that at the O.K. Corral in Tombstone, Arizona, in 1881—featuring the legendary characters Doc Holliday and Wyatt Earp—became the stuff of pop culture legend in their own day. In some instances, the scale of the conflicts within communities came to resemble warfare. Of particular note was the feud between big cattlemen and their smaller rivals in Wyoming at the start of the 1890s, which became known as the Johnson County War. Ultimately, though, as populations in the West grew, so did the extent of governance within the territories. A series of fully-fledged states emerged and gradually the tide of extra-legal violence began to turn. As the century came to an end, the West was starting to become a more established part of the wider nation.

Many of the popular histories of the West often neglect one final crucial set of actors in the settlement of the region: women. Early texts often portrayed the West as an area conquered and settled by men alone. Perhaps some of this was due to the fact that men made up the vast majority of the settlers in the various boom towns that were the focus of much popular literature. Yet, demographic studies have shown that, although this was true of mining towns, it was not true of the West as a whole. The State of Nebraska, for instance, had a fairly even gender balance from the outset (Jensen & Miller, 2004: 18–19). Despite this, few western women have been subjected to significant historical scrutiny. Perhaps the best-known exception to this rule is Martha Canary, better known as Calamity Jane. As a figure who accompanied military expeditions, entered Deadwood with Wild Bill Hickok, and joined the mining rush to the Black Hills, she might well have been selected for attention precisely because of her supposedly "masculine" experiences. However, she was also a mother, a cook, and a businesswoman, all of which are rarely mentioned in popular portrayals (McLaird, 2005: 3–6). Calamity Jane is a useful example of an individual who represented a number of different things to different audiences, a little like the West itself. However, with the gradual integration of this diverse and complex West, the idea of the "frontier" which it had once represented seemed to be slipping away.

In 1890, the U.S. Census Bureau suggested that there was no longer an American frontier—the imagined boundary between settled and unsettled land that had existed since the nation's founding had disappeared. In this sense, 1890 was a landmark year for unity. The nation's population now spanned the continent. Yet, for historian Frederick Jackson Turner, it also marked another juncture in American history. His famous essay, *The Significance of the Frontier in American History* (1893), not only popularized the idea of the end of the frontier, but also reviewed its importance in the development of the United States to that point. For Turner, the United States' continuous westward expansion had helped forge a peculiarly American character. Westward expansion and settlement had helped the U.S. move away from Europe to a new 'growth of independence on American lines' [*Doc. 9, p135*]. The closing of the frontier thus posed new questions about what would continue to make the United States "American".

Since the time Turner's "**frontier thesis**" was first advanced, generations of historians and commentators have attempted to define what precisely the West and the "frontier" represented in U.S. history. Where Turner saw the West as the 'the meeting point between savagery and civilization' [*Doc. 9, p135*], subsequent interpretations have regarded the region less as a borderland and more as a cultural crossroads. The Wild West of dime novels was a land full of adversity, adventure, and violence, and many commentators and historians in the twentieth century continued to portray the West along just such lines. However, more recent interpretations have moved on to consider the region as one of diverse communities sometimes compromising, sometimes conflicting, but almost always interacting and intermingling (Etulain, 2004: 509). Either way, it would be hard to conclude that by 1890 the West had brought about a clearer national unity in anything other than a geographical or demographic sense. The region had been conquered and sparsely settled, but new divisions had already arisen along ethnic and economic lines. Indeed, as the region's longstanding tension—that between the U.S. and Native Americans—had been largely subdued, divisions familiar to the rest of the nation had soon come to rise in its place.

5 Party politics in the Gilded Age

In 1873, Mark Twain and Charles Dudley Warner published a satirical novel called *The Gilded Age: A Tale of Today*. Since then, the term has most often been used to characterize a period of stagnation, **laissez-faire** economic policies, and endemic corruption in U.S. politics. It is easy to identify many of these features in the presidency of Ulysses Grant (1869–1877). During his two terms, the dominant Republican Party's reputation began to deteriorate among northern voters. This was not helped by the national press revealing a series of scandals implicating numerous high-profile members of Grant's administration. The years that followed saw a number of lesser-known figures ascend to the presidency, but each of them was held back by party divisions over key issues such as political reform and economic policy.

By the late 1870s, the nation had become more divided in their voting intentions. Yet, for many voters, there was little to help tell the parties apart, at least on an ideological level. In the 1860s and early Reconstruction era, political battles over civil rights, citizenship, and states' rights had been fiercely and clearly contested between the Republicans and Democrats. However, with the end of Congressional Reconstruction, more practical issues such as currency reform came to the fore, and such issues often divided both of the main parties and their supporters.

In 1884, **Grover Cleveland** became the first Democrat elected to the presidency since the end of Congressional Reconstruction. Rather than marking a turn of the political tide, his presidency further exacerbated political divisions. Cleveland was a strong advocate of the **gold standard** as a basis for the U.S. economy, putting him at odds with many in his own party. By 1892, the electorate's increasing frustration with the divided and discredited major parties was beginning to show more clearly. New groups, like the Populist (or People's) Party, began to win seats in Congress under an electoral system that favored only two parties. It looked like the stale politics of the Republicans and Democrats might finally have driven the nation to look for answers elsewhere.

Reestablishing Republican governance

In 1869, after the chaos of Andrew Johnson's presidency, Grant called upon citizens to do their share 'toward cementing a happy union' (Grant, 1869). Yet, to achieve a successful reunion, Grant believed the South had to accept a very Republican view of post-war harmony. His administration oversaw the ratification of the Fifteenth Amendment, defended African American rights, and firmly cracked down on the Ku Klux Klan. However, Grant's punitive approach toward the South led to breaks within his own party and the brief insurgency of the so-called "Liberal Republicans" who favored a more moderate approach to white southern views. Ultimately, these insurgents ran a joint campaign with the Democrats behind Horace Greeley. Though Grant easily triumphed in his campaign for re-election, the seeds of internal discord had already been sown (see Chapter 2).

Grant, as one of his biographers puts it, though regularly celebrated 'as one of the Republic's greatest generals', is also 'denigrated as one of its worst presidents' (Simpson, 1991: xiii). This sense that Grant's administration was so disappointing is largely down to the series of corruption scandals that arose during his time in office. The first symptoms of this problem arose during the so-called "Gold Ring" scandal of 1869. Grant's brother-in-law was involved in a scheme that manipulated the price of gold for the profit of a select few by using insider knowledge of government economic policies. By the time of the 1872 election, however, the more infamous Crédit Mobilier scandal had broken. Congressional investigations into this episode, which saw the Union Pacific Railroad Company use a "dummy corporation" to funnel cash to politicians, led to the censure of two members of the House and the expulsion of a U.S. senator (see Figure 5.1). Thereafter, the scandals just kept coming. There was the "Whiskey Ring" scandal of the mid-1870s, which saw Grant's personal secretary linked to an illegal operation that paid off tax collectors to avoid alcohol duties. Then there was the "Indian Ring" scandal, which led to Grant's secretary of war being impeached—and later acquitted—for his involvement in a scheme that saw Native American trading post concessions sold for secret kickbacks (Nester, 2013: 251–252).

By 1876, the idea that Grant had allowed such widespread corruption within his administration to go unchecked made some regard the president as the guilty party. After all, how could the president have been so consistently blind to the actions of those around him? Of course, there were other factors working against the Republicans in 1876. The nation was still recovering from the "Panic of 1873"—an international banking crisis that had dealt a strong blow to the U.S. economy. Outside of the South, the rest of the nation had grown increasingly weary of Reconstruction, with Grant's interventionist approach going thoroughly out of fashion. Faced with a divided and seemingly corrupt administration, an economic downturn, and strong public skepticism about continued federal intervention in the South, the Republicans faced an uphill battle in 1876.

Figure 5.1 Uncle Sam directs U.S. Senators (and Representatives) implicated in the Crédit Mobilier of America scandal to commit Hari-Kari. Carl Schurz and Charles Sumner peer out from behind a screen (1873)

Niday Picture Library/Alamy Stock Photo

If the taint of corruption already loomed heavily over the final days of Grant's presidency, the election of 1876 did nothing to help matters. Rutherford B. Hayes' election was anything but straightforward and required him to strike a "corrupt bargain" in 1877 before he was able to take office (see Chapter 2). Many regarded him as a pretender to the office. Some even mockingly referred to him as "His Fraudulency" (De Santis, 1963: 97). Despite this, Hayes had been nominated as a reform candidate by the Republicans in 1876 and, as such, he faced fierce opposition from the Grant loyalists within his own party. This faction was nicknamed the "**Stalwarts**". Led by New York senator **Roscoe Conkling**, they exemplified an increasingly damaging rise of internal division within the Republican Party.

The Stalwarts detested Hayes' talk of civil service reform, or, as they called it, "snivel service reform". Any attempt to meddle with the existing system and make appointments more meritocratic was bad news for figures like Conkling. He had made his political career from distributing such offices for "favors" in what was known as the "**spoils system**". Hayes' struggle with his own party did not end with the Stalwarts though, as another faction within the **"Grand Old Party"** (**G.O.P.**) seemed equally set on frustrating their new leader. This faction, labelled the "**Half-Breeds,**" was led by a discontented presidential candidate from 1876, Senator **James G. Blaine**. In addition to these internal party splits, Hayes faced a divided government—where Congress and the White House were not controlled by the same party. "Division" appeared to be the defining feature of Hayes' early days in office.

In recognition of the challenges before him, Hayes sounded a conciliatory tone in his 1877 inaugural address. He called upon citizens to unite in order to achieve 'a union depending not upon the constraint of force, but upon the loving devotion of a free people' [*Doc. 10, p136*]. For his supporters, Hayes' moderation, reformism, and ability to stand aside from factionalism made him an ideal figure to unite the nation. However, his compromise cabinet appointees—including a Democratic southerner as postmaster general and the "Liberal Republican" Carl Schurz as secretary of the interior—did little to satisfy his most prominent Republican critics. They not only disliked these appointees but loathed the fact that their spoilsmen had not been appointed instead. Blaine and Conkling were so disgruntled that they attempted to use congressional checking powers to block the president's appointees, only relenting when press and public attention turned against them (Vazzano, 2006: 523–529).

Where Hayes' cabinet appointments frustrated his critics, his determination to reform the civil service infuriated them. In his inaugural address, Hayes called for 'a reform that shall be thorough, radical, and complete; a return to the principles and practices of the founders of the Government' (Williams, 1914: 8). Good to his word, Hayes successfully lobbied for the removal of **Chester A. Arthur** as the collector of the Port of New York. Arthur was one of Conkling's protégés and the president's move, predictably, enraged the senator. However, though this was a high-profile move that gained a good deal of press attention, it also proved to be an exception to the rule. Wholesale reform of the civil service never really regained this momentum during the rest of Hayes' term (Hoogenboom, 2003: 109).

Aside from taking on the factions within his own party, Hayes also challenged the Democrats who controlled the House of Representatives. He used his presidential veto to frustrate appropriations bills that contained "riders" aimed at undermining black voting rights in the South. In this regard, the president was good to his inaugural address and its talk of universal male suffrage and rights. Nevertheless, one should not forget that Hayes also withdrew federal troops from Louisiana and South Carolina who were there to ensure such voting laws were respected (Vazzano, 2006: 535–536). When it came to other minority ethnic groups, Hayes also appeared to take a relatively progressive approach. He favored Grant's advocacy of assimilation—rather than extermination—of Native Americans, and he vetoed a bill that aimed to specifically prevent Chinese immigration in 1879. However, assimilation was certainly not the preference of most Native Americans, and Hayes vetoed the Chinese exclusion bill over a matter of treaty commitments, rather than because he supported continued migration. Indeed, Hayes went on to negotiate treaty changes that achieved most of what the vetoed bill had suggested in the first place (Hoogenboom, 2003: 108–110).

Hayes' record on civil rights and immigration could be interpreted generously as somewhat progressive but, in reality, represented a continued loss of momentum that had started during Grant's second term.

Under Hayes the economy finally started to recover from the Panic of 1873. Yet, the Panic had brought the nation's monetary policy back to the top of the political agenda. Grant's administration had stopped coining silver in 1873 and soon began to withdraw paper money (greenbacks) from circulation as well. The aim was to return the nation to a more restricted "gold standard," and Hayes was a firm supporter of these moves. However, greenbacks and silver coinage were popular with farmers, as they increased the amount of money in circulation and made it easier to get credit. In the 1876 elections a "Greenback–Labor" Party challenged both major parties, running on a platform in favor of increasing the amount of paper currency in circulation. In 1878, with Congress divided on the matter and mindful of the numerous votes on offer, they passed the Bland–Allison Act, overturning President Hayes' veto to do so. Although the Republicans controlled the Senate, many had backed the measure, especially those from states with large silver mining industries. The new law made silver dollars full legal tender (even if in limited amounts), made permanent the existing greenbacks in circulation, and catalyzed a debate about currency that would run on and on through this period (McCulley, 2012: 22–24). The Republicans were punished at the polls later that year, losing control of the Senate to the Democrats. However, the midterms also saw the Greenback Party make gains in the House at the expense of both parties. Though the Republicans were the main losers in these elections, neither party was pleased to see the Greenback Party making progress on the back of this tricky and divisive issue.

Republican factionalism grows

As the 1880 elections approached, the Republican Party's factions saw their chance to restore the old order of things, particularly when it came to the spoils system. Hayes had committed to serving only one term and therefore there was every chance a more compliant replacement could be found. The Stalwarts put their weight behind Ulysses Grant and the Half-Breeds backed their factional leader James Blaine. However, when the convention reached a stalemate, it was **James Garfield**, the senator-elect for Ohio, who became the unlikely compromise candidate. The Stalwarts were initially reluctant to support Garfield, so he offered to consult Conkling when it came to future federal appointments in order to win them over (Shaw, 2003: 134–136). The Stalwarts could also take heart from the nomination of Chester Arthur as Garfield's running mate—the Conkling protégé whom Hayes had removed from the New York Customhouse. Blaine, though on better terms with Garfield, was also placated when later offered the role of secretary of state in Garfield's cabinet. In the end, the result that November saw an incredibly tight popular vote, with Democratic war veteran Winfield

Scott Hancock running Garfield extremely close. Though Garfield won the Electoral College vote more convincingly, the national voting map showed a clear sectional split between north and south. Once again, a deeply divided Republican Party had opted for a compromise leader, and this candidate had, in turn, received a very limited popular mandate.

Garfield used his inaugural address to set out an agenda quite similar to Hayes', at least when it came to democratic reforms. Like Hayes, he called for civil service reform—an issue that had already proved so divisive for the Republican Party. Garfield also criticized states that unfairly denied African Americans their voting rights—a traditional Republican refrain. However, Garfield departed from Hayes' support for the gold standard. He called instead for **bimetallism** (the coinage of both gold and silver), a move that would undercut the Greenback Party and win back support from rural voters in the West. It was these issues that looked set to dominate Garfield's first year in office. However, that July, things took an unexpected turn when Charles Guiteau shot the new president. The would-be assassin infamously proclaimed: 'I did it. I will go to jail for it; Arthur is president, and I am a Stalwart'. As word of the president's shooting spread, both the public and press speculated wildly as to Guiteau's motivations. Did he have mental health issues? Was this the act of an immigrant nihilist? Perhaps it was all part of a factional plot (Rosenburg, 1968: 4–7)? Whatever Guiteau's true motivations, Garfield finally succumbed to infection in September and the assassin had indeed put Arthur in the Executive Mansion.

One of the new president's first high-profile moves suggested that he was not going to be a passive placeholder of the nation's top office. In 1882, President Arthur vetoed the Chinese Exclusion Bill—a measure that a divided Congress had endorsed with ease. The bill suggested that Chinese labor endangered 'the good order of certain localities', as many working class Americans feared Chinese competition for low-paid work (Chinese Exclusion Act, 1882). Arthur's veto message retorted that a two-decade ban on Chinese labor migration was unwise and would likely send the wrong message to nations of East Asia. 'No one can say that the country has not profited by their work', Arthur argued, and though unpopular in some areas of the country (such as California), this was not reason enough for such a ban (Arthur, 1882) (see Figure 5.2). However, though the president had used his executive veto, Congress was largely unmoved. The only significant modification Congress made to the bill was to reduce the initial period of exclusion to ten years, at the end of which the act would have to be renewed. With this minor concession, the bill became law. The president had acted, but with little consequence given that the Democrats had a plurality in the House and the Republicans remained divided on the matter.

On top of a divided government, Arthur—like Hayes and Grant before him—faced a divided party during his term. A clear example of the continuing divisions came with Republican nominations for the New York gubernatorial race in 1882. Conkling's Stalwarts backed Treasury Secretary

Figure 5.2 "The Only One Barred Out" (1882)
Niday Picture Library/Alamy Stock Photo

Charles Folger. Meanwhile, the Half-Breeds and independents backed the incumbent governor Alonzo Cornell. When Folger won the nomination, it did not take much for Arthur—a former protégé of Conkling—to be tainted with the brush of favoritism. To make things worse, Folger was later defeated by the Democratic candidate Grover Cleveland (Greenberger, 2017: 204–206).

The 1882 midterm congressional elections saw the electorate torn between the two parties as much as ever. The Democrats, who had been the largest party in the House before the election, retained an overall majority there, though the Republicans managed to maintain marginal control of the Senate. In his annual message the following month, Arthur called for decisive action to reform the spoils system. When he came to office the year before, Arthur had seemed the 'least likely reformer' of the system which had made his career (Karabell, 2004: 9). Yet, during the second half of his term, he ended up supporting the passage of the reforming 1883 Pendleton Act. The legislation created a salaried Civil Service Commission to oversee a more meritocratic appointment system. It also required some officeholders to pass an exam to prove their competence, rather than relying on political bosses to pick their favorites. However, despite its reformist aims, the Pendleton Act only partially reformed the spoils system, and only a minority of posts were subject to the meritocratic provisions of the new law.

If the Pendleton Act was a limited reform, the **tariff** revisions that followed in 1883 were a disappointment to all concerned. Politicians were so divided on what to do about the high tariffs levied on goods entering the nation from overseas that it was almost impossible for them to take a coherent line. Nicknamed the "Mongrel Tariff," the resulting measure made only the most marginal reductions, and Arthur was unable to benefit from any sense of momentum behind his administration. Added to this, the president's health was in decline. Arthur had been diagnosed with Bright's Disease the previous year and, despite his own ambition to run again in 1884, the key powerbrokers in his party did not feel able or willing to support him (Gould, 2014: 77). These factors conspired to create yet another contentious election year. With Arthur unwanted by his party, the Republicans turned to perhaps their party's biggest name: James Blaine. The Democrats, meanwhile, nominated New York Governor Grover Cleveland—the reformer who had beaten the Stalwart-backed Folger in the gubernatorial race of 1882.

Blaine was an eloquent speaker and popular with his Half-Breed followers. However, press coverage, particularly in Democratic-leaning sections, routinely presented Blaine as an inveterate liar who represented the very worst of the spoils system and profiteering from office [*Doc. 11, p137*]. Added to this, Blaine's ill-chosen epithet for the Democrats as the party of "Rum, Romanism, and Rebellion," supposedly cost his party any chance of winning over the Irish vote (a significant factor in swing states like New York). Further damage was done by a formal split in the G.O.P., echoing the splits that had ebbed and flowed since Grant's time. A group of Republicans who felt Blaine was simply too unprincipled to lead their party in Washington switched to the Democrats, preferring Cleveland to the "Con-tinental liar from the state of Maine!" Their detractors called these splitters "**Mugwumps**" and saw them as self-righteous idealists whose aspirations for meritocracy and non-partisanship promised only electoral suicide (McFarland, 1975: 2). These factors combined, along with the increasing Democratic grip over the southern states, to win the election for Cleveland. This was in spite of the revelations that Cleveland had fathered a child out of wedlock, which became a staple anecdote for his critics. The result in the Electoral

College that November saw Cleveland victorious, but only with the help of his own state of New York. Blaine might well have rued offending the Irish voters of that state, which Cleveland secured by the tiniest of margins: just over a thousand votes.

The Cleveland era

The 1884 election represented a breakthrough for the Democrats—their first presidential election win since the Civil War. However, Democratic success did not bring to power a party any more united than the outgoing Republicans. After the end of Republican Reconstruction, much of the South gradually fell under the control of conservative Bourbon Democrats, who proudly stood as the party of white supremacy (see Chapter 3). In the rest of the country, where denying African Americans the vote did not have the same electoral benefits, the Democrats seemed to offer different things to different people. For some, they represented a party with a more reform-minded agenda; an image that had spurred on the Mugwumps to join them. Others, such as Congressman William Steele Holman of Indiana, liked to see the party as one which sought a fair deal for all, not just the rich (Baker, 1998: 33–35). In New York City, dating back to the corrupt politics of Boss William Tweed, the party had long courted Irish American voters, and by the 1880s this link had become increasingly solid. Thus, the Democrats were—depending on the city or state in which they ran—the party of white supremacy, political reform, the Irish, and the working class.

With such a broad spectrum of voters supporting his party, it helped that Cleveland had something to offer many different groups. When it came to the South, the president was not an advocate of social equality for African Americans and did little to interfere with this vital region of Democratic support. During his campaign, Cleveland had made clear his commitment to cleaning up politics and continuing civil service reform, in turn attracting the Mugwumps from the Republican Party, along with many other opponents of the spoils system. His support for the gold standard and laissez-faire economics appealed to many economic conservatives (and Republicans), while his support for lower tariffs appealed to a wide variety of working class voters. Meanwhile, in cities like New York, with large European migrant populations, the president's opposition to alcohol restrictions was also widely appreciated. If the Democrats could appear almost as a different party in different parts of the country, so too could their president.

One of the few areas where Cleveland did attempt action during his first term was in regard to economic policy. First, he tried to reverse moves toward bimetallism but was ultimately stopped by Congress (Crockett, 2012: 893). However, he gained more traction when it came to tariff reform. By the late 1880s, the federal government was working at a surplus, and tariffs were one of the key sources of government income. In Cleveland's mind, this situation was leading the country to the verge of another economic panic. For the president, tariff reduction would help reduce the surplus and remain in line with his laissez-faire principles when it came to government interference in trade. The president's 1887 annual message was essentially a lecture on tariff reform, and he made it clear that he felt high tariffs were antithetical to both laissez-faire governance and to the welfare of the common man. He called the existing system of high protectionist tariffs a 'vicious, inequitable, and illogical source of unnecessary taxation' (Reitano, 1994: 9–10).

The tariff question provided the clearest dividing line between the two parties and was an issue that united a good number of Democratic voters. However, some of the president's other executive actions started to cause concern among the electorate. Cleveland vetoed large numbers of Civil War veterans' pensions and even some emergency aid bills—never the wisest strategy for winning the nation's hearts. The president had his reasons, of course. First, when it came to veterans' pensions, he believed that Republicans were abusing the system to buy votes. Second, the president felt that Congress was exceeding its constitutional powers when providing federal funding for state aid. He even vetoed the so-called "Seed Bill" that sought to provide $10,000 to aid 'drought-stricken farmers' in Texas. Though a small number of voters might have understood his reasoning, to many the president's actions looked heartless (Pafford, 2013: x).

Though Cleveland certainly believed in limited government, this did not mean he did not think some government was necessary. In 1887, the president approved a measure that had a significant impact on the nation's relatively unregulated economic growth: the Interstate Commerce Act. This law attempted to stop price fixing and the growth of monopolies among railroad companies by bringing them under federal regulatory supervision. It even established a new regulatory agency, the Interstate Commerce Commission (ICC). The ICC was the first of its kind, an independent governmental body that could serve as a check on big business. Though Cleveland's first term had proved somewhat mixed in terms of satisfying those who voted for him, the party was united in re-nominating him as its candidate for the 1888 presidential election.

While the Democrats had an incumbent candidate for the presidency in the form of Cleveland, the Republicans lacked a clear frontrunner for their nomination. The party's biggest name, James Blaine, ruled himself out, leaving the field wide open. That summer saw yet another divided Republican Convention and, once more, this led to a compromise candidate. This time, it was the former governor of Indiana, **Benjamin Harrison**. Harrison raised a variety of issues during his campaign, such as cleaning up electoral processes and railroad regulation, but such reformist measures would hardly mark him out from his Democratic rival. When it came to the issue of the tariff, however, Harrison advocated a high protectionist measure, drawing a clear line between the two parties. He also raised the issue of Cleveland's

Civil War pension vetoes, something that drew large crowds of veterans to his home in Indianapolis, where he campaigned from his "**front porch**". The fact that Harrison was the grandson of the famous general and short-lived president William Henry Harrison did not hurt his cause with the large veteran electorate either (Bourdon, 2014: 249). The election result that November was incredibly tight. Cleveland won a plurality of the popular vote, with a very strong showing in the South. However, it was Harrison who secured the win in the Electoral College. Harrison won back not only the crucial state of New York that had proved so costly four years earlier, but also his home state of Indiana.

The 1888 presidential election was the third in a row in which neither the Republicans nor the Democrats attracted half of the votes cast. Not only was a north–south split showing signs of continuing, but smaller parties were increasingly drawing votes away from both main parties. In this election, parties committed to "single issue" platforms—such as the prohibition of alcohol or the rights of workers—attracted thousands of voters. The main parties might have differed when it came to tariff reform, but when it came to broader social issues, they seemed just as ideologically bereft as they had since the end of Republican Reconstruction. With the parties so hard to tell apart on so many issues of the day, it seemed that perhaps the time for a new party was fast approaching.

Harrison's presidency is perhaps the most under-studied in even this period of "lesser-known" presidents. Historian Sean Cashman (1993: 267) characterizes Harrison's term as something of an "interregnum," during which the nation was led by Congress rather than the president. However, biographer Charles Calhoun argues that Harrison deserves more credit than this. He claims that Harrison 'racked up a long list of accomplishments' and was committed to a strong and active federal government, especially in contrast to Cleveland. He also maintains that Harrison had an important role in shaping congressional legislation, through a mixture of threatened veto action, public statements, and informal meetings (Calhoun, 2005: 1–4). However, though Harrison might have believed in bigger government and voiced his opinions, most of the action during his time in office undoubtedly played out in Congress.

Perhaps the most influential Republican in the U.S. Senate, especially after the departure of Blaine and Conkling in 1881, was John Sherman of Ohio. Sherman had been treasury secretary during the Hayes administration and an unsuccessful presidential nominee at the G.O.P. conventions in 1880, 1884, and 1888. It should come as no surprise, therefore, that it was his name that was attached to the two most high-profile measures of Harrison's term. Congress passed both the Sherman Antitrust Act and the Sherman Silver Purchase Act in 1890 while they still had majorities in both the House and the Senate. The Antitrust Act sounded radical with its mission to break up **trusts** and threaten over-powerful businesses. In reality, it was a compromise measure, vague enough so as to be easily subverted by shrewd businessmen. The Silver Purchase Act was also a concessionary measure, reflecting the ongoing divide between "silverites" and "goldbugs" in the Senate. The act increased the amount of silver that the government purchased (from the lower levels of the earlier Bland–Allison Act) and provided for the coinage of silver. Thus, the two key acts that bore the Republican senator's name appeared, on the face of it, to work against the interests of big business. However, like the Antitrust Act, the Silver Purchase Act was unlikely to be taken too seriously, and the law left the decision about silver coinage in the hands of the incumbent administration (White, 2017: 633–634).

Both Republican measures gave the appearance of reform without actually assuring any would happen. Businesses could remain safe in the knowledge that, so long as the government did not act upon them wholeheartedly, little would change. Meanwhile supporters of silver—especially in the many new states in the West, recently given full representation in the Senate—could see that Harrison's administration remained a clearer friend than the "goldbug" Cleveland would ever be. Just as with previous administrations in this period, the internal divisions within the main parties made it all but impossible for strong reform legislation to pass through Congress without being watered down.

Though Republicans in the West might have been enthusiastic about the Silver Purchase Act, there were many elsewhere that were far less keen on the legislation. However, these more economically conservative Republicans were willing to compromise on the issue of silver—for a price. In return, they expected western support for a strongly protectionist tariff (Poole & Rosenthal, 1997: 103). The proposed McKinley Tariff was so high that its sponsor, Representative **William McKinley** of Ohio, earned the moniker of the "Napoleon of protection". Once successfully pushed through the legislature, the act raised general tariff duties from thirty-eight to almost fifty percent—though this varied depending on the product. Some items, such as imported tinplate, became almost unaffordable in order to protect domestic industries, while others—such as sugar—remained duty free. The act also allowed for reciprocal trade treaties to be drawn up with other countries to allow for the importation of goods at lower rates on a case-by-case basis.

Despite sponsoring the most significant tariff change for years, McKinley lost his House seat in the congressional midterms that year. Indeed, McKinley was only one of several Republicans to be unseated that November, and the Democrats regained control of the House in the next session. The Democrats had successfully managed to paint the tariff as a sign of the Republican Party's distain for the average working man (Reitano, 1994: 129–130). However, Cleveland and his fellow "gold Democrats" had their own policy that proved unpopular with many other working men in the form of the gold standard. Though the Democrats benefitted in these midterms, they were not alone in doing so. 1880 saw the first representatives of the Populist Party enter Congress. Although they were small in number at this point, the Populists represented a brand of politics popular with farmers and potentially with the wider working class (see Chapter 6). Perhaps they would finally be the party to gain traction within the increasingly stale and factional two-party system.

The 1892 contest between Democrats and the Republicans was, in many senses, a rerun of the 1888 election campaign. Both Cleveland and Harrison were duly re-nominated by their respective parties, and the election campaign appeared to be largely a referendum on the McKinley Tariff. Cleveland called for lower tariffs, and Harrison stood behind his party's protectionist measure. That summer, however, an outbreak of labor unrest at the Homestead Steel Works outside Pittsburgh, Pennsylvania, and the government's dysfunctional reaction to it, helped to bolster Democratic claims that the Republicans were the party of big business (see Chapter 6). With momentum now in their favor, and the Democrats' ever tighter grip on the South guaranteeing them a bloc of electoral votes from that section, Cleveland looked the favorite to win. There was, though, the growing threat of the Populist Party to consider.

The Populists held their first national convention in 1892, in Omaha, Nebraska. They demanded greater democracy, workers' rights and silver coinage, while denouncing the power of big businesses. They also presented the two main political parties as chronically corrupt. The United States was, the Populists suggested: 'a nation brought to the verge of moral, political, and material ruin' [*Doc. 12, p138*]. In the end, the party's message went across best in the West and the South, areas with the largest rural populations. The Populists' presidential candidate, James B. Weaver—a former Greenback–Labor candidate—managed to pick up more than eight percent of the popular vote, as well as the electoral votes of a handful of western states. However, in Congress, many Populists—particularly in the West—had opted to run on "**fusion** tickets" with one of the main parties in order to avoid splitting the vote. Though a few managed to win seats in Congress, the nature of the first-past-the-post electoral system made challenging the two main parties an uphill struggle.

Despite the growth of the Populist vote, Cleveland managed to secure victory in November and his party secured both chambers of Congress. From 1893, the Democrats would control the executive and both chambers of Congress for the first time since the Civil War. The electorate, however, looked more divided than ever. The nation was split beyond party lines on a variety of issues, such as the tariff, coinage, and workers' rights. Many of these issues echoed an increasing sense of class and urban–rural division that is detailed in the next chapter. The two main parties' vote shares were in steady decline and national election results continued to be tight, with neither party able to command an absolute majority of public support. Added to this, the electoral map continued to look increasingly divided along regional lines. Southern white voters opted overwhelmingly for the

Democrats while African Americans in the region were being squeezed ever further to the margins. The Populists, meanwhile, were making visible breakthroughs, but only really in the West. If the decades that had passed since the end of the Civil War were supposed to have helped soothe the nation's differences, the electoral map of 1892 painted a very different picture of where the nation stood.

6 Robber barons and Knights of Labor

The decades after the Civil War were characterized by unprecedented industrial and economic growth in the United States. Between 1870 and the 1890s, the country transformed from being centered mainly upon agriculture, to one increasingly made up of vast urban metropolises, especially in areas outside of the South (Bensel, 2000: 5). This "second" industrial revolution accelerated in the last few decades of the nineteenth century as businesses found their way around obstructive laws restricting business ownership across multiple states (Risjord, 2005: 3). Soon the development of trusts and holding companies facilitated the expansion of corporations into behemoths that controlled newly dominant industries, such as steel and oil. At the helm of these great business enterprises were a tiny cabal of plutocrats who made vast fortunes, truly putting the "gild" into the **Gilded Age**.

The transformations wrought by the Civil War, rapid expansion into the West, and mass immigration (see Chapter 8), combined to propel this industrial growth by connecting new markets, and bringing in much needed resources and workers. Meanwhile, technological innovations allowed this growth to accelerate even further. Yet, this second industrial revolution was not simply a story about inventors and business tycoons. It was also one about the working classes across the country who powered these changes. The United States might have undergone its formative moves toward becoming the industrial and financial powerhouse of the twentieth century, but there was a sense that this rapid progress was creating deep fissures across the country. The growing gap between the wealthiest in the nation and the masses of American farmers, miners, and factory workers led to increased unrest. In both rural and urban communities, labor began to organize, strike, and protest at a whole new level. By the mid-1880s, these social divisions seemed to threaten the very stability of the nation.

Technology

The most famous figure of the technological age that followed the Civil War would have to be Thomas Alva Edison. Along with his assistants at his base in Menlo Park, New Jersey, Edison helped pioneer an efficient incandescent light bulb and the phonograph (a sound recording device), made improvements to the telegraph (invented before the war by Samuel Morse), and aided the development of the nascent moving pictures industry. However, it was commercial electric light for which he was most loudly trumpeted—seen as a clean and modern technology altering Americans' relationship to the natural world and even their very culture (Freeberg, 2014: 2–8). Building on his time working at one of Edison's centers, Serbo-Croat immigrant Nikola Tesla led yet further breakthroughs in electricity generation using alternating current (rather than Edison's preferred direct current) (Carlson, 2013: 3–5). Another immigrant, Alexander Graham Bell, was credited with the invention of yet more transformative technology in the guise of the telephone. These technological advances helped power and connect the nation during its period of phenomenal growth, as well as making a name for the United States as a center of innovation. Meanwhile, great expositions in Philadelphia (1876) and Chicago (1893) showcased this modernization to the nation and the wider world.

Technological change, and the ensuing industrialization of the United States, did, of course, have less positive consequences. As the latter part of this chapter shows, it had serious social ramifications and led to an underlying sense of social injustice among many working class Americans. However, there was also a clear set of environmental consequences that should not be ignored. Even in the South, which saw the smallest impact of this second industrial revolution, the extraction of raw materials and the intensification of farming methods wrought environmental consequences, akin to those faced by the farmers, miners, and cattlemen of the West (Cowdrey, 1996: 103). In the North, the vast factories, refineries, and other industrial hubs created environmental pollution on an unprecedented scale.

The growth of cities and their ever-expanding peripheries, especially the very largest ones such as New York and Chicago, helped create what William Cronon (1991: 265) calls, 'the single most powerful environmental force reshaping the American landscape since the glaciers began their long retreat to the north'. The increasing need for fossil fuels brought changes to the nation's rural landscapes, created new jobs, and polluted the air. Meanwhile, the cities themselves grew into distinctive new environments. They simultaneously became marvels of electrification and production, while also creating a new type of "wilderness," comprising numerous poor, crowded, and neglected neighborhoods (Merchant, 2007: 112–118). However, the case for environmentalism had to wait. It was not until the early twentieth century that the progressive movement had gained sufficient momentum to bring governmental attention to the impacts of the nation's growth on both rural and urban environments. During the Gilded Age, the sorts of regulation that the environmental movement would require were kept firmly at bay by big businesses, which saw such regulation (like anti-trust legislation) as a barrier to higher profits.

Even though some moves were made to regulate businesses—most notably the 1890 Sherman Antitrust Act—such measures were not proactively pursued. Financiers and businessmen kept the wheels of growth turning by exploiting legal loopholes and often through simple bribery. This was the era of laissez-faire government when it came to the expansion of business and industry, allowing favorable conditions to be exploited to their maximum potential with minimal interference. There was some measure of government intervention in the economy—for example, via high tariffs and infrastructure spending—but these instances mainly helped to further facilitate business growth. The Republican Party soon became the most closely associated with this approach, while the Democrats took several decades to define themselves as offering something different. Even in the early days of this industrial boom, the links between business leaders and politicians seemed too close for some, and the scandals of the Grant administration publicized such engagements on a national scale. In this age of economic growth, some men became fantastically rich, but—as the latter part of this chapter illustrates—for the majority of the working class, the trickle down impact of this affluence was slow in making itself felt. As historian Jack Beatty put it in the title of his 2007 book, the 'triumph of money' in this period represented an 'age of betrayal'.

The robber barons

Just as the phrase "Gilded Age" became associated with wanton greed and corruption, so too did the names of those who led this exceptional growth in business, finance, and industry. These figures—invariably men—are frequently labelled the "**robber barons**" of the age. Writers such as Matthew Josephson in his 1934 book of that title, popularized the term as representing the owners of vast business empires built with little concern for those they trampled upon along the way. Though many of these figures sought to improve their reputations later in life through acts of philanthropy, the memory of *how* many of them made their fortunes never fully faded. Yet, despite often being portrayed in a negative light, these robber barons could well be credited with leading the United States to a position in the world where its manufacturing output and overall finances were now equal to—if not ahead of—their European counterparts (George, 1982: 31). Indeed, whereas in the past critics dubbed them "robber barons," as time has passed many have started to regard them as 'farsighted entrepreneurs' (White, 2017: 7).

For the earliest examples of robber barons, one need look no further than what was fast becoming the bedrock of industrial growth after the Civil War: the railroad network. As vital arteries controlling the flow of the nation's commerce, control of the railroads allowed businessmen potential for not only profit, but considerable influence across a range of interdependent industries. For example, where would the western cattle barons be without their iron roads and refrigerated rail cars? The most noteworthy figure in this domain was the former steamship magnate Cornelius Vanderbilt. Sometimes called the "Commodore," Vanderbilt got involved with the railroad industry in the immediate aftermath of the war, acquiring the Hudson River Railroad—stretching from Manhattan to Albany in New York State—then the New York Central that connected on from Albany to Lake Erie. In the years that followed, Vanderbilt continued to add to his network, using all means necessary to outsmart or sabotage his rivals. Ultimately, Vanderbilt came to build a route linking Chicago to his magnificent hub at Grand Central Depot in New York City (not to be confused with the later Grand Central Terminal which replaced it in 1913). However, there were suspicions among some at the time that, on the road to amassing his fortune, Vanderbilt not only hurt his rivals' pockets but also cut corners on the lines themselves. It was claimed that such actions led to the collapse of a rail bridge in late 1876, which resulted in the death of ninety-two people aboard the *Pacific Express* (Martin, 1992: 56–57).

Despite this controversy, it was Jay Gould, an important speculator and one of Vanderbilt's key competitors for control of rail lines in these early years, who was far easier to link to corruption than the Commodore. These railroad tycoons typified the wealth and economic dynamism of the period, as well as a limited consideration toward workers or ethics. After all, it was Gould, along with his business partner James Fisk, who had devised the gold cornering scheme in 1869 to help push up the value of his Erie Railroad's freight revenues. The dubious dealings of the "Gold Ring" led to the Black Friday panic in the gold market and subsequent economic turmoil (Morris, 2005: 69–79).

Another leading robber baron, who saw that to prosper in this period one needed to invest in and control technologies, was Scottish immigrant **Andrew Carnegie**. An entrepreneur who had made his early wealth via shrewd investments in railroads, Carnegie moved into the iron and steel industries when he had accumulated sufficient capital. In the aftermath of the Civil War, Carnegie invested in companies that produced iron (Union Iron Mills) and then purchased it to build railroad bridges (Keystone Bridge Company). He stayed ahead of competitors by adopting cutting edge technologies, such as the Bessemer process (first used in England), which produced less brittle steel and was soon introduced into Carnegie's operations in the United States. By the 1890s, Carnegie perfected the system of "vertical integration" that saw him invest in all aspects of the process, including the iron ore itself (Nasaw, 2007). Ultimately, in 1901, Carnegie sold off his steel empire to a fellow robber baron, financier John Pierpoint "J. P." Morgan.

J. P. Morgan had built his reputation by facilitating mergers between the great industries of the day. By 1895, his renamed company (J. P. Morgan & Co.) began a period of almost unparalleled influence over not only industrial fortunes, but the nation's finances. As Ron Chernow (1990: 720) puts it, Morgan 'exercised powers that today are dispersed among vast global banking conglomerates'. When called before the House of Representatives in 1912 to explain 'his alleged role in the monopolization of financial capital in the United States', Morgan told the committee: 'I do not feel that I have vast power … . I am not seeking it, either'. Yet, Morgan, credited with masterminding the end to the Panic of 1907, certainly did have power (Pak, 2013: 1–2). By the turn of the century, figures like Morgan appeared to wield the sort of influence most politicians could only dream of.

Though Morgan was powerful, the wealthiest robber baron of them all was John D. Rockefeller. Like the others, the nature of Rockefeller's huge success divided (and still divides) opinion. His biographer, Ron Chernow (1998: xv), offers a reason for this when he claims that Rockefeller was 'an implausible blend of sin and sanctity'. Rockefeller made his first waves in Ohio, gradually building up his collection of oil refineries until, in 1870, he established Standard Oil, along with his business partner Henry M. Flagler. As the company grew ever larger, swallowing up its competitors by any means necessary, it became the key provider to many rail lines. As such, even in its early days, Standard Oil was accused of using its market domination to drive competition out of business through offering companies their oil at significantly lower prices.

As the years went by, Standard Oil grew well beyond the reaches of Ohio through the use of holding companies, making Rockefeller's empire national, and one that seemed to continually expand into associated industries. His business empire was, for its critics, an "octopus"—a term popularized by the Frank Norris novel of that name. The callous nature of Rockefeller's consolidation of power featured in social reformer, **Ida Tarbell's**, *The History of the Standard Oil Company* some years later (Weinberg, 2008: 46–48). In the conclusion to her two-volume book, Tarbell (1904: 291) describes her feelings about the company's actions across the years: 'it is always fighting measures which equalise privileges and which make it more necessary for men to start fair and play fair in doing business'. Such measures, however, were few and far between for much of the Gilded Age as both the Republicans and Democrats avoided open confrontation with big business.

To many it seemed that the robber barons, a small band of industrial and financial giants, had everything sewn up to work for their further profit. For Carnegie, however, the inevitable inequalities of the system could yet be overcome. Not, he reasoned, by some dramatic change to the system but by the generosity of the wealthy. In his 1889 article "Wealth," Carnegie explained that the man of wealth should act as 'the mere agent and trustee for his poorer brethren, bringing to their service his superior wisdom, experience and ability to administer, doing for them better than they would or could do for themselves' [*Doc. 13, p139*]. However, such ideas did not sit well with many working class Americans, who felt that perhaps a dramatic change to the system was exactly what was needed. As a result, across the country, in both the countryside and the sprawling towns and cities, popular movements arose to challenge the status quo.

Agrarian reaction

As the nation grew ever more urban, it became increasingly divided between those who lived in vast conurbations and those who remained on the nation's farms and plantations. In many senses, the attempts by the working class to challenge the plutocracy of the day were held back by this very division. Though attempts were made to unite agricultural and industrial workers across the period, they seldom lasted. What generally happened is that the rural workers moved in one set of circles and the urban workers in another. Both scored some successes, yet their failure to coalesce might well have limited their overall impact. Despite this, rural laborers and urban workers were often united in feeling that little was being done for them by the two main political parties. As a result, disgruntled interest groups began to form collectives, pressure groups, and even political parties of their own in order to make their voices heard. The remainder of this chapter will explore the developments of such movements within first the rural communities of America and then the urban worker communities of the nation's expanding cities.

For Richard Bensel (2000: 5), one of the primary reasons why the nation was able to grow so far and so fast in the late nineteenth century was the subsidization of industrial expansion via profits from agricultural exports. These exports often came from the very southern plantations where industrialization was least visible. Yet, although agricultural output rose to meet the nation's ever higher demands, the economic situation of U.S. farmers deteriorated, leading to increased disillusionment with the existing party system. As ever, farmers remained susceptible to the vagaries of drought and crop failures, but the Gilded Age brought with it newer threats. As the average value of crops fell between the 1870s and 1890s, the price of rail freight transportation continued to rise, putting a further strain on farmers (Smith, 1984: 422). At the same time, the perceived status of American farmers went into decline. As Jack Beatty (2007: 108) puts it, farmers went from being the 'representative American of the 1860s', to 'the "hayseed" of 1890'. For some, there was a clear villain here, and it was the railroad monopolies.

In response to the pressure that big business was bringing to bear upon small farmers, citizens in farming states began to organize resistance. One of the best known examples of such action arose in the late 1860s with the foundation of the National Grange of the Order of Patrons of Husbandry—better known as the Grange, or the Grangers. It has been described by historian Gretchen Ritter (1999: 51) as 'an agrarian self-help group' that sought to use its collective power to challenge the railroad rates and bring attention back to the often-overlooked farming communities it represented. By the 1870s, some of the Grangers had begun to move towards forming their own political party—the Greenback Party—that, as its name suggests, aimed to fight for an increase in the money supply through supporting paper currency. Spurred on by the Panic of 1873, the Greenback Party's efforts to oppose the gradual withdrawal of paper currency led to some success for the party (see Chapter 5) and it even gained support from laborers outside of the rural communities it was established within. The party name—which evolved toward the Greenback–Labor Party—represented this brief period of unity between its two main worker bases (urban and rural). The party's peak probably came in 1878, when it gained 13.8 percent of the national vote (Ritter, 1999: 49). By 1880, however, support had swiftly ebbed and the party's presidential candidate, James Weaver, captured only around 300,000 votes. This was mirrored in Congressional elections that year, where the party received only around four percent of the national vote. The party's lack of traction in the two-party system, along with the rise of other competing movements, led to its gradual erosion in the early 1880s.

In the place of the Grangers and Greenbackers arose the Farmers' Alliance. Despite its name, it was really a loose assortment of three "alliances" which varied significantly in makeup on a regional and racial basis: the Northern, Southern, and Colored Farmers' Alliances. Like the Grangers they aimed to combat the power of distant businessmen and favor the lot of the average farmer through collective action. One of the leaders of the movement, Charles Macune had, some years earlier, set up the Farmers' Alliance Exchange in Texas where farmers could work collectively to cut out middle men (Postel, 2007: 33). The Southern Alliance, organized in Texas in the late 1870s, aimed to work cooperatively against big money and cattle barons and therefore appealed across racial lines. Even when working to the same ends though, race proved a key obstacle in uniting the voices of farmers and the idea of racial cooperation with black farmers proved a step too far for most white southerners. By 1886, excluded by the Southern Alliance, black farmers decided to form their own Colored Alliance.

Racial division was not the only factor that served to limit the size and scope of the Alliances. Unlike the urban labor movements discussed later, there was a sense that the Farmers' Alliance was less of a class-based movement, and more of an interest group, in that they rarely discriminated on the basis of landownership (Woodward, 1971: 188–193). Perhaps this offers some answer as to why the rural and urban movements often worked separately to improve the conditions of their members. Nevertheless, there were those who sought to create a social movement that could bridge this divide. The most successful movement along such lines was an effective successor to both the Greenback–Labor Party and the Farmers' Alliance: the Populist Party (also known as the People's Party).

The successes of the Populist Party as a political force in federal elections are explored elsewhere in this book, but it is useful to also consider the extent to which it was a true workers' party that might span divisions that existed between urban and rural workers. For historian Charles Postel (2007: 19), the Populist Party was initially conceived as an "industrial confederation": 'a multiclass alliance uniting "industrial orders" across the rural–urban divide'. Such a vision was outlined and expanded upon in the party's 1892 Omaha Platform [*Doc. 12, p138*]. Yet, this vision failed to create a long term union between the urban and rural working classes. Postel (2007: 19) rejects the argument that this was largely down to a 'cultural or ideological divide' along an urban–rural axis. After all, the Populists fared well in Midwestern states among urban workers.

The populist movement did, however, appear to be split in terms of how best to bring about economic changes that would benefit such a wide variety of supporters. For Michael Pierce (2012: 97), populists ended up splitting into three distinct and competing groups along these lines: those who focused on silver currency, those who felt the platform should be far wider, and the "socialists" who called for government ownership of the destructive monopolies. Pierce argues that leading figures in the first two groups, such as James Weaver (a silverite and former Greenback presidential candidate) and Tom Watson of Georgia (who wanted a broader appeal), unified to push out those with more socialistic tendencies. With this in mind, it is perhaps not surprising that urban workers might not have felt all that welcome in the populist movement. By the mid-1890s, many of them had moved into the third group: those with socialistic tendencies.

Urban reaction

Just as there was a long and winding road toward mass organization of rural interests that led to the formation of the Populist Party, there was an equally complex journey toward mobilizing the nation's industrial and urban workers. The urban story can be traced back to 1866 when, only months after the end of the war, Baltimore, Maryland, witnessed the birth of the National Labor Union (NLU). Under the leadership of William H. Sylvis, the NLU acted as an umbrella organization that hosted a yearly conference of smaller unions (Montgomery, 1987: 11–13). However, soon after the NLU's establishment, another urban labor movement of far greater consequence arose in the form of the elaborately named Noble and Holy Order of the Knights of Labor.

The Knights of Labor, established in 1869, drew in skilled industrial workers from the cities, miners from the West, and even small businessmen. Like the Grangers before it, it began as a secretive and fraternal organization, while building on the earlier efforts of the NLU (Smith, 1984: 227). However, as Leon Fink (1985: xii) notes, unlike the NLU, the Knights of Labor was the 'quintessential expression of the labor movement in the Gilded Age, the first mass organization of the American working class'. It was an industrial union, meaning that it sought to combine the collective bargaining power of both skilled and unskilled workers within a specific industry in order to effect change. The most significant leader within the organization was probably its second president, Terence Powderly, who saw the Knights as a way to unite all workers 'in a great universal redemptive enterprise' (Smith, 1984: 227). At the start of the 1870s, it seemed that unionism was gathering significant momentum in the nation's cities.

The depression of 1873, though, proved a severe setback to the development of the union movement. Thousands lost their jobs and incomes declined for most workers. The existing trade unions, meanwhile, appeared powerless to help and soon enough their memberships went into significant decline. As the depression lingered on, the trade union movement's reputation took a further blow thanks to the actions of a secret Irish American "terrorist" group, the Molly Maguires. The Molly Maguires led a campaign of assassinations and industrial sabotage in Pennsylvania in the mid-1870s. Unfortunately for the labor movement, many of the Molly Maguires had close links with trade unions. Anti-labor voices soon began to focus on these connections, undermining the trade unions' already tarnished reputations (Kenny, 1998: 10). By the middle of the decade, the early momentum of trade unionism had been halted.

Despite the steady decline in early trade unions' memberships, it was not long before workers united in strike action—and this time on a national scale. In 1877, a small rail strike in West Virginia rapidly became a nationwide phenomenon. As it spread into other cities and states, it often managed to unite a diverse array of workers, from across ethnic and industry lines. However, it also managed to unite the forces of big business and the nation's elite, who helped organize "citizen militias" to help fight back against the forces of labor. In the end, the federal government had to take charge and restore order (Foner, 1988/2002: 583–585). The Great Strike illustrated that the working class was growing increasingly militant and, because the North's attention turned toward this new unrest, it also helped hasten the abandonment of federal-led Reconstruction in the South (Stowell, 2008: 8).

The years that followed the Great Strike saw a renewed growth in both unionism and radicalism. In the early 1880s German immigrant Johann Most gained traction with workers through a series of speaking tours, bringing more members into a growing Socialist Labor Party and leading to calls for greater unity among American socialists (Smith, 1984: 231–235). However, in early 1886, it looked as though the more conservative side of the labor movement was in the ascendency. That year saw the Knights of Labor call one of its most significant strike actions—in a departure from its earlier stance on avoiding such measures. As a result, its membership grew to a height of almost 750,000 (Fink, 1985: xiii–xvi). The Knights' more aggressive posture appeared to be paying off. The early success of meetings between its leader Terrance Powderly and the robber baron Jay Gould over their railroad strike action seemed to support this sense of progress. However, for some, the failure of the Knights to secure lasting change during this strike action meant that just as quickly as they attracted a mass membership, so they lost it upon the longer-term failure of that action (Phelan, 2000: 171).

The activities of the Knights in 1886, however, were just the tip of the iceberg. Continued labor disruption that year grew so widespread it became known as the "Great Upheaval". The most notorious event of 1886 occurred in Chicago that May. During a mass meeting, convened to consider the violence that had broken out between strikers and police at the McCormick Reaper Works, a bomb was thrown at the gathered crowd and police, and chaos ensued. The Haymarket bombing was the work of anarchists with links to Europe, and it set off what might be seen as an early "Red Scare" in the United States that had a deep and lasting impact on the Left. The hysteria it created pushed trade unions toward an even more conservative approach to direct action. Furthermore, Haymarket marked the beginning of the end for the Knights of Labor, who appeared to lack a clear voice or decisive direction in response to the events. Although, for more radical leftists, the anarchists of Haymarket became 'heroic figures' and their subsequent executions raised 'critical questions about American society in the industrial age', the event is generally seen as yet another setback for the labor movement as a whole (Green, 2006: 301).

Though 1886 saw both a renaissance and then rapid decline of the Knights of Labor, it also saw the rebirth of another union movement, which—that same year—renamed itself the American Federation of Labor (AFL). Unlike the Knights, the AFL was decidedly a craft union, which meant that rather than all workers within an industry being represented collectively, they were grouped and lobbied instead based on their craft or skillset (and thus might come from different industries). Their bargaining power came from being able to restrict the availability of all workers in a specific field. The AFL's leader, **Samuel Gompers**, claimed that he wanted his union to be free from partisan alliances. However, Julie Greene's (2004: 2–3) recent research has shown that the AFL, though remaining officially non-partisan, in reality formed a close—if vacillating—relationship with the Democratic Party.

During the chaos of 1886, the AFL focused on better wages and an eight-hour working day as its primary goals. For Gompers, as he told a Senate Committee a few years earlier, limiting the working day to eight hours would have wide-ranging effects: 'it would create a better spirit in the working man; it would make him a better citizen ... A man who works but eight hours a day possesses more independence both economically and politically'. Such a change in spirit, Gompers felt, would stop workingmen's votes being bought and, from a social perspective, leave them less likely to resort to alcohol [*Doc. 14, p140*]. Added to his popular messages, the events of the turbulent year 1886 helped further bolster Gompers' credentials. Where the Knights had appeared directionless in the wake of Haymarket, Gompers and the AFL were lauded by many labor activists for campaigning for clemency on behalf of those arrested (Smith, 1984: 242–255). The AFL became the primary force among organized labor after the fall of the Knights. However, they did meet some competition in the West, where a somewhat different union controlled many of the mineral mining industries: the Western Federation of Miners (WFM)—an organization founded in 1892 by those imprisoned after the Coeur d'Alene miners' strike of 1889. The WFM, unlike the AFL, moved in a more socialist direction as the 1890s progressed (Dubofsky, 2000: 42–48). Though the Knights were severely diminished after the Great Upheaval, unionism was still very much alive.

The final major labor clash of the period came in 1892, at the Homestead steel plant situated on the outskirts of Pittsburgh, Pennsylvania. Andrew Carnegie owned Homestead but it was his protégé, Henry Frick, who ran it. Frick made changes at the plant that enraged workers, including wage reductions, which the union rejected. Frick then imposed a lockout of the recalcitrant workers and later fired them. The workers' union organized a mass response, which met with violent armed force in the guise of 300 private detectives—or "Pinkertons"—hired by Frick to quell the unrest. What resulted was carnage. In the end, 8,500 National Guardsmen were called in to end the rioting. The situation escalated still further when a Russian anarchist émigré, Alexander Berkman, attempted to assassinate Frick. However, Frick survived, Berkman was imprisoned, and the strike gradually dissolved as a combined result of growing economic pressure on the workers and successful court actions brought by Carnegie's company (Smith, 1984: 469–479). Paul Krause (1992: 4) sees the Homestead strike as a 'quasi-mythical epic that pitted the aspirations of organized labor against the heartless rule of greedy tyrants', and it ended with labor being roundly defeated.

The decades after the Civil War did see some evidence of increased national unity when it came to industrial growth. Technology linked the nation in a more physical sense—through improved transportation and communication links. New farmers' movements grew in the shape of the Grangers and the Farmers' Alliance, while miners unionized and the Knights of Labor and American Federation of Labor drew in workers from the industrializing cities and beyond. Workers were uniting on an unprecedented scale. However, what marks this period out more than growing unity, is an increased sense of division. The rise of the robber barons seemed to herald an increasing divide between the rich and poor. But even the working class movements that rose in opposition to big business were often at odds with one another—be this on an urban–rural basis, a skilled–unskilled basis, racial grounds, or even over the nature of action to be taken. The Great Strike, Great Upheaval, and the violence at Haymarket and Homestead, were not signs of great unity, but symptoms of a wider malaise. By 1892, the nation was deeply divided in many respects.

However, the rising Populist Party, even with its own internal divisions, seemed to offer a way forward: a third way. It seemed that the Populist Party might appeal widely enough to really challenge the two main parties, which too often seemed bereft of ideology or principle. As Chapter 9 goes on to explore, though the populist movement failed to break the two-party system, it and its successor—the progressive movement—did manage to change the course that the two main parties had charted from the end of the Civil War through to the re-election of Grover Cleveland in 1892. From this point onward, the character of the two main parties underwent some truly significant shifts. This in turn led to the rise of two (or three) progressive presidents who would lead the modernization, reinvigoration, and growth of the presidency at the dawn of the twentieth century.

7 The United States and the world

As a former European colony surrounded by other European colonies, the "Old World" affairs of Europe loomed large when the United States first became a republic. North of the border was the vast expanse of British North America (Canada) and Russian-owned Alaska. To the South were Spanish Mexico and Florida, along with a series of island nations in the Caribbean that were under the sway of various European powers. The U.S. did not take long, though, to consider itself the predominant power in the Americas. As early as 1823 the U.S. went so far as to expound the so-called **Monroe Doctrine**, which expressed the United States' ambition to halt any further European annexations or interference in the Americas. As many of Spain's colonies achieved their independence around this time, it appeared the U.S. was embracing the role of first among equals when it came to republics in the Americas. Though largely aspirational in 1823, the United States proved increasingly willing and able to act upon this hemispheric hegemony as the century progressed, and not always with the support of its neighboring republics.

After the Civil War, the U.S. looked to continue its expansion west toward the Pacific and maybe even beyond (see Chapter 4). Meanwhile, the nation's growing economic and industrial prominence saw the U.S. beginning to surpass its European rivals in wealth and output. As a result, some in the U.S. called for what was described as a "**large policy**," which would see the United States take on a greater role in world affairs. For those like Republican Senator **Henry Cabot Lodge**, this might take the form of a formal overseas territorial or strategic presence. For others, a diplomatic or primarily economic role was preferable. Yet, whatever method was to be employed, the United States made far greater efforts to project its power beyond its borders. This more active course significantly strained its diplomatic relationships with European powers, the nations of the Americas, and with East Asia. At the same time, public opinion at home began to diverge quite markedly, with many questioning the wisdom of the United States' new direction.

Relations with the European empires

Russian interest in a North American empire had never really taken off, and migration and investment from Saint Petersburg in their existing colony of Alaska had remained stagnant for years. Following defeat in the Crimean War (1853–1856) at the hands of a coalition that included the British, Russia's straitened financial situation led it to reconsider the future viability of its North American territory. This combination of Anglo–Russian tension and Russia's new interest in offloading its North American possessions created the ideal situation for expansionists in the United States (Goldfrank, 2013: 294–295). In 1867, Secretary of State **William Seward** secured the purchase of Russian Alaska at what appeared to him a bargain price. However, for many in the U.S., Seward's purchase was sheer folly. Jibes were leveled at Seward for purchasing a seemingly barren and frozen wilderness: it might be useful only as a national "icebox" or a polar bear garden his critics mocked (Hinckley, 1973: 1–2). The purchase, however, not only secured the United States control of a significant portion of the Pacific Coast (and kept it out of the hands of the British), but also proved quite farsighted as, in decades to come, the mineral and oil wealth of the territory was discovered and exploited.

U.S. relations with Britain, which still controlled most of the territory north of the United States, had been complex and difficult from the earliest days of the nation's history. Although the British remained officially neutral during the American Civil War, the relationship between the British and the Union government had been strained. The United States criticized the British for allowing Confederates to travel in British North America and for allowing the construction of ships in Britain which were destined for the Confederate navy. Indeed, after the war, the U.S. effort to seek damages for the carnage wreaked by the British-built CSS *Alabama* provided a high-profile source of tension between the nations. At the same time, groups of Irish nationalists (often simply termed "Fenians") sought to agitate along the U.S.–British North American border in order to help bargain for Irish independence from Britain.

Sympathy for the Irish cause was fairly widespread, not least among the now substantial Irish American population. Keen to secure the support of this growing group of voters, President Johnson made overtures toward the Irish nationalists, suggesting potential governmental support for their cause. In British North America, these increased tensions, along with the U.S. annexation of Alaska, led to genuine fears of a full-scale invasion by the only recently demobilized U.S. army. Yet, despite this troubled period, from 1869 onward, these tensions swiftly dissipated. The incoming Grant administration, less concerned with the Irish American vote than Johnson, sought to ease tensions. In 1871, the U.S. and Britain negotiated the Treaty of Washington that sought to firm up neutrality between the two nations going forward (Sim, 2011: 275–279). Though this was not the last Anglo–American wrangle prior to the Great War, it was the last time a full-scale war looked anything like a genuine possibility.

Though the purchase of Alaska had marked a significant expansion of U.S territory not connected to the existing United States, by the 1880s the United States' overseas possessions were virtually non-existent. In terms of an "overseas empire," the U.S. laid claim only to some tiny, scattered, and largely uninhabited islands in the Pacific that were mined for the much sought-after fertilizer, guano (bird and bat droppings). Meanwhile, the United States' commercial rivals, especially Britain and France, were making rapid headway in consolidating and expanding their control of overseas territories across the globe. Nowhere was this more apparent than in the so-called "Scramble for Africa," a continent where the United States had withdrawn from its only pseudo-colony of Liberia (previously controlled by the American Colonization Society) in 1847.

To stop complete Anglo–French domination of Africa, in 1884 the chancellor of the recently unified state of Germany, Otto von Bismarck, called interested nations together in Berlin to consider the continent's future. The U.S. sent representatives along in the hope of securing an international resolution that would support free trade along key rivers in Africa and to support the Belgian king's supposedly humanitarian effort to set up a vast state in Central Africa under a "benevolent" association (and not under British or French control). However, the victory of the anti-imperialist Grover Cleveland in the 1884 presidential election and a virtual deadlock in the U.S. Senate meant the Berlin Treaty was never ratified by the United States. Nevertheless, its actions to support the freedom of all nations to trade in Africa proved a useful early sign of what later became known as the "Open Door" trade policy (Munene, 1990: 73–79).

Although negotiation and diplomacy characterized many U.S. interactions with Europe in the years after the Civil War, 1898 saw the United States take up arms to achieve its foreign policy goals. In that year, the U.S. declared war on Spain, a declining world power which had been fighting increasingly brutal wars against its colonies in Cuba and the Philippines. Keen to stimulate newspaper sales, the so-called "Yellow Press" in the United States ran sensational headlines focusing on Spanish war crimes (including their use of concentration camps in Cuba). After the "unexplained" sinking of the USS *Maine* in Havana harbor, pressure mounted on President William McKinley to take action. Nevertheless, many in Congress remained reluctant to join the war in Cuba if its goal appeared to involve taking possession of Spain's empire. These reservations were largely appeased with the Teller Amendment to the proposed declaration of war, which pledged that the U.S. would not annex Cuba if it was victorious. By the end of April, Congress and the president were onboard and the U.S. formally declared war on a European power for the first time since the 1812–1815 war with Great Britain.

The Spanish–American War offered many of those too young to fight in the Civil War their first chance to fight for the U.S. in a major conflict.

Among this younger generation was the assistant secretary of the Navy, **Theodore Roosevelt**. Once the war began, Roosevelt resigned his position and raised his own regiment to fight in Cuba. Nicknamed the "Rough Riders," Roosevelt's regiment contained a mixture of soldiers from across the nation, including northerners (like him), western frontiersmen, and former Confederates (see Figure 7.1). The Rough Riders were symbolic of Republican hopes that this new war would help finalize national reconciliation, and the rapid and one-sided U.S. victory over Spain proved a triumph for McKinley's party. Yet, where sectional divisions appeared to be easing during the war, new divisions soon emerged over whether or not the U.S. should run an overseas empire when the fighting ceased. Though Cuba had been promised independence, the rest of Spain's empire in the Caribbean and Pacific remained up for negotiation. Of course, this new projection of U.S. power and its potential to forge an overseas empire did not only cause concern on the mainland United States and across the former Spanish Empire. The other imperial powers of the day also looked on with a great deal of interest.

Many European powers were understandably shaken by the scale of U.S. success in the Spanish–American War, but a key exception to this trend appeared to be Britain. Indeed, there were suggestions that the British might

Figure 7.1 Colonel Roosevelt and his Rough Riders (1898)
GL Archive/Alamy Stock Photo

have intervened in the Pacific to aid the Americans during the war, and quietly supported the U.S. post-war annexation of much of Spain's former empire (Smith, 1994: 229). The U.S. seemed to reciprocate this growing rapprochement when, in 1899, the British got involved in a protracted conflict with the Boers in South Africa. The Second Boer War (1899–1902) provided ample opportunity for Britain's rivals to condemn them for war crimes in South Africa. Yet, though many in the U.S. were critical of British actions, official government and business reaction seemed to offer quiet support. U.S. trade with the British expanded significantly during the conflict, and loans from American bankers underwrote around twenty percent of British costs in the war. The McKinley administration, and later that of Theodore Roosevelt, opted to pursue a course of tactical neutrality (Wilson, 2014: 112–119). Roosevelt was of Dutch ancestry and perhaps more likely to sympathize with the Dutch-descended Boers than most. However, he also felt there was more advantage to keeping Britain fully aware that the U.S.—if not a formal ally—was one of the few nations in the world that was not a natural enemy. Indeed, when it came to negotiations over the Alaskan–Canadian border shortly afterwards, the U.S. was able to extract repayment for its goodwill.

Where the Berlin Conference and Spanish–American War had shown the U.S. take quite different routes to oppose unchecked European imperialism, in a number of other instances the U.S. resorted to its long-held hemispheric foreign policy paradigm, encapsulated by the Monroe Doctrine. This policy was reiterated wholeheartedly by Grover Cleveland's secretary of state, Richard Olney, in 1895 when he suggested that the U.S. was 'practically sovereign' over the Americas (Maass, 2009: 384). The Venezuela Crisis of 1895 put Olney's words to the test when Britain supported their colony of Guiana in a boundary dispute with the neighboring republic of Venezuela. The U.S. objected and the British backed down, more concerned with maintaining U.S. friendship and the growing threat of Germany. Venezuela again came to the fore in U.S. policymaking between 1902 and 1903 when Britain and Germany notified the U.S. that they planned an "intervention" in the country in order to force Venezuela to make good on its debts. The United States intervened to avoid further European meddling and successfully advocated a negotiated settlement.

In 1902, the growing bonhomie between the United States and Britain played a major role in diffusing the potentially awkward issue of defining the border between Canada and Alaska. Following the Klondike Gold Rush of the mid-1890s (in Canada's Yukon Territory), access to the Pacific Coast became more important. The United States, keen to redeem something from their relatively benign stance toward the British in the Second Boer War, saw a chance to capitalize in terms of territorial gains. A tribunal was established and organized in such a way as to assure Anglo–American rapprochement would trump over Canadian interests. It was composed of three Americans, two Canadians, and one Englishman. Lord Alverstone, the British representative, sided with the U.S. delegates, securing a peaceful outcome that simultaneously enraged many in Canada. Further progress toward settling Anglo–American disputes in North America came in 1909, when the Permanent Court of Arbitration in The Hague settled a long-running dispute over access to fishing rights off the British Dominion of Newfoundland. Overall, the prevailing sense in the early twentieth century was that Britain and the United States were fast becoming strategic allies, albeit on a strictly informal basis.

Successful projection of U.S. diplomatic power in the early twentieth century was, of course, not restricted to the Anglo–American relationship. One clear example was President Roosevelt's involvement in bringing about an end to the Russo–Japanese War (1904–1905), with the resulting peace conference being held in the United States and leading to the 1905 Treaty of Portsmouth. The following year, Kaiser Wilhelm II of Germany invited Roosevelt to mediate a potential Franco–German conflict in Morocco. Acting as a power broker in European imperial affairs was certainly a sign of the growing, if grudging, respect the U.S. had established by the early twentieth century. When the Nobel Committee awarded Roosevelt their Peace Prize for his diplomatic efforts in 1906, it served as yet another sign of growing U.S. influence in world affairs.

Roosevelt's successor, **William Howard Taft**, was a less significant figure in European affairs, though he did seek to negotiate arbitration treaties to help see off disputes with key European powers going forward. Taft was not the first to try this, but every earlier attempt during the McKinley and Roosevelt administrations had been frustrated in the U.S. Senate. Taft's 1911 attempts to secure treaties that 'mean something' with both the British and the French failed to break this pattern. Once again, the U.S. Senate amended the proposed treaties until they were no longer worth ratifying (Coates, 2016: 101–102). Many in the Senate feared being bound by decisions that were not made fully in its own interests (a fear that reappeared with the Treaty of Versailles in 1919, see Chapter 10). Nevertheless, between 1865 and 1913, the United States had worked determinedly through force, threat, and negotiation, to assert its right to a seat at the table of the European empires. Where prior to 1865 most Europeans saw the U.S. as a truly second-rate world power, by the eve of the Great War, this perception had shifted significantly, if not entirely.

Relations with Latin American nations

Secretary of State William Seward had grand ambitions for territorial expansion in the Western Hemisphere, well beyond his Alaska Purchase. Indeed, for historian Brenda Gayle Plummer, Seward was a continuous driving force for U.S. 'territorial expansion and the pursuit of privileges in Latin America' during his time as the head of the State Department (1861–1869). He had dreams of a U.S. canal across the Panamanian isthmus, wanted to purchase the Danish West Indies, annex the Dominican Republic, and establish a naval base in Haiti (Plummer, 1992: 50). However, Seward's wholehearted expansionist zeal was not widely shared by his countrymen and women, nor in the republics and empires that he wished to prevail upon in order to achieve his vision. Indeed, though some of his dreams were ultimately realized (the canal and the annexation of the Danish West Indies), their fulfilment came long after his death in 1872.

One of Seward's successors, James G. Blaine, who served briefly as secretary of state in 1881, and then again from 1889 to 1892, held a far more economically-focused vision for the United States' role in Latin America. Blaine, himself a convert to the concept of **trade reciprocity** (mutual concessions), advocated increased free trade in Latin America to open up markets and increase U.S. exports. He even supported the idea of an inter-American customs union. Blaine believed that such ventures would not only help increase U.S. trade, but also cement his country's place as the dominant nation in the Americas ahead of any European or hemispheric rivals. In his second term as secretary of state, Blaine also pressed the idea of "Pan-Americanism" and increased inter-American cooperation. In line with this policy, the U.S. hosted the first International Conference of American States between 1889 and 1890 in Washington D.C. (Crapol, 2000: 118–119).

However, not all U.S. efforts to exert authority over the Western Hemisphere led to the harmony Blaine envisaged. Between 1891 and 1892, relations between the U.S. and Chile sank to an all-time low. U.S. sailors from the USS *Baltimore* and Chilean locals came to blows in the Chilean port city of Valparaíso, resulting in the death of two U.S. sailors. When added to pre-existing tensions between the two nations, the *Baltimore* incident deteriorated to such an extent that the two nations very nearly went to war. Indeed, Chile's eleventh-hour climb-down, when it agreed to pay reparations to the U.S., was the only thing that averted it (Sater, 1990: 53–68). The U.S. might have envisaged a closer union between the nations of the Americas, but it was also clear that the U.S. saw itself in the driver's seat in any such arrangement.

Though the idea of annexing territories in the Americas was widely spoken of in the second half of the nineteenth century (even the more economically-focused Blaine felt that Canada was a viable candidate for annexation), such moves were first realized only following the Spanish–American War of 1898. Following the war, the United States took control of two of Spain's former Caribbean colonies: Cuba and Puerto Rico. Though Cuba had long been the object of U.S. expansionists' desires, the U.S. had promised not to annex the island, and the nation became independent in 1902. However, the U.S. did secure for itself the valuable naval base of Guantanamo Bay, and the Platt Amendment of 1901 made clear that—should the U.S. deem the Cuban government "unstable" in the future—it maintained the right to intervene to ensure Cuban stability. In the years that followed, the U.S. occupied the island on several occasions to restore "stability," and this stability was often closely linked to assuring U.S. business interests were fully secured (Burns, 2018). Puerto Rico, however, was annexed by the United States and became among the first "unincorporated territories" of the United States. This new classification of territory became defined more clearly by a series of Supreme Court decisions known as the *Insular Cases* in the years that followed. Unlike previously annexed territories (such as Alaska), Puerto Rico and the other acquisitions from the Spanish–American War were not on a direct path to becoming U.S. states, but instead remained colonies of the United States, without automatic rights or protections under the U.S. Constitution.

With the acquisition of a two-ocean insular empire from 1898 onward, calls for a greater naval capacity (in the form of bases and an improved fleet) were redoubled. One of the leading advocates of such a course was Alfred Thayer Mahan, the author of the influential work, *The Influence of Sea Power upon History* (1890). Mahan looked to the British Navy for lessons on power projection and his work proved an influential manual for expansionists such as Theodore Roosevelt. In this regard, a trans-isthmian canal (for both trade and military purposes) was vital, though earlier plans for such had failed despite the concerted efforts of both Seward and Blaine. Under President Roosevelt, a man convinced that such a canal would help support a "large policy" for the United States, the idea was given yet another try.

After some debate over whether the better route would be through Nicaragua (which Blaine had favored) or Panama (which Seward had favored), the U.S. Congress eventually opted for Panama—at the time under the rule of Columbia. The Columbian Senate, however, rejected the idea in 1903. Undeterred, Roosevelt decided to back a Panamanian independence movement and, that same year, recognized the newly independent nation of Panama. He then proceeded to sign a new canal treaty (the Hay–Bunau-Varilla Treaty) with Panama rather than Columbia. Historians have long debated whether Roosevelt's move to recognize an independent Panama and then secure territory in the new nation through which it could build a canal (the Panama Canal Zone) was a dastardly act or simply a straightforward piece of understandable diplomacy (Friedlander, 1961). Regardless of his tactics, the president had certainly secured a vital strategic and trading conduit through the Americas that would enable the U.S. to fully develop into a two-ocean power when the waterway was finally completed in 1914.

When it came to European imperial intervention in the Americas, instances such as the two Venezuela disputes had made clear the U.S. commitment to preventing European nations from occupying more lands within its hemisphere. However, as the U.S. occupations of Cuba and the annexation of Puerto Rico made clear, the U.S. did not feel obliged to abide by the rules it set for its European imperial peers. By 1904, Theodore Roosevelt no longer seemed keen to annex further territories, but he did feel that U.S. policy toward the Americas needed further clarification. That year, he added his own "corollary" to the 1823 Monroe Doctrine. Roosevelt maintained the traditional U.S. commitment to keeping European powers out of the hemisphere but added that the United States might have to enforce stability in these nations by acting as 'an international police power' [*Doc. 15, p141*].

The years that followed the Roosevelt Corollary made clear that this stance was no idle threat and the United States went on to send troops into a number of American nations (especially in the Caribbean). These "interventions," like those in Cuba under the remit of the Platt Amendment, seemed more focused on economic than political stability. As such, many in the U.S. and its neighboring republics deemed U.S. economic intervention across the Americas as "imperialist" in intent. By the dawn of the twentieth century, U.S. business interests (foremost among them the United Fruit Company) had invested so heavily in the Caribbean and Latin America that many of these nations' economies were effectively controlled by U.S. capital.

Despite many precedents for U.S. economic intervention in the Americas, it is Roosevelt's successor, William Howard Taft, who is most often portrayed by historians as the president who initiated an overtly economic approach to U.S. foreign relations in the form of his so-called "**Dollar Diplomacy**". Led by his secretary of state, Philander Knox, Taft's administration built upon his predecessor's foundations when it came to both economic expansion and interventionist "stabilization" in Latin America. However, this continued U.S. economic dominance—coupled with military interventions and occupations—severely undermined the sort of Pan-American ideals of earlier figures like Blaine. To most Latin American nations, the U.S. seemed far more like a successor to the European empires it had sought to deter from the region than the chief protector of their liberty. Indeed, between 1865 and 1913, the U.S. appeared to have transformed itself from being the ideological defender of the Americas, to the economic hegemon and self-titled policeman of two continents.

Relations with the Asia–Pacific region

Though the United States' relations with European empires—especially Britain and France—dated back to the very genesis of the nation, and relations with Latin America and the Caribbean had been central to the nation's early years, the same cannot be said of the United States' relationships in the Asia–Pacific region. That said, there was some history to U.S.–Asian relations prior to the Civil War. For example, Commodore Matthew Perry's "opening" of Japan in 1853, saw a nation—previously almost wholly closed to international trade—agree to open two of its ports to U.S. ships. Added to this, another important Asian connection was slowly forming through significant Chinese immigration to the U.S. in the mid-nineteenth century, especially around the time of the California Gold Rush. However, in the second half of the nineteenth century, the U.S. started to engage with its Pacific neighbors on an entirely new level.

After the Civil War, the issue of Chinese immigration to the United States arose relatively quickly as a political issue and resulted in the two nations signing the 1868 Burlingame Treaty. This treaty provided that the U.S. would continue to allow free immigration for Chinese nationals traveling to the United States and for their protection under the Fourteenth Amendment—a policy designed to help provide workers for the construction of the transcontinental railroads. Yet, soon enough the tide of public opinion—especially in California—turned in favor of immigration restriction. This came first with the 1880 Angell Treaty and then shortly afterwards with the passage of the infamous 1882 Chinese Exclusion Act (Keohane, 2002: 72–74). The political ramifications of U.S. public opinion weighed far more heavily on U.S. legislators than any passing concern for the pride of China (see Chapter 8). From 1882 onward, the United States marked China as a nation whose citizens were singularly undesirable. Yet, Chinese government protests met with continued frustration as the exclusion legislation was extended for a decade after it first expired in 1892 and was then enforced indefinitely in 1902.

With Chinese immigration restrictions firmly in place, U.S. relations with China became almost fully focused upon increasing trade. As the century came to a close and the vast majority of Asia came under formal European imperial sway, China remained as the largest uncolonized nation in the region. Despite this, many nations had established their own spheres of interest, which the United States perceived as a potential threat. With China's huge population, the competition was on for control, not so much of Chinese territory but of access to its burgeoning markets. In 1899, McKinley's secretary of state, John Hay, issued the first of two "Open Door" notes [*Doc. 16, p142*], expressing the U.S. desire to keep China "open" for commercial expansion. This put the United States in line with Britain's approach to China, though McKinley politely refused a more formal alliance with Britain that might press home their mutual interests (Cullinane & Goodall, 2017: 18–19).

The doctrine of the Open Door was soon reiterated when the United States formed part of a multinational force that occupied parts of China during the Boxer Rebellion of 1900. The U.S. sent forces from the Philippines to quell anti-foreign tensions in Peking (Beijing), and some military leaders suggested taking the opportunity to establish a more permanent presence there. However, McKinley and Hay stuck to their principles, issuing a second "Open Door" note, and rejecting any formal occupation (Meiser, 2015: 74–75). President Taft and Secretary of State Knox made further moves to keep the Open Door fully ajar by negotiating their way into a significant international mining venture (the Hukuang loan) in the Chinese region of Manchuria. Furthermore, the U.S. also supported recognition of the new Chinese republic, declared in 1912. Though China remained frustrated by formal anti-Chinese discrimination and outbursts of violence in the United States toward Chinese immigrants, the U.S. stance on Chinese territorial sovereignty made them an awkward ally of sorts.

Though the United States was ready to assert the independence of China, it proved less forthright in securing the sovereignty of other Pacific nations in the late nineteenth century. U.S. interests in Hawaii had developed across the nineteenth century, with efforts to annex the territory predating the Civil War. However, the American presence in the islands continued to grow, through both missionary action and growing investment in the islands' sugar plantations. Indeed, it was U.S. citizens in the Hawaiian Islands who eventually managed to secure the removal of the Hawaiian monarch. Yet, the anti-imperialist president of the time, Grover Cleveland, was unwilling to take the final step of full occupation. However, with a different administration in control in Washington, in 1898 the U.S. finally took the step of formally annexing the Hawaiian Islands. Historians still differ as to whether this was done for economic reasons or military contingency, but the war with Spain was certainly on policymakers' minds (Osborne, 1981). After the annexation of the islands in 1898, the U.S. presence in the Pacific expanded swiftly. The smaller eastern archipelago of the Samoan Islands was annexed as "American Samoa" within a few short years, and—as a result of the Spanish–American War—the small island of Guam was soon earmarked as a key base for the U.S. Navy. Unlike these relatively small insular possessions, however, annexation of the far more populous Philippine Islands divided U.S. popular opinion far more markedly.

In the wake of Spanish defeat in 1898, Filipino independence fighters proclaimed the formation of a Philippine Republic under the leadership of Emilio Aguinaldo [*Doc. 17, p143*]. As the year progressed, however, Aguinaldo and his followers began to sense the U.S. was set on permanently replacing—rather than simply removing—the Spanish. As a result, at the start of 1899, a protracted war broke out between the U.S. and Filipino nationalists. The resulting Philippine–American War "officially" came to an end only in 1902, though fighting continued in outlying islands well after this. The Philippine–American War brought much negative attention to the U.S. presence in the islands, with reports of war crimes being investigated by the U.S. Senate. Despite far greater opposition to annexation than was found in Guam or American Samoa, the U.S. administration of Theodore Roosevelt maintained its official stance that it was in the Philippines for the good of the Filipino people, and the United States remained in control of the islands for decades to come.

From the late 1890s onward, with the annexations of Hawaii and the Philippines in particular, a growing number of American citizens began to coalesce into what became an anti-imperialist movement. However, the term "movement" might go too far in suggesting that the various figures involved were united. The movement was ideologically diverse: combining Democrats and Republicans (such as former presidents Grover Cleveland and Benjamin Harrison), robber barons and trade unionists (such as Andrew Carnegie and AFL leader Samuel Gompers), as well as white supremacists and voting rights advocates (such as Benjamin Tillman and **Jane Addams**).

Some argued that the annexation of overseas territories, especially the clearly reluctant Philippines, was undemocratic and went against the founding principles of the United States. Others feared an influx of cheap labor, or what some regarded as "inferior" racial stock. The motivations behind anti-imperialism might have varied, but the movement clearly failed to stop the spate of annexations at the turn of the century. Nevertheless, as recent historical studies have suggested, the movement might well have marked up success in the longer term. When the anti-imperialist movement finally disintegrated around 1909, the United States appeared to have all but abandoned formal overseas expansion (Cullinane, 2012: 1–10).

By the turn of the century, Pacific-bound tensions began to emerge between the U.S. and Japan. Like the U.S., Japan was an empire on the rise in the region. Between 1894 and 1895, Japan had gone to war with neighboring China and the result had been very much in Japan's favor. What might have been a passing interest, however, became a pressing concern for the United States after 1898, as many of their new insular possessions (particularly the Philippines) lay far closer to Japan than the United States. Added to this, California became a hotbed of anti-Japanese sentiment in the early years of the twentieth century. There were real fears that the U.S. and Japan might well come to blows, and Japanese victory in the Russo–Japanese War only further stoked such concerns (Hajimu, 2009). If such a war did arise, the fate of the new U.S. empire in the Pacific looked bleak. In 1905, Secretary of War William Howard Taft visited Japan to calm these tensions. The resulting U.S.–Japanese memorandum confirmed that the U.S. would accept Japanese ascendency in Korea and in return the Japanese confirmed support for continued U.S. sovereignty in the Philippines. In 1907, Secretary of State Elihu Root negotiated another agreement with Japan to assuage tensions over Japanese immigration. This so-called "Gentlemen's Agreement" saw the Japanese agree to limit emigration in return for formal U.S. moves to reverse the rise of discriminatory measures in California. The following year, Secretary Root came to another agreement that reiterated U.S. support for Japanese hegemony in Korea. However, the United States did not want to appear entirely on the defensive. In 1907, President Roosevelt sent his modern "Great White" naval fleet on a world tour, which just happened to call in on the Japanese in 1908. Such a gesture was fully in line with Roosevelt's belief that one should always "speak softly and carry a big stick" in such affairs. By 1911, when the two nations signed a Treaty of Commerce and Navigation that assured trade between them would continue well into the coming decade, tensions appeared to be ebbing. However, many in the U.S., including Roosevelt himself, had come to question whether an overseas empire (especially in the Philippines) was more of an Achilles' heel than a benefit to the United States (Burns, 2020).

In some senses, U.S. foreign policy after the Civil War had helped to reunite the nation. The Spanish–American War and U.S. expansion overseas helped take attention away from sectional bitterness and provided avenues for the North and South to work together once again. Yet, in many other ways, these same actions made the U.S. increasingly divided. Its new disjoined and unintegrated overseas colonies created a physical dislocation, as well as new legal divisions. It also caused rifts on the U.S. mainland, where citizens grew increasingly divided between those who saw imperial expansion as a good thing, and those who felt the U.S. had abandoned its republican and democratic principles. When **Woodrow Wilson** entered the White House in March 1913, he inherited an overseas empire that the Republicans had built and a nation which had more fully become a "two-ocean" power. It was now physically, diplomatically, and economically integrated among or within other distant nations to a far greater extent than ever before. With tensions between the European empires nearing breaking point, Wilson took charge of a nation that had traditionally tried to insulate itself from internal European spats, but it remained to be seen whether the U.S. could maintain such distance now it had taken on a far greater role in world affairs.

8 Immigration, ethnicity, and the changing face of the nation

Ethnic tensions, and the question of who could be a full citizen of the United States, certainly did not disappear with the post-war amendments to the Constitution. Yet, it was not only the South that comprised a heterogeneous population. In the years after the war, mass immigration to other parts of the United States made ethnic diversity even more marked. Though Europe had always been the origin of the majority of newcomers to the United States, huge numbers were arriving from countries that were increasingly regarded as undesirable, such as Ireland and Italy. Meanwhile, in the West, the arrival of thousands of Chinese, initially attracted by the Gold Rush of 1849 and offers of railroad construction jobs, also continued apace. In response, just as the South had seen social discord flare up between its white and black populations, the rest of the nation also witnessed a rise in ethnic conflict.

"**Nativism**," a sense that something needed to be done to protect a pre-existing American identity amid an immigrant flood, had grown strong in the years before the Civil War. The 1850s, for example, had seen the rise of a short-lived, anti-Irish Catholic "American Party," often called the "Know Nothings". However, as the war came to an end, not only was there a renaissance in nativism, but its proponents felt they were increasingly on firmer "scientific" ground. Far from being the preserve of southern Democrats, the notion of the superiority of the so-called "Anglo-Saxon race" became increasingly popular across the country. Indeed, leading Republican politicians began speaking openly about the need to protect a distinct white, Anglo-Saxon, Protestant (WASP) "race".

Despite the upward trend of racism and white supremacy, the years after the war also witnessed the growth of a reaction to this prevailing narrative. African Americans, led by civil rights advocates such as W. E. B. Du Bois, began to organize outside of the South and call not only for greater consideration, but for the rights they felt had too long been denied them. Yet, though the turn of the century saw the birth of the modern civil rights movement, the main political parties did little to support this new drive for equality. Where the question of race relations had proved so divisive and destructive in the South during the decades after the war, it appeared that the rest of the nation was not so far removed from such tensions as it might have seemed.

Scientific racism

Whether the focus was westward expansion, overseas expansion, African American citizenship, or immigration, an underlying current that helped or hindered a multitude of policy decisions in the late nineteenth century was a growing acceptance of racial hierarchy and WASP superiority. While expanding westwards, policymakers were guided by the concept of Manifest Destiny, a divine right to rule from coast to coast and subdue the supposedly less civilized people who inhabited the otherwise pristine wilderness. Overseas, the United States annexed the Philippines against the will of many people in those islands, and a large part of this decision rested on the belief among many white supremacists that the Filipino people were helpless wards in need of U.S. guidance. In the South (and beyond) the widespread belief that African Americans were an inherently inferior race remained unshaken by the abolition of slavery or Republican Reconstruction. Finally, when it came to immigration, the idea that the United States was in essence a WASP nation grew ever more potent as the century came to a close. Concepts of who was and was not a desirable American became evermore guided by concerns over one's ethnic origins, rather than the practical benefits that one brought to the United States.

It is clear that concepts of "race," and with them racism, were not born in the nineteenth century. However, this period arguably saw them peak in the guise of pseudo-scientific theories that appeared to bolster pre-existing notions of racial superiority and inferiority. In the years leading up to the Civil War, an idea that gained traction with southern white supremacists, especially those keen to bolster the continuing validity of slavery, was the concept of polygenesis: the idea that not all human beings were of the same origin or "species". This pseudo-scientific concept had links to the Bible, with the idea that where white people were descended from Adam, other races must descend from other biblical figures. The idea gained support from otherwise seemingly credible scientists, such as the Swiss biologist Louis Agassiz (who migrated to the United States) and the anthropologist Samuel Morton. Morton and Agassiz, building on the ideas of earlier philosophers, argued that different races had, over the course of centuries, shown quite distinct qualities and abilities. For example, they argued, sub-Saharan Africans had failed to create great civilizations, whereas white Europeans had excelled in this area (Sussman, 2014: 32–34). For some, such observations, from otherwise credible sources, fit well with the otherwise hard to prove theory of polygenesis.

Combining aspects of science, philosophy, and homespun wisdom to create alternative justifications for racial separation and hierarchy was a growth industry in the years after the Civil War. For example, Charles

Darwin's famous *On the Origin of Species* (1859), which outlined his theory of evolution by natural selection, leading to differing species of flora and fauna, became yet another text adopted and adapted by white supremacists. Though it rejected polygenesis, it was interpreted as supporting the idea that humans might instead have *evolved* into separate and unequal species. Around the same time, the English philosopher Herbert Spencer developed his own ideas about evolution and with them the concept of the "survival of the fittest" (or "social Darwinism"). With Spencer's suggestion that the "strong" inevitably win out over the "weak" in nature, his theory soon became a favorite among white supremacists. Yet, a more sinister mixing of science and racism was still to come. Darwin's cousin, Francis Galton, pioneered the pseudo-science of eugenics, which argued that human beings could be improved by selective breeding of those with desirable traits. Eugenics represented a logical extension of white supremacist readings of Darwinism and Spencerianism and, for its most extreme advocates, offered support not only for WASP racial purity but also the elimination of the weaker races. By the start of the twentieth century, these various (mis)readings of science to explain and even endorse racism, were accepted to varying degrees across much of WASP America.

The emergence of social Darwinism and eugenics were clear examples of a hardening of racial lines in the late nineteenth century, supposedly underpinned by scientific proof. Inevitably, though, such ideas soon slipped from the realms of academia into the popular consciousness. Thomas Dixon, the white supremacist author best known for his novel and play *The Clansman* (1905), which was later made into the film *The Birth of a Nation* (1915), adopted just such arguments in his earlier novel *The Leopard's Spots* (1902). This overtly racist work sees one character explain, for example, the supposed futility of educating African Americans: 'The Ethiopian can not change his skin, or the leopard his spots ... You don't believe that any amount of education can fit a negro to rule an Anglo-Saxon, or to marry his daughter' [*Doc. 18, p143*]. In the United States, such ideas helped many federal and state politicians to justify racially-guided policies such as Chinese exclusion, the continued ill-treatment and disenfranchisement of African Americans, the assimilationist policies forced upon many Native Americans, and the annexation of distant overseas colonies.

When the U.S. annexed Hawaii in 1898, there was a sense among many imperialists that the ease with which the United States had taken control over the islands, like the territories of Native Americans before, represented WASP superiority and their natural right to rule. Many imperialists and anti-imperialists agreed that when Hawaii was annexed, the Hawaiian people would need to be civilized in an American style, or else they might prove to be a constant burden on the United States (Hunt, 1987: 80–81). When applied to the Philippines, this message resounded even louder. White supremacists were extremely concerned about absorbing the much larger and even more racially diverse population of the Philippines. Therefore, not only was the idea of U.S. citizenship placed on the backburner for Filipinos, but the bulk of Filipinos were overtly portrayed as backward and in need of significant education to enable them to form a civilized society. At the 1904 World's Fair in St. Louis, Missouri, the United States constructed a Filipino village, so that U.S. citizens could come to observe their new imperial wards. However, rather than foster understanding, the human zoo that the fair's organizers created, effectively portrayed Filipinos as lower down an evolutionary chain. Newspapers wrote widely of the savage Filipinos at St. Louis, even suggesting that they had eaten the dogs which had gone missing from nearby neighborhoods (Kramer, 2006: 266–274). From the contiguous states, all the way out to the distant South China Sea, there was a growing sense that U.S. policy was guided overtly by a sense of racial superiority.

Though many pseudo-scientific concepts could be adapted by those wishing to discriminate against non-white peoples in the United States, the same period also saw an increasing line drawn between different classifications of white immigrants. The idea of Anglo-Saxon culture as a high point in natural selection, with the United States at the pinnacle, shaped the ideas of those in the most powerful positions in politics. President Theodore Roosevelt spoke of the superior racial stock of Northwestern Europe, when compared with less desirable immigrants pouring into the United States from elsewhere. Roosevelt feared that the continued dilution of WASP Americans could lead to a form of "race suicide". As historian Gail Bederman (1996: 203–204) notes, this led to numerous WASP citizens sending letters to Roosevelt with pictures of their large families, proclaiming that there would be 'No race suicide here!'

With even the president adhering to such concepts, it is not hard to see why the turn-of-the-century United States was such a racially stratified country with a hierarchy of races descending—in the eyes of white supremacists—from the so-called Anglo-Saxon down to the sub-Saharan African. For many southern politicians, such racial hierarchies were fixed, but for others there was potential for other races to advance. Roosevelt, for example, subscribed to the idea of gradual racial progress over time—an idea linked to the late eighteenth century theories of Jean-Baptiste Lamarck. Even so, Roosevelt felt that such progress would take a great deal of time to achieve and he believed that African Americans had been given the vote too soon (Dyer, 1980: 106). Notions of racial superiority (and inferiority) certainly varied across the country by the time of Roosevelt's presidency, but there is no doubt that such ideas served to keep many sections of the country divided along ethnic lines well into the twentieth century.

Immigration and new minorities

In the four decades prior to the Civil War, around ninety-five percent of immigration to the United States was from Northwestern Europe. Between 1861 and 1900, however, this proportion dropped to sixty-eight percent, with the bulk of the remainder—around twenty-two percent—coming from Southeastern Europe. It should also be noted that the volume of immigration after the Civil War was far higher than that in the early decades of the nineteenth century (Daniels, 1991: 122). Though the European regions and nations from which the majority of immigrants came did evolve between the Civil War and the end of the century, the change did not come immediately. Indeed, it was not until the 1880s that Southeastern European immigration really took off. Most of these newcomers—from all parts of Europe—tended to gravitate to areas where there was a pre-existing presence of their countrymen and women, be that in farming communities out west or in the ever-expanding industrial urban areas (Higham, 1955/2002: 15). However, it was the gradual evolution of where different immigrants came *from* that became central to much of the anti-immigrant discourse across the period and helped support the ethnically targeted and draconian restrictions on immigration that were to follow in the 1920s.

Though migration from German-speaking Europe had been taking place since before the United States came into existence, the numbers of German immigrants increased significantly in the nineteenth century. Between 1816 and 1914 nearly five and a half million Germans migrated to the U.S., moving the Germans ahead of the Irish as the largest immigrant group after the Civil War. Historian Klaus Bade (1997: 4–7) sees the bulk of this nineteenth century German migration as 'primarily a socioeconomic mass movement', catalyzed first and foremost by economic conditions in Europe rather than idealism. Unlike Irish immigrants, most (but by no means all) Germans moved to rural areas rather than big cities, and much of this migration was to states in the Midwest around the Great Lakes. Around a quarter of German men worked in agriculture and more than a third worked in skilled trades, while German women were expected to take on the role of mothers, housewives or domestic servants. There were, of course, divisions based around religion (Lutheran, Catholic or Jewish) and regions of origin, but there was also a sense that German–American culture was something recognizable. German language newspapers dominated the foreign language press in the U.S. and some schools allowed instruction in German. As well as this, the music and beer hall social culture often associated with German communities took root in the American mindset (Daniels, 1991: 148–164). Yet, despite the continuance of distinctive cultural identities in many German communities, the nativist reception of German Americans prior to 1913 was relatively muted, with Germans being seen as more traditional (and desirable) American stock.

Other "traditional" Northwestern Europeans that made up a large number of immigrants to the United States in the mid- to late nineteenth century were those from Great Britain and Scandinavian countries. The British, however, rarely formed "ethnic" communities or published British newspapers and journals, and records of their migration are very poor. As a result, they are relatively understudied by historians. Nevertheless, as William Van

Vugt (1999) notes, we do know that a disproportionate number of British migrants were farmers and unskilled laborers, and among Welsh migrants a particularly large number were miners. Scandinavian migration followed a pattern more akin to the Germans than the British, with many establishing quite distinct communities, especially in midwestern farming states. The majority of Scandinavian migration came from Sweden where, until the 1890s, most migrants were farmers leaving a country where a rising population, and consequent surplus of manpower, led many to seek agricultural work in the United States (Ljungmark, 2008: 28–30). As a result, these more "Anglo-Saxon" migrants from Northwestern Europe ended up quite dispersed across the United States, largely in rural communities.

Nativists, particularly in the early years after the Civil War, continued to respond in a far more hostile manner toward a final Northwestern European migrant group: the Irish. Immigration from Ireland had expanded rapidly during the Great Famine (c.1846–1852) but this only represented the beginning of the arrivals—indeed, immigration between 1855 and 1921 accounted for almost half of Irish immigration to the U.S. since 1700. The bulk of this later migration came from southern Ireland, the vast majority being Roman Catholic, and often from the poorest Gaelic-speaking areas of the island. By the end of the war, most Irish Americans, unlike the majority of German Americans, settled in large urban areas such as New York City or Boston. However, a smaller number, largely men, moved west to California and the cities of Denver in Colorado and Butte in Montana (Kenny, 2000: 131–143).

The bulk of these Irish migrants had very limited education or skills and therefore took on low-paid, low-skilled labor in the cities where they settled. Many women were forced to take on paid work as domestic servants, to such an extent that Irish American women became depicted in popular culture, derogatively, as the domestic character of "Bridget" or "Biddy". Such critical caricatures presented Irish domestics as ill-mannered, unable to speak English, and sometimes violent (Urban, 2009). Pre-war stereotypes of Irish men as uncouth, work-shy, whiskey drinkers never disappeared either, and nor did a strong strain of WASP anti-Catholicism. However, by the later decades of the century, the Irish were a very significant electorate in many eastern cities and politicians did not overlook their potential voting power. For example, the Democratic Party machine in New York City (**Tammany Hall**) offered a significant opportunity for Irish Americans to become part of the political establishment. By the turn of the century, Irish Americans appeared to be firmly part of the fabric of the northeastern districts they dominated.

For the supposedly "new" Southern and Eastern European migrants who started to arrive in greater numbers at the turn of the century, things looked challenging from the outset. Like the Irish, they moved primarily to the cities of the urban Northeast and Midwest and, for nativists, they were just as unwelcome. The largest of these newer groups of migrants from Southern and Eastern Europe was the Italians. The four decades before the Great War (First World War) represented the greatest period of emigration in Italian history. Fourteen million left Italy, with twenty-nine percent of these moving to the United States. However, migration was very regional and a far greater number of Italians left southern parts of the country. Most of these migrants were male agricultural workers or laborers, and the majority moved to big cities such as New York and Chicago. Despite these Italians' almost universal Catholicism, Irish Catholics—who were already well established in various northeastern cities—gave scant welcome to what they saw as more laissez-faire coreligionists (Daniels, 1991: 194–198). Of course, as with any newer immigrant group, the existing working classes feared competitors who might offer to do the same jobs as them for lower pay. Anti-immigration sentiment was not wholly racial or ethnic in its basis, and economic hardship was a significant contributing factor to growing xenophobia.

Alongside the Italians, the turn of the century also saw a significant influx of Poles and Jews who came from across Southeastern Europe, especially from the Austro–Hungarian and Russian Empires. By 1910, foreign-born Polish speakers accounted for almost one million people in the U.S., in addition to more than a million and a half second generation Polish Americans. The majority of Poles settled in the Great Lakes region, in cities such as Chicago, Pittsburgh, and Detroit, though a significant number also settled in New York City. Like the Italians, Polish immigrants were mainly Catholic, often from rural backgrounds and commonly took on among the lowest paid jobs in manual industries (Daniels, 1991: 214–222).

Like other migrants from Southern and Eastern Europe, most Jewish immigrants of the late nineteenth and early twentieth century moved in the hope of better economic conditions. However, in addition to economic pull factors, many Jews also sought to escape increasing religious persecution in Eastern Europe, especially the pogroms (massacres) in Russia. Around three million Eastern European Jews had settled in the United States by the early 1920s, where before 1880 there had been only around a quarter of a million. Almost all Jewish immigration was to the Northeast, but New York City proved a particular magnet. There they joined the increasingly diverse urban workforce in manual and unskilled jobs and formed close-knit communities (Daniels, 1991: 223–226). By 1918, New York City was the exemplar of the changing face of the nation. Its staggering population of 5.6 million people included two million immigrants, comprising roughly: 600,000 Eastern European Jews, 400,000 Italians, 200,000 Irish, and 200,000 Germans, along with many, many more (Anbinder, 2016: 304).

The first experience of a new life in America for almost all of this later wave of arrivals came at the immigration hub of Ellis Island in New York Harbor. The federal government established Ellis Island in 1892 as an inspection station to administer checks on newcomers and, soon enough, nearly eighty percent of immigrants to the U.S. were sorted through this gateway. New arrivals were inspected for what were regarded as physical and mental shortcomings, but formal discrimination against Southeastern Europeans on the basis of ethnic origins would not become law until the 1920s. Indeed, between 1892 and 1924, immigration boomed and around twelve million migrants passed through the checks at Ellis Island (Cannato, 2010: 6–14). Ellis Island was, of course, not the only port of entrance for new migrants. The port of Galveston in Texas served as an alternate route for a minority of immigrants accounting for, among others, about 10,000 Jewish immigrants between 1907 and 1914 (Marinbach, 1983: xviii). In 1910, San Francisco's Angel Island opened as a Pacific immigration gateway, although it had been acting as a Chinese inspection point since 1882 (Lee & Yung, 2010: 10). New York's entryway, however, was by far the busiest of the period and was a veritable rite of passage for millions of "new" Americans by the turn of the century.

Though Irish and Southeastern European migrants often suffered a lot of discrimination in the period explored here, there was a sense that—unlike Native Americans, African Americans or migrants from Asia—they could eventually be assimilated and could become American by virtue not of their internal ethnic identity, but their external "whiteness" (DiAngelo, 2018: 18). Civil rights activists, like the African American scholar W. E. B. Du Bois, had harsh words for Italian Americans who sought to assert their "whiteness" and draw their own color line against non-white minorities, despite the discrimination many Italians faced themselves (Guglielmo, 2003: 1–2). Yet, the option of full assimilation, whether or not one opted to take it, was generally only open to those who fit the skin color preference of the era.

The first wide-ranging measure to restrict immigration came with the 1882 Chinese Exclusion Act. In one sweep, an entire nation was dismissed as unwanted on a very public level. Yet, it was a while until further official anti-Asian policy was enacted at a federal level. Another restrictionist measure that came in 1882 was far broader. The Immigration Act passed that August excluded criminals, those with mental health problems, and those likely to be a burden on the state. In 1885, the government acted once more to control migration, passing the Alien Contract Labor Law (also known as the Foran Act), aimed at preventing the importation of laborers on prearranged contracts. Further measures at the turn of the century went on to exclude polygamists, anarchists, and prostitutes. Yet, by the turn of the century, it was Asian migrants who once again came under increased scrutiny (Lee & Yung, 2010: 7).

A clear sign of increasing hostility toward Asian migrants came in 1902, when Congress renewed the Chinese Exclusion Act indefinitely. Labor leaders like Samuel Gompers had long campaigned against Chinese migration. For him and many other white working class men and women, especially on the West Coast, the Chinese represented 'an unpleasant, "indigestible," and perhaps threating yellow mass' (Krenn, 2006: 55). Yet the indefinite ban on Chinese immigration did not satisfy nativists. If anything, it spurred them on to demand similar restrictions on other Asian minority groups. Soon enough, an Asiatic Exclusion League was formed in San Francisco, looking to end Japanese and Korean immigration. In 1906, San Francisco formally attempted to segregate its schools, a move aimed firmly at appeasing voters who were unhappy with Japanese immigration. The following year, immigrants from the Indian subcontinent were swept out of the town of Bellingham in Washington State, in a fit of anti-Asian fervor that showed it was not just the Japanese who were being targeted.

In 1907 the federal government intervened in the situation on the West Coast which, as well as appearing to divide its residents, was also threatening diplomatic relations with Japan (see Chapter 7). The U.S. came to a bilateral "Gentleman's Agreement" with Japan, which put an effective end to Japanese immigration without the need for a formal ban like that which applied to China. Though respecting Japan as a growing military power, many nativist citizens on the West Coast came to see the Japanese as part of a wider threat to their societies. The Japanese were perceived as part of a so-called "yellow peril" sweeping in across the Pacific. However, despite Asians bearing the brunt of official exclusionary policies prior to the First World War, there were already moves afoot to exclude other groups deemed as undesirable.

The U.S. government decided that action needed to be taken to address not only Asian immigration, but the continuing high levels of immigration from Europe. In 1907, Congress established an investigatory commission to undertake a comprehensive review of the immigration situation across the nation. In 1911, the Dillingham Commission's report was finally published. It began by focusing on the shift from the so-called "old" European migration to the "new". The commission characterized the former as groups who 'mingled freely' in the West and 'were quickly assimilated' (such as the Germans and the Scandinavians), in contrast to the latter who 'have congested together' in cities and where 'assimilation has been slow' (such as the Italians and Poles) [*Doc. 19, p145*]. The commission went on to recommend restrictions to immigration that would best serve the United States' economic interests.

For Katherine Benton-Cohen (2018: 1–5), the Dillingham Commission's report was fundamental to the characterization of immigration as a *problem* that needed fixing. This was a notion, she argues, that dominated the century that followed. Mass immigration, of the type seen in the decades after the Civil War, certainly created increased tensions across the nation, but particularly in its large urban areas in the Northeast, Midwest, and California. Increasingly, anti-immigration antagonism moved from being localized in different cities to being a concern for the federal government. Though the United States had been forged and populated by immigrants from day one, by the dawn of the twentieth century it became increasingly ill at ease with continued high levels of immigration. Where white supremacists in the South of the nation began to draw "color lines" to segregate and discriminate against African Americans, elsewhere across the nation hostility toward Asians and Eastern Europeans began to divide urban communities on a new level.

The growth of black activism

Amidst growing WASP acceptance of scientific racism and Anglo-Saxon supremacy, mass African American disenfranchisement in the South, and growing hostility toward blacks within many urban environments in the North, things did not look promising for those advocating greater racial equality. Though the Reconstruction-era Republicans had focused strongly on the interlinked issues of race and rights, by the end of the nineteenth century it appeared that the Republican Party had abandoned southern blacks to Jim Crow in the South and were doing little to stop increased discrimination toward African Americans in the North. The same, however, could not be said for many black intellectuals and activists who had grown increasingly disappointed and disillusioned with their politicians in the years since Radical Reconstruction ended. Despite all the obstacles that non-white Americans faced by the turn of the century, these same decades also saw the rise of African American activism and organizations that would form the foundations for the broader civil rights movement of the 1950s and 60s.

At the end of the nineteenth century, despite the theoretical potential for African Americans to move to the North, roughly ninety percent still lived in the South. Indeed, it was not until the outbreak of the Great War in Europe in 1914 that African Americans began to move north in great numbers, largely to fill the labor gaps left by an inevitable slowdown in European immigration (Jackson, 1991: xiv–xv). However, even prior to the so-called "**Great Migration**," black activism in the North was slowly growing and starting to challenge the pre-existing influence of southern-based African American political figurehead Booker T. Washington. For an increasing number of African Americans in the North, Washington seemed to have grown overly powerful on the basis of broadly accepting the status quo, that blacks and whites could be "separate but equal". Washington's recent biographer, Robert Norrell (2009: 14–16), argues that to accept the view that Booker T. Washington was a self-serving sell-out who was too keen to compromise with white American politicians is unfair. He suggests, instead, that Washington worked successfully within a restrictive society to gain the ear of presidents, and that his messages of optimism and hope should not be disregarded lightly. Yet, in spite of such re-evaluation, the more critical image of Washington did not come from nowhere. Though Washington offered one route forward, there were others who sought more rapid and wide-ranging change.

W. E. B. Du Bois, a Harvard-educated academic born in Massachusetts after the Civil War, felt that where Washington's message had once had purpose and direction, the twentieth century needed a new message. Where Washington focused on manual and industrial training for African Americans, Du Bois called for higher education as well. Du Bois advocated a better educated "talented tenth" of black Americans to 'guide the mass away from the contamination and death of the worst' [*Doc. 20, p146*]. However,

Washington already dominated the key black organizations and networks at the turn of the century: the National Afro–American Council and the National Negro Business League. In some senses he appeared to his rivals not unlike a big city "boss," who controlled black patronage and influence across the nation.

In 1905, Du Bois met with fellow activists near Niagara Falls and together they formed what became known as the Niagara Movement, which sought to challenge Washington's dominance. Though it existed for only a few short years, the Niagara Movement's radicalism, in contrast to Washington's "Atlanta Compromise" [*Doc. 7, p133*], was clear. The black-run organization called for proper recognition of the rights enshrined by the Fourteenth and Fifteenth Amendments to the Constitution, as well as equal economic and educational opportunities. However, the Niagara Movement had a very restricted membership and was riven by internal disagreements, such as that between Du Bois and William Monroe Trotter, an influential Boston newspaper editor. Added to these difficulties, it was also chronically short of funds, and this fact was exacerbated by the efforts of Booker T. Washington to dissuade wealthy donors from supporting a movement openly challenging his own supremacy (Carle, 2013: 175–177; Rudwick, 1957). In 1909, the Niagara Movement was superseded by another Du Bois-led endeavor, the far more successful **National Association for the Advancement of Colored People (NAACP)**.

The NAACP carried on pressing for the constitutional rights of African Americans across the nation, and its efforts became increasingly directed toward the nation's courthouses. Du Bois sought to amass greater funds and support by leading the publicity efforts of the new organization, primarily through its magazine *The Crisis*. Building on the earlier work of Ida B. Wells, the organization also led efforts to combat the crime of lynching, seeking to do this through backing legal action in state courts. It was this method, as the years progressed and the organization grew in influence, that would help lead to the groundbreaking court decision of *Brown v. Board of Education, Topeka* in 1954 (Meier & Bracey, 1993). However, despite growing success in organizing legal challenges to the status quo, African Americans were often left out of, or segregated within, the greater reform movements of the period known as the Progressive Era. Also, in spite of a succession of supposedly "progressive" presidents in the early twentieth century, foremost among them Theodore Roosevelt, neither the Republicans nor the Democrats did much to help African Americans in their struggle against widespread injustice.

Where President Roosevelt spoke of justice and meritocracy regardless of race, and even invited Booker T. Washington to the White House in 1901, he did very little in practice to support African American efforts to regain infringed constitutional rights. The Republican Roosevelt coveted white southern votes, which at this stage went almost universally to the rival Democratic Party. He was fully aware that to win over white voters (who made up the vast majority of voters across the South by this point), further "interference" in southern affairs on behalf of disenfranchised African Americans would prove entirely counterproductive (Burns, 2019). W. E. B. Du Bois became so dissatisfied with Republican inaction that, by 1912, he encouraged African Americans to vote for the Democrats (though few did so at this stage). However, the southern-born Democrat Woodrow Wilson, who won the presidency in 1912, went on to prove even more detrimental to African American rights than his predecessors had (see Chapter 10).

Though the 1910s saw a significant move forward in African American organization, with the NAACP's growth and its increasing legal challenges to the status quo, there was certainly a long way to go. Indeed, the state of the national mood on the thorny issue of race (in all its pseudo-scientific guises) seemed to stand out as a clear shortcoming of the otherwise quite transformative reform movements at the start of the twentieth century. By the time Wilson took office in 1913, the United States was an increasingly segregated and ethnically divided society. Sadly, the progressive movement of the early twentieth century, which sought to solve so many social divisions, did little to challenge those related to race and ethnicity (see Chapter 9).

9 Bryan, Roosevelt, and the evolution of party politics

The U.S. elected Democrat Grover Cleveland as their president for the second time in November 1892 without any great enthusiasm. Cleveland secured forty-six percent of the popular vote, while his Republican opponent, Benjamin Harrison, garnered only forty-three. Although neither candidate had secured fifty percent of the vote four years earlier, both saw their share of the vote drop in 1892. Despite growing challenges from third parties such as the Populists (see Chapter 5), both major parties had continued to avoid any coherent ideological focus on matters of social or political reform. The 1890s, however, saw the beginning of radical change in this situation.

By the 1890s, economic disparity and related sociopolitical developments led to increasing unrest and division in both rural and urban communities (see Chapter 6). The Democrats and Republicans seemed broken: ideologically deficient and internally divided. Meanwhile two broad reform movements—populism and **progressivism**—sought to challenge the status quo. In response, the next two decades saw both the Democrats and the Republicans rebrand. More radical and vocal politicians in the form of **William Jennings Bryan** and Theodore Roosevelt re-energized interest in the established parties by capitalizing on the zeitgeist of the popular reform movements. Yet, such changes did not come without putting enormous strains on their already fractious parties and the electorate more generally. By 1912, the divisions within the Republican Party, and the divided loyalties of the electorate, resulted in an election like no other. The period between 1892 and 1912 saw significant change in the main political parties, but the result of the 1912 election seemed to indicate a nation more politically divided than at any time since the Civil War.

Populism and the rise of William Jennings Bryan

No sooner had Cleveland retaken control of the Executive Mansion than his nascent second term suffered a mortal blow: the depression of 1893. For years Cleveland had made clear that he believed silver coinage was the root of the nation's economic woes and it was no surprise, therefore, that his administration turned to gold for a solution to the crisis. In 1893, Congress repealed the Sherman Silver Purchase Act of 1890, which—though it had not allowed for unlimited coinage of silver—had moved the nation's monetary policy toward bimetallism, as well as leading to a depletion in the country's gold reserves. The repeal angered many Democratic voters who had long advocated bimetallism, especially farmers and miners in the South and West. Worse still for Cleveland, the repeal did not appear to have any clear impact on the ongoing depression.

Along with increasing antagonism from miners and agricultural workers, urban labor unrest also began to resurface. In 1894 Jacob Coxey, an Ohio businessman, led a march of unemployed workers across the country to protest in the nation's capital—they were nicknamed "Coxey's Army". Only months later, the socialist **Eugene V. Debs** led a damaging strike of railroad workers in response to mass dismissals and wage cuts at the Pullman railcar company. Cleveland acted strongly to suppress the Pullman Strike. The president sent the Army to quell the unrest but, in so doing, alienated yet another set of key Democratic supporters (Schneirov, Stromquist & Salvatore, 1999: 4–5). In this time of ongoing economic hardship and growing unrest, Congress opted to turn to the always thorny issue of tariff revision. Cleveland had been elected on a platform that had promised to lower tariffs, a policy that might yet have saved his image with some disenchanted voters. However, in the summer of 1894, Senate Republicans amended the proposed tariff legislation so heavily that the resulting Wilson–Gorman Act did very little to lower tariffs at all. Even if the Democrats had attempted tariff reform, they had failed to deliver. Only two years into Cleveland's second term, his popularity appeared to be entering a nosedive among key groups of Democratic voters and, to make things worse, the deepest depression in U.S. history to that point showed no signs of abating.

In his first term (1885–1889) Cleveland had managed to attract new supporters to the Democratic Party, drawing the Mugwumps away from the Republicans. According to his biographer Richard E. Welch (1988: 215), he even helped to soothe the divisions between the northern and southern wings of his party. However, Cleveland's continuing anti-silver stance, his firm stand against labor, and the party's failed tariff revisions not only saw the divisions within his party start burning brightly once again, but also saw the party's support base decline significantly. The 1894 midterms were a disaster for the Democrats, as the Republicans regained control of the House of Representatives in a landslide. With things moving in the wrong direction at the polls, the chastened Democratic Party knew that it needed to change tack to avoid doing even worse in the rapidly approaching election year of 1896. In June 1896, the Republican Party nominated the safely conservative former governor of Ohio, William McKinley, to run for the presidency. It also adopted a platform committed to high tariffs and the gold standard. When the Democrats met to adopt their platform the following month, what happened has been described by historian Michael Kazin (2007: 55) as 'an act of protest and transformation'.

The Democratic Convention of 1896 was electrified by the oratorical skills of William Jennings Bryan of Nebraska, who roused the gathered delegates with a speech attacking Cleveland's favored gold standard. Bryan declared to those present: '… you shall not press down upon the brow of labor this crown of thorns. You shall not crucify mankind upon a cross of gold' [*Doc. 21, p147*]. The convention adopted an even more pro-silver platform than previous iterations, describing the gold standard as a British policy that was fundamentally un-American. The platform also proposed avoiding further tariff revision, and looked instead to federal taxation, a move that had recently been struck down by the Supreme Court and which (like silver coinage) had been opposed by Cleveland. The party's platform described a move toward taxation that 'may be equally and impartially laid, to the end that wealth may bear its due proportion of the expense of the Government' (Democratic Party Platform, 1896). When the Democrats nominated Bryan as their presidential candidate for the upcoming presidential election, the repudiation of the Cleveland era was complete.

While the Republican Party was moving toward a gold standard stance by 1896, the Democrats were not the only party running on a clear pro-silver platform. The Populist Party, which had taken votes from both parties in earlier elections, had already made silver coinage a key plank of their increasingly popular platform. However, in 1896, with two parties running on a "silver" platform, some in the Populist Party thought that the best route forward might be to join forces with the Democrats and offer fusion candidates. They reasoned that in a three-way race, the "silver" vote would split between Democrats and Populists in many areas of the nation and allow the Republicans easy victory by default. However, in the South, where in many states there was little effective opposition to the Democrats anyway, others wanted to remain a separate third party (Postel, 2007: 269–272).

In the end, the fusion advocates won the day, and the Populist Party nominated William Jennings Bryan as its presidential candidate, with the Populist Tom Watson of Georgia as his running mate. Some "Gold Democrats" left the Democratic Party and nominated John Palmer to run under the banner of a "National Democratic Party," but their efforts proved largely inconsequential. Bryan was now the presidential candidate on two parties' tickets, meaning that there was now little to distinguish the Populist Party from the Democrats. Anti-fusion figures believed that, in the long run, fusion would spell the end of the Populist Party, rendering it obsolete. However, though this is the fate of many large pressure groups, this result could be seen as a type of success. The Democrats, after all, had now adopted a firmer ideological platform—this time supported by their presidential candidate—and one which addressed key Populist demands: silver coinage and a better deal for the working classes.

Once nominated, Bryan took to touring the country, enthusing crowds in key marginal states, and laying the groundwork for what many would see as a very modern political campaign (Kazin, 2007: 72–78). Meanwhile,

Figure 9.1 President William McKinley on the porch of his Canton home
World History Archive/Alamy Stock Photo

McKinley's Republican campaign appeared stuck in the past. While Bryan buzzed around the nation, the far more sedate McKinley appeared on his "front porch" to address journalists from his home in Canton, Ohio (see Figure 9.1). There was, however, more to the 1896 Republican campaign than met the eye. Mark Hanna, a leading Republican in McKinley's home state of Ohio, busily won McKinley the backing of important businessmen like John D. Rockefeller and J. P. Morgan by "educating" them about the dangers of a Bryan victory. Between them (and their business interests) Rockefeller and Morgan donated in excess of half a million dollars to the Republican campaign. For historian Robert Merry (2017: 137), Hanna's political education strategy 'transformed American politics'. Just as Bryan's national tours and speeches represented one part of the modern presidential campaign, Hanna's systematic grooming of influential supporters and donors behind the scenes represented another.

To some, the election of 1896 might appear to have represented a binary ideological choice quite unlike previous post-war elections: between the big business-backed status quo of McKinley and the transformative Democratic populism of Bryan. However, as William Harpine (2006: 18) notes, such a presentation does something of an injustice to McKinley. Though it is easy to present McKinley as the dollar-rich Goliath relying on scheming and financial clout to win the day against Bryan's intrepid David, such a characterization is not entirely fair. Bryan was, after all, backed by both the influential Tammany Hall political machine in New York City and by the states of the Solid South, where the suppression of African American voters made the result all but inevitable in that region. Nevertheless, that November, it was William McKinley who became the first presidential candidate since Ulysses Grant in 1872 to win over fifty percent of the popular vote. He was swept to victory on the back of strong showings across the Northeast and Midwest. Bryan was equally convincing in the South and West, where he won convincingly, but where—sadly for him—fewer people lived. The 1896 election had seen a significant shift in the offering from the Democratic Party, but it had also seen its rejection.

For Robert Merry (2017: 455), McKinley's first term (1897–1901) was 'among the most momentous presidential terms in a generation'—though, as previous chapters have indicated, this was perhaps not as lofty a claim as it might seem. In addition to leading the nation into its first war with a foreign power for half a century, McKinley's administration finally made a decisive impact on the nation's economic policy. The Dingley Tariff of 1897 was far more transformative than the Wilson–Gorman Tariff that preceded it and what it achieved was precisely the opposite of what Cleveland's Democrats had attempted in 1894. The Dingley Tariff saw tariffs on imported goods reach new highs—a triumph for protectionism. As his term progressed McKinley also led a decisive break in his party's previous lukewarm approach to bimetallism. Furthermore, in 1900, the Republican-controlled Congress passed the Gold Standard Act, making gold the basis of the U.S. dollar. Along with this, McKinley continued along the lines of the, by now familiar, Gilded Age laissez-faire approach to big business and industry. By the end of his term, the economy seemed to have recovered from the depression that had started back in 1893 and the Republican administration was happy to take the credit. However, while many voters were pleased with the improved economic outlook and the new vigor shown by the United States in its imperial ventures overseas, not everyone was so convinced. For those who wanted radical change or reform to the socio-economic or political status quo, the smooth ride of the conservative McKinley toward re-election in 1900 suggested that the chances of such alterations were becoming increasingly remote.

The progressive movement

Among those with most cause to be gloomy about the prospect of a second McKinley term were the progressives. The progressive movement is something which historians have often struggled to define because, in many respects, there was no coherent or united movement at all. As historian

Maureen Flanagan notes, the progressives were a diverse and not always harmonious group—a little like the anti-imperialists—and often fought for quite different "progressivisms". Progressives came from a range of classes, despite often being portrayed as almost wholly middle class. They were also often at odds over how to achieve their differing agendas. Yet, as Flanagan (2007: vi) also argues, there is no doubt that the progressives and their many reform agendas 'convulsed U.S. society from the 1890s through the 1920s', and 'produced fundamental changes to American society that altered both government and citizenship'.

If one narrows the scope of what progressives were demanding into three major domestic concerns, the following were certainly among the most high profile: business and industrial regulation; social welfare; and political reform. In some senses, these areas of concern were nothing new, and many earlier movements (especially the populists) might be regarded as the forerunners of progressivism. However, though the influential historian Richard Hofstadter appeared to portray the populists as too provincial, nativist, and anti-Semitic to be true progressives, others, like Norman Pollack, saw populism as a positive and far-reaching response to industrialization (Collins, 1989: 15). The populists had, after all, sought democratic reforms and curbs on the excesses of big business—some of the key issues that were taken up by the progressives who followed in their stead. Though populism and progressivism were by no means the same movement, there were certainly overlaps and parallels that are hard to ignore.

When it came to business regulation, not only did the progressives raise familiar cries for a curb on the growth of monopolies, they also called for measures to make businesses more responsible, humane, and even environmentally conscious in their practices. Campaigners like Ida Tarbell used their voices to highlight the dark side of how the great plutocrats of the day (like Rockefeller) made their money. Others, such as the investigative reporter Upton Sinclair, highlighted the endemic bad practice and lack of care for health and safety perpetrated by these industrial giants. In his novel, *The Jungle* (1906), Sinclair denounced the meatpacking industry and depicted the hard lives of those who worked within it. Yet, though some socialists might have wanted to take dramatic action to change the state of the nation's economic affairs, the bulk of Americans wished for more moderate, government-led reforms to the system. Activists like the lawyer Louis Brandeis favored greater government intervention to break up monopolies, while progressive journalists like Herbert Croly felt that the government needed to take greater control of regulating businesses (McGerr, 2003: 153). Either way, most progressives felt that the government needed to play a far more active role to right the perceived wrongs of the Gilded Age.

Aside from calls for action to be taken against big business, another significant plank of the broad progressive agenda was reform of the nation's urban environments. In 1890, at the start of the Progressive Era, police reporter Jacob Riis published his influential book, *How the Other Half Lives*. Built

Figure 9.2 "Bandit's Roost," by Jacob Riis (1888)
World History Archive/Alamy Stock Photo

around Riis' vivid photographs of crowded and squalid tenement houses in New York, the book caused a sensation among reformers (see Figure 9.2). The impact came not so much from the idea of poverty in the city, which had been raised by many in earlier years, but from seeing its gritty reality in Riis' powerful images (Pascal, 2005: 6–8). The industrialization of the Gilded Age may have enriched an elite few but it had also created an ever-growing underclass, most noticeable in the nation's vast metropolises. For many progressives, not only did action need to be taken against the elite, but also to help the poorest in society.

Alongside calling for government intervention to tackle urban poverty and address the neglected condition of many cities' poorest districts, numerous progressives took action themselves. Perhaps the most well-known example of this was when Jane Addams and Ellen Gates Starr set up Hull House in Chicago. Their settlement house provided unmarried women with accommodation and childcare, while also encouraging newer immigrants to acclimatize to life in the United States. The model was copied across the country in many urban areas, and by the mid-1910s there were over 400 such projects (Traxel, 2006: 10). Others formed pressure groups to push against what they saw as the causes of poverty and, for a significant number of progressives, the biggest culprit was alcohol. The Anti-Saloon League, established in the 1890s, believed that alcoholism among the poorest in the nation exacerbated domestic abuse and poverty, as well as limiting the effectiveness of the workforce. In just these two examples—settlement houses and campaigns for the prohibition of alcohol—one can begin to see the diversity of issues and actions that drove reformers in this period. However, alongside calls for government support to help cut big business down to size and address poverty in the nation's industrial centers, many progressives felt that in order to achieve any real progress, the government itself needed cleaning up.

By the turn of the century, some states had started to experiment more widely with direct democracy in order to break the two main parties' almost total control of the nation's political system. Initiatives and referendums increasingly allowed the public a direct voice in law-making decisions. However, the bulk of changes came via reforms to the existing systems of representative government. Recall elections allowed voters the option to remove elected officials before the end of their terms, if they were seen to be acting against voters' interests. In Wisconsin, Governor Robert La Follette consulted academics to devise a reform agenda that resulted in the introduction of direct primary elections, taking the choice of political candidates out of the hands of party bosses and giving it to a wider electorate (Unger, 2000: 120–131).

While democratic reform was making clear inroads on a local and state basis, there were also calls for reform to national politics. For some, this meant the direct election of U.S. senators, while others advocated universal votes for women. Although efforts for women's suffrage had been ongoing throughout the Gilded Age—led by figures such as Susan B. Anthony—only a handful of states allowed women to vote by the end of the nineteenth century. The U.S. Congress continually rejected calls for a constitutional amendment that would end gender discrimination when it came to the ballot box. Despite women leading so many facets of the progressive movement, it took several more years, and the Great War, before the federal government finally took action to end gender-based voting discrimination across the rest of the country (see Chapter 10).

Theodore Roosevelt: the accidental president

As the 1900 election approached, politicians like Robert La Follette in Wisconsin and the new governor of New York, Theodore Roosevelt, were making their names on a growing progressive wing of the Republican Party. Though it was the role of Roosevelt's "Rough Riders" in the Spanish–American War that catapulted him to national fame (see Figure 7.1), Roosevelt had spent many years prior to that establishing his progressive credentials. As a Civil Service Commissioner and Police Commissioner in New

York City in the 1890s, Roosevelt had built a reputation as a man committed to cleaning up politics and tackling urban injustice. When looking for a new vice presidential candidate to replace the recently deceased Garret Hobart, many progressives in the party felt Roosevelt was the perfect man for the job. However, to conservatives in the party, Roosevelt seemed too unpredictable and independent-minded. As the president's chief advisor, Mark Hanna, famously put it—allowing Roosevelt to join the ticket would mean that only McKinley stood between a "madman" and the presidency.

Despite conservative reservations, Roosevelt's national profile made him too valuable to discard and Hanna failed to stop his nomination as McKinley's vice presidential running mate. With Roosevelt as McKinley's youthful and reform-minded running mate, the Republicans won a handsome victory in the 1900 presidential election over William Jennings Bryan and Adlai Stevenson (Cleveland's second term vice president). However, Hanna's warning words proved to be prophetic. In September 1901, only a few months into his second term, President McKinley was shot during a visit to the Pan-American Exposition in Buffalo, New York and died a few days later. Roosevelt described the assassin, Leon Czolgosz, as a dangerous anarchist, while others felt that the inequalities of the Gilded Age had driven him to madness and murder (Rauchway, 2003: 94–96). Regardless of his motivations, Czolgosz brought to office someone who appeared to be quite different from the assassinated president. Of course, people had assumed this would be the case when Arthur assumed the presidency in 1881, but no significant policy changes had been forthcoming. In 1901, there was no immediate seismic shift either. After all, despite his reformist credentials, Roosevelt knew he was running the nation largely on McKinley's mandate. However, Roosevelt's ascendency marked a far more significant changing of the guard than that twenty years earlier. Although Roosevelt remained somewhat constrained by his accidental rise to the presidency at first, as the months passed, he soon laid the groundwork for the far more proactive leadership he would come to exemplify.

In 1902, Roosevelt took a big step toward increased activism when he intervened directly in a labor dispute between anthracite coal miners and their bosses in Pennsylvania, forcing both sides to accept mediation. Where previously the government had tended to favor the industrialists in strike action (like Cleveland and the Pullman Strike of 1894), Roosevelt appeared to be giving equal consideration to the workers. Not only did this bolster his progressive credentials, it made clear he was willing to take decisive action, beyond what most considered to be his constitutional powers. Historian James Holmes (2006: 45) describes this as a model for future 'federal police action'. Roosevelt's progressive activism was also on show in his early efforts to break up monopolies ("trust-busting," as it came to be known). He urged the Justice Department to take on a high-profile case early on in his first term: Northern Securities, a railroad monopoly that involved a number of well-known tycoons including Rockefeller and Morgan. Though the businessmen fought back, the U.S. Supreme Court eventually held that the trust's dissolution was legal. In 1903, Congress established the Department of Commerce and Labor to assist the increased trust-busting business of the federal government, showing a gathering of pace in this new direction. Roosevelt appeared once more to be the champion of the average American. To hammer the message home, Roosevelt promised U.S. citizens a "square deal," and it appeared, on the face of it, that he was the one who could and would deliver it.

In the presidential election of November 1904, Roosevelt saw off the challenge of his Democratic rival, the relatively obscure judge Alton B. Parker, in what amounted to a landslide in both the popular vote and the Electoral College. The anti-silverite Parker managed to carry the reliable southern states, but Roosevelt won those western states which had been more partial to the pro-silver Democratic candidate of 1896 and 1900, William Jennings Bryan. With his own strong mandate, and majorities in both chambers of Congress, Roosevelt's second term saw the Republicans build significantly on the more modest moves made during his first. For example, whereas in 1903 the Elkins Act had bolstered some of the powers of the Interstate Commerce Commission (ICC) regarding rebates, the 1906 Hepburn Act extended its remit much further and even gave the ICC the power to set railroad rates, placing further checks on the power of big business. For historian Peri Arnold (2009: 2–5), Roosevelt's second term represented a clear break with what he calls the 'party president period' that preceded it. Instead of working within traditional party networks, Roosevelt expanded his own executive powers and used what is often called the "bully pulpit" of his office to speak directly to the nation instead. Roosevelt was looking to be just the sort of disruptive "madman" that Hanna (who died in 1904) had feared.

As Roosevelt's second term continued, further interventionist reforms piled up. In 1906, Congress passed the Meat Inspection Act and the Pure Food and Drug Act, bringing in sweeping new federal regulations regarding the manufacturing and processing of food and drugs, which sought to protect consumer health. Such legislation spoke clearly to the fears raised by Upton Sinclair's progressive exposé, *The Jungle*. Yet, though Roosevelt kept delivering when it came to the progressive aim of regulating big business, there was somewhat less movement on social welfare or increasing levels of direct democracy. Indeed, by 1906, Roosevelt felt that those crying out for such reforms should quieten down. These "**muckrakers**," he claimed, were obsessing over the most negative aspects of U.S. life and tarnishing the reputations of otherwise good men. Though 'often indispensable to the well being of society' the president felt they needed to learn 'when to stop raking the muck' [*Doc. 22, p148*].

One area of reform that really marked Roosevelt out was his strong commitment to safeguarding the environment (which again could be seen as part of his wider moves to regulate big business). After all, it was the unfettered exploitation of natural resources and the exhaustion of land through intensive farming that posed some of the most severe environmental threats for the future. Roosevelt, who had spent a great deal of time in the West earlier in his life, was keen that the great American outdoors should be preserved for future generations. Though Roosevelt was not the first to set aside lands for the future (Yellowstone National Park was established back in 1872), he did so on an unprecedented scale. The president worked closely with the head of the newly created U.S. Forest Service, Gifford Pinchot, who historian Ian Tyrrell (2015: 5) describes as Roosevelt's 'de facto second in command for domestic affairs'. Together they set aside vast tracts of land to create new national parks, forests, and wildlife reserves. However, the close relationship between Roosevelt and Pinchot was not entirely positive for the Republican Party going forward—instead, it sparked an almighty split in the G.O.P. that would ruin them in 1912.

Taft and the Republican split of 1912

Roosevelt had ruled out being his party's nominee in 1908, suggesting that his success in November 1904 would represent his second term and that he would follow in the tradition of his predecessors and stand down upon its completion. With the party in need of a new candidate, Roosevelt endorsed his Secretary of War William Howard Taft. Taft, a former federal judge and civil governor of the Philippines, appeared to be a solid Roosevelt loyalist whom the president could trust to carry on in his stead. Roosevelt's preferred choice was formalized at the party's 1908 convention, and in November, Taft saw off the third attempt by William Jennings Bryan to win the White House for the Democrats. Though Bryan picked up a handful of western states that Parker had failed to win in 1904, and once again swept the South, he fell way behind in the overall popular vote and the Electoral College.

Everything looked set for Roosevelt to retire from the national political scene on a high, with his handpicked successor set for at least another four years in the White House to continue building upon his legacy. Taft's presidency, however, hit a significant hurdle in its very early months. He raised the issue of tariff revision for the first time since 1897, but his party was more divided than ever on what form any revisions should take. The party's conservatives favored maintaining high tariffs, but progressive reformers in the party (whose ranks had swelled under Roosevelt) wanted lower tariffs. Largely as a result of these increasing ideological splits within the Republican Party, the Payne–Aldrich Tariff of 1909 ended up as a compromise measure that satisfied virtually nobody, including the president. Most of all, however, it angered Republican reformers. Their early hopes for Taft's presidency turned to increasing suspicion that the new president was set to become a tool of the party's conservative wing rather than a true successor to the reforming Roosevelt (Chace, 2005: 17).

Despite this early setback, Taft's presidency was not without its successes, and many of these should have heartened his progressive doubters. From 1909 onwards, Taft strongly supported the passage of the Sixteenth Amendment to the U.S. Constitution, which provided for a federal income tax (a measure that was eventually ratified in 1913). Populists and progressives had long lobbied for such a tax, seeing it as a way to force the wealthier in society to contribute more to government revenue. In 1910, the Mann–Elkins Act further expanded the remit of the ICC, allowing it to take charge of regulating a host of communication industries. Finally, perhaps the clearest sign of Taft's progressive credentials could be seen in his continuing to "bust" trusts at a rate that outpaced even Roosevelt himself. Nevertheless, to his critics, Taft's reformism always appeared to be far more limited in its scope than Roosevelt's (Coletta, 1973: 255–258).

Taft had sincere reservations about Roosevelt's generous interpretation of executive power and was also reluctant to advocate significant changes to the longstanding political traditions of the country. He was, for instance, fairly grudging in his support for the Seventeenth Amendment, which provided for the direct election of senators (also ratified in 1913). He also vetoed a bill that would have secured Arizona's admission as a state of the union because its provisional constitution allowed for judicial recall. Ultimately, Arizona was forced to remove the recall measure to gain Taft's approval. In 1912, Arizona and New Mexico became the last of contiguous forty-eight states to join the union. Taft's lukewarm approach to reform of political processes certainly served to feed the suspicions of progressives in his party. However, it was Taft's relationship with his predecessor which proved the final straw that finally drove the progressive wing of his party to leave.

The split between Roosevelt and Taft began in a rather roundabout way. Upon assuming office, Taft appointed a new secretary of the interior, Richard Ballinger, while leaving Roosevelt's close ally Gifford Pinchot in place at the head of the Forest Service. Unlike the devout conservationist Pinchot, Ballinger was far more open to commercial exploitation of the nation's natural resources, leading to a very public row between the two. In the end, Taft intervened and fired Pinchot. This act allowed an already restless and disgruntled Roosevelt to mobilize efforts to wrest back control of his party (Chace, 2005: 15). From early 1910 onward, Roosevelt increasingly sounded out supporters within the G.O.P. about a future challenge to Taft, and the party's disappointing midterm election results later that year provided Roosevelt with the necessary momentum. The Democrats made gains in both chambers of Congress, taking control of the House of Representatives for the first time since 1895. For Taft, November 1910 was the beginning of the end.

By 1912, the increasingly public divide between Taft and his former friend Roosevelt looked set to divide the Republican Party along ideological lines. At the party's convention that year, the conservatives—who had always seen Roosevelt as far more of a threat than Taft—rallied behind the incumbent.

Progressives, disappointed with what they saw as a slowing down of reform under Taft, gave their backing to Roosevelt. Building on the work of progressive thinkers like Herbert Croly (the author of the 1910 work, *The Promise of American Life*), Roosevelt called his proposed activist program the "New Nationalism". In addition to his previous reform record, Roosevelt called for even greater federal intervention, welfare provision, and democratic innovation. Though the National Convention's vote that summer was close, in the end, Republican Party delegates nominated Taft as their presidential candidate. Infuriated, Roosevelt denounced Taft's victory as reliant on the corrupt spoils system and decided to run a third-party campaign under the banner of the newly-formed Progressive Party that November. With Roosevelt running as a progressive and the Republican Taft running as a "progressive conservative" (as historian Jonathan Lurie's 2012 biography put it), there seemed little space for a third progressive in 1912. Yet, with the Democrats' choice of Woodrow Wilson and his progressive "New Freedom" program, and the Socialist Party's candidate, Eugene Debs, promising a host of even more radical progressive reforms, it was ultimately a four-way race to win the progressive vote.

That November, Debs' Socialists attracted nearly one million votes, a high point for a party running so far to the left of the political spectrum in the United States. With the "progressive vote" well and truly split, however, it was the division of former Republican Party supporters between Roosevelt and Taft that proved decisive. Neither Roosevelt nor Taft managed to win even a third of the popular vote, leaving Wilson—with more than forty percent—a runaway winner in the Electoral College (taking forty of the forty-eight states). Roosevelt might have bettered Taft in the election, but between them they had handed control of the White House and Congress to the Democrats. In March 1913, Woodrow Wilson became the first Democratic president of the twentieth century. However, though a landslide winner in the Electoral College, Wilson won his election with the smallest proportion of the popular vote since Abraham Lincoln in 1860. If one were looking for signs of increased national political unity, the most divided popular vote in half a century did not seem to bode all that well.

10 Wilson and the Great War

Woodrow Wilson and his Democratic Party walked away the undisputed winners of the divisive election of November 1912. By the following March, Wilson occupied the White House and his party held a large majority in the House and a narrow one in the Senate. In theory, Wilson was well positioned to enact his progressive New Freedom program. However, though Wilson might have campaigned on a broadly progressive platform, both his party and the nation itself were no less divided than they had been during the preceding decades. With the first Democratic president since 1897 in charge of patronage and appointments, the party's diverse nature soon became apparent as different factions wanted reward for their loyalty during the years in the political wilderness. Many of his southern Democratic colleagues were more noted for a form of race-baiting conservatism than by their liberal progressivism. If Wilson wished to maintain power for more than a single term, he needed to appease his party's solid southern factions, as well as progressives elsewhere in the nation who had edged him to victory in states divided between the rival ex-presidents Roosevelt and Taft.

If Wilson faced an uphill struggle in domestic terms, it was foreign policy that would prove his overriding challenge. Even before his party faced the midterm elections in 1914, the long-standing rivalries among the empires of Europe had finally led to all-out war and, for the United States, a cautious neutrality would prove a challenge to its national unity. The war, Wilson's approach to it, and its outcome, would come to define his presidency. He won re-election in 1916 with a promise to keep the United States out of the war but ended his second term as an out-and-out internationalist. Wilson might have led his nation to victory in 1918, but in 1920 he saw his party decimated in the presidential and congressional elections. This chapter will trace both the domestic and foreign policy fortunes of Wilson's presidency, and reveal just how difficult a job the president had in keeping his divided party, and his divided country, together during a truly tumultuous period both at home and abroad.

The New Freedom: domestic affairs before the war

The 1912 election appeared to many voters to be a choice between various shades of progressivism. Wilson's biographer John Milton Cooper (2009: 105–107) presents Wilson's turn away from his previous conservative positions as somewhat opportunist in nature. Nevertheless, as Governor of New Jersey (1911–1913), he had managed to reposition himself along progressive lines and defined himself as a politician who would respond to the people and not the factions of his party (Clements, 1999: 53–59). Wilson's 1912 brand of progressivism was based firmly upon the ideas of the brilliant lawyer Louis Brandeis. What made the "New Freedom" of Wilson distinct from the "New Nationalism" of Theodore Roosevelt was a core Brandeis idea. Where the New Nationalism accepted the inevitability of financial monopolies, the New Freedom sought to root them out entirely. For Wilson and Brandeis, this was not only good for the nation's economic future but also for its democracy (Rosen, 2016: 62–64).

Despite his promises, when Wilson first took office there were signs that progressivism might actually be slowing down in some areas. Where Roosevelt and Taft had been very proactive in their trust-busting pursuits, Wilson's administration was somewhat less convincing. His party's antitrust legislation, the Clayton Antitrust Act and Federal Trade Commission Act of 1914, appeared to carry on the momentum of Roosevelt and Taft, building on the Sherman Antitrust Act of 1890. However, as John Milton Cooper (2009: 234) notes, the labor provisions in the Clayton Act were very limited and the Federal Trade Commission—as a force to regulate business—did not become a potent one until the 1930s. On paper, Wilson's first years in office seems to have offered progress but, in reality, it offered little in terms of pro-labor and antitrust activism.

Wilson's administration had more success when it came to tariffs and banking. In October 1913, the Democrat-controlled Congress passed the Underwood–Simmons (Revenue) Act. For the first time in decades, duties on a variety of goods were lowered substantially in line with the party's promises. The timing of this was helped significantly by the ratification of the Sixteenth Amendment during the final days of the Taft administration, allowing for a federal income tax to compensate for the loss of revenue from tariffs. When it came to banking reform, rural southerners and many western Democrats wanted to ensure that big business was not put in charge of any new banking system—an idea that had been under consideration for some years—and that any changes would benefit small farmers. In the end, the Democrat-controlled Congress passed the Federal Reserve Act of December 1913. It set up the Federal Reserve System, providing the U.S. with a central bank that could more effectively control the nation's money supply. However, the Democrats did not enact some of the more radical proposals aimed at challenging big business, nor did they provide much direct relief for farmers (Flanagan, 2007: 153–154).

The limits of Wilson's progressive zeal during his first term are partially down to the divisions within the Democratic Party. By this time, the party's already distinctive southern wing had itself split into two broad factions: the Bourbons and the agrarians. The former was the traditional conservative wing and the latter the more radical, agrarian wing. Both factions sought greater influence now a southern Democrat was in the White House. Wilson acquiesced, appointing numerous southerners to his cabinet. The agrarians, under the unofficial leadership of Representative Claude Kitchin, encouraged progressive reform. However, the already dominant Bourbons gained the bulk of high level positions and put a brake on such reforms. The Democratic Party's longstanding North–South divisions had not disappeared, but deeper divisions had arisen within the South itself (Keith, 2004: 24).

Despite the Bourbon–agrarian division, there was one issue on which both southern factions largely agreed, and that was white supremacy. Here, southern Democrats did not have to push their new president too hard to gain his tacit support. Southerners William McAdoo (Treasury Secretary) and Albert Burleson (Postmaster General) swiftly moved to reintroduce segregation within their departments in the federal government. Meanwhile, Wilson expressed admiration for D. W. Griffith's white supremacist reimagining of Reconstruction in the film *The Birth of a Nation* (1915) during a private screening of the film at the White House. For a presidential candidate who had offered a "fair deal" for African Americans, and even convinced influential black leaders like W. E. B. Du Bois to support him, the reality of Wilson's first term soon drove away what little black support he had mustered. Despite the recent scholarship of Patricia O'Toole (2018: 77–79), which presents him as a reluctant enabler in the rolling back of black rights in exchange for southern support, Wilson's administration proved even more disappointing for black citizens than those that had come before.

Another group disheartened by the president's first term was the women's suffrage movement. In 1890, Elizabeth Cady Stanton and other civil rights campaigners had led a renewed effort to secure the vote, when existing campaign groups merged to form the American Woman Suffrage Association (AWSA). In 1913, representatives of the movement met with Wilson in the Oval Office. Among their number was journalist and veteran suffrage campaigner Susan B. Anthony who had helped form the American Equal Rights Association way back in 1866 and had been arrested after voting in New York State in 1872. Despite their compelling arguments to the president, Wilson gave only lukewarm reassurances that he would consider their case. He fell back upon one of the core arguments against an amendment to the U.S. Constitution—that the issue of voting rights for women was one for individual states to decide. After all, some states already allowed women the vote, and this "solution" allowed Wilson to avoid appearing to threaten states' rights (Cassidy, 2019: 63–66).

Despite the limitations of his administration's early years when it came to social reform, the final year of Wilson's first term witnessed a renaissance of progressive activism. In 1916, Congress passed the Farm Loan Act, targeting agricultural workers, as well as several labor acts, including the Adamson Act (which set out an eight-hour day for rail workers) and the Keating–Owen Child Labor Act (which took limited action to discourage the employment of children). Furthermore, Wilson appointed a key progressive thinker, Louis Brandeis, to the U.S. Supreme Court. However, it should not go unremarked that this renewed progressive vigor came in an election year, when the Democrats faced a Republican Party far less divided than four years earlier. Some credited this move as winning over vital progressive support in Wilson's fight to beat the Republican candidate Charles Evans Hughes. Yet, Wilson's 1916 victory could be credited even more narrowly to his winning in California. Whereas the progressive Republican candidate for the U.S. Senate, Hiram Johnson, won election in California that November by almost 300,000 votes, Hughes lost the presidential election in the same state by a narrow 4,000 votes (Henretta, 2006: 144). Had Hughes won the electoral votes of California, he would have been replacing Wilson in Washington the following year—as it turned out, the Democrats' late progressive revival had secured Wilson's re-election instead.

Wilson, Latin America, and neutrality

As the 1912 election campaign made clear, Wilson was not elected as a foreign policy president. However, external factors—particularly in Latin America—drew Wilson into foreign affairs quite early on in his first term. Wilson wanted to set a tone in foreign policy that repudiated Roosevelt's militaristic (and Taft's economic) interventionism. Wilson called for a focus on 'morality' rather than 'expediency', with a move toward a more reciprocal and balanced relationship with the nations of the western hemisphere (Burton, 2003: 56). However, Wilson's approach still held a strong dose of paternalism. In order for the nations of the Americas to become equal democratic states, he believed that sometimes the United States would have to push them forcefully in the right direction. Though anti-imperialist in theory, in reality Wilson's foreign policy resulted in continued, and in some cases increased, intervention in Latin America.

Some of Wilson's early foreign policy moves suggested that the new president really would herald a change of direction. Wilson's new secretary of state, the anti-imperialist William Jennings Bryan, helped spearhead this change of tack. The administration agreed a new treaty with Colombia to improve their fractured relations since the Panama Canal episode, with the U.S. offering both an apology and $25 million in compensation. Wilson also backed the idea of a Pan-American Pact—a sort of League of Nations for the Americas—though such talk ultimately came to nothing (Cooper, 2009: 245–247). Outside of the Americas, Wilson also made moves that heralded a reformist tone. His administration withdrew from a loan agreement in China (agreed under Taft), which Wilson felt would see the U.S. compromise

Chinese independence (Clements, 1999: 137). Furthermore, thanks to the efforts of Democratic Representative William Jones, in 1916 the United States formally confirmed that its goal for the Philippine Islands was their eventual independence from U.S. rule. The following year, back in the Americas, Jones also lent his name to an act that granted increased citizenship rights to Puerto Ricans. Taken alone, these examples might suggest a real change of direction, but they were not the end of the story.

Where the Roosevelt and Taft administrations had overseen military interventions in Latin America to assure "stability" or, for critics, to ensure that governments upholding U.S. economic interests were maintained, Wilson seemed little different. Though critical of his predecessors' actions, Wilson actually increased the scale of Caribbean intervention, overseeing the occupation of Haiti and the Dominican Republic during his first term (Burns, 2017: 139–146). Between 1916 and 1917, the U.S. went on to negotiate the purchase of the Danish Virgin Islands in the Caribbean. Only a year after promising the Philippines future independence, the U.S. had annexed a new overseas colony. Despite all of these instances, though, perhaps the most telling evidence that Wilson's new direction for foreign relations was not really all that "new" came in Mexico.

At the start of 1913, Victoriano Huerta took power in a coup during a particularly tumultuous part of the ongoing Mexican Revolution. That summer, in line with his conviction that the U.S. had to instill greater stability and democracy in Latin America, President Wilson called for an embargo on arms sales to Huerta's authoritarian regime. Relations continued to sour in the months that followed until April 1914. That month, Mexican authorities briefly arrested some U.S. sailors in the port of Tampico leading to a diplomatic incident, while a German ship made its way to nearby Veracruz with a cache of arms destined for Huerta. In response, Wilson ordered the occupation of the Mexican port of Veracruz and the subsequent military escalation helped lead to Huerta's resignation and replacement that summer. However, though a new, more democratic government was formed under Venustiano Carranza, things did not remain quiet for long.

Huerta's rule might have temporarily united his internal enemies, but these grudging alliances soon frayed once he was gone. Francisco "Pancho" Villa, who had unsuccessfully challenged the U.S.-backed Carranza's rule in 1915, initiated a series of raids across the U.S.–Mexican border the following year. After several U.S. citizens had been killed during these raids, in March, Wilson ordered in troops under the command of General **John "Black Jack" Pershing**. Despite his antipathy toward Villa, Carranza was outraged at U.S. forces venturing unilaterally into Mexican territory. For the second time in a year, the United States had intervened militarily in Mexico against the wishes of its leaders. Wilson's Mexican policy illustrated, much like his interventions in the Caribbean, that a new, more amicable U.S. hemispheric policy proved easier in theory than in practice. However, as the hunt for Villa continued, U.S. attention was increasingly drawn to affairs much further afield.

Expectations of some sort of European imperial conflict were not new in 1914—after all, President Roosevelt had intervened to calm tensions between Germany and France over Morocco only a few years earlier. War had already shaken the Balkans between 1912 and 1913 and, by the summer of 1914, the larger European powers were drawn into this volatile region: first Germany and Russia, and then France. The Great War had begun. On 4 August 1914, Britain declared war on Germany and the United States broke its silence. Pointing out that, with such diverse origins, the American population might have sympathies with different sides in this war, President Wilson called for his country to 'be neutral in fact, as well as in name, during these days that are to try men's souls' (Wilson, 1914). Nevertheless, tens of thousands of sympathetic U.S. citizens went on to serve in French and British imperial armies in order to take part. By the end of 1914, two sprawling alliances had emerged. On one side were the Allied Powers—Britain, France, and Russia (along with several Balkan states and Japan)—and, on the other side, the Central Powers of Germany, Austria–Hungary, and the Ottoman Empire. Wilson had set forth neutrality as the favored policy of the United States and, for more than two years, he managed to keep the United States out of the war.

Though at its outset the United States was, to some extent, able to view the Great War as a distant conflict between European empires, as 1915 progressed, the isolation of the United States was becoming increasingly compromised. The British attempted to block German access to the Atlantic, placing mines in the ocean and conducting stop-and-search checks on neutral shipping, including that of the United States. Wilson, reluctant to escalate matters, downplayed British actions (Sheffield, 2002: 66). Meanwhile the German Navy's increased attacks on merchant shipping crossing the Atlantic, a crucial supply route for Germany's enemies and a counterpunch to the British blockade, was more difficult for Wilson to ignore.

Though German U-boats would hardly consider attacking U.S. vessels at this stage, this did not stop them attacking British vessels carrying U.S. citizens. Such was the case when a German torpedo sank the RMS *Lusitania* on 7 May 1915, a British ship carrying among its large passenger list over 100 U.S. citizens. Though not the first sinking of its kind, the *Lusitania* became something of a *cause célèbre* in the United States and posed a significant stumbling block to continued U.S. neutrality. Some in the Wilson administration, such as Secretary of State Bryan, felt that it would be best to warn U.S. citizens against traveling on combatant vessels. Instead, the president formally condemned Germany's actions and expressed his support for U.S. citizens to continue traveling as they wished. A spurned Bryan quit the cabinet the following month. Wilson's words showed that the United States was willing to take a stand if necessary and he left it down to Germany to ensure that U.S. neutrality remained unbroken. At first, this stance met with success: a month after the sinking of the *Lusitania,* Kaiser Wilhelm secretly instructed his Navy to cease firing on any large passenger ships. However, Wilhelm's retreat was an obstacle for German strategic goals in the Atlantic and the cessation of such attacks looked unlikely to survive if the war continued for any great length of time (Doenecke, 2011: 77–79).

Aside from the threat to U.S. lives in the Atlantic, there were significant domestic political factors guiding Wilson's policy of neutrality. Firstly, U.S. businesses had made it clear they did not want the conflict to interfere with trade and, of course, there was an excellent opportunity for the U.S. to benefit while its rivals were busy. However, such a policy was not without its dangers, as increasing trade during a foreign war—particularly with Britain—put inevitable pressure on Germany's reluctant decision to cease attacks on non-military Atlantic shipping (Floyd, 2013: 3–5). Added to these economic considerations were the deep-seated divisions among the American populace regarding the war's combatants, a factor Wilson had acknowledged in his August 1914 declaration of neutrality. Many Irish American voters, who had supported Wilson in 1912, strongly opposed joining a war to support the British whom they regarded as denying the right of Ireland to self-government. In addition, many German Americans and others from the Austro-Hungarian and Ottoman empires were reluctant to support action that might see them take up arms against the countries of their ancestors. To join the Great War in the election year of 1916 would have been, to put it mildly, electorally difficult.

Many First World War historians have presented Wilson as 'instinctively sympathetic to Britain on cultural grounds', and have regarded his actions as tending, marginally, toward the Allied nations (Sheffield, 2002: 65). M. Ryan Floyd's recent work explores in detail what he regards as Wilson's drift, by late 1915, away from neutrality in all but name. For Floyd, the failure of repeated diplomatic overtures, combined with the various U-boat infractions in the Atlantic, saw Wilson increasingly come to believe that Germany was a 'militaristic state'. The British, for their part, did all they could to support such a shift in direction, making tactically timed concessions to the U.S. while becoming increasingly bound to them economically (Floyd, 2013: 5–6). Yet, despite a growing shift toward the Allied cause within the Wilson administration, when he campaigned for re-election in 1916, his party used the slogan "He kept us out of war!" So clear was the anti-war sentiment among the American people that the Republican Party's platform in June 1916 proclaimed its commitment to peace and neutrality as well. Though progressivism and domestic affairs certainly played their part in the election that November, it was clear that a vote for Wilson was still widely regarded as a vote for continued neutrality, and his narrow victory gave him a mandate to continue along that path.

The end of neutrality and peace without victory

Despite being heralded as the figure who kept the U.S. out of the Great War, the election of 1916 perversely ensured that Wilson would also be the one to take the United States into the conflict. In January of 1917, after huge losses disillusionment with Wilson's administration. Nevertheless, Cox's campaign reiterated both Wilson's progressive domestic agenda and his commitment to joining the League of Nations. The party nominated the assistant secretary of the Navy, Franklin Delano Roosevelt, as Cox's running mate. Roosevelt helped to boost Cox's progressive credentials, as well as adding a famous surname to the ticket (Cross, 2012: 85). However, the public appetite in 1920 was not in favor of four more years of Wilsonian policy. That November, Harding secured over sixty percent of the popular vote, the highest proportion since the Civil War ended. A return to normalcy was the order of the day and the rejection of Wilson's legacy was resounding. Yet, though the majority of the nation appeared to have united in rejecting Woodrow Wilson's brand of progressive internationalism by the end of 1920, it was harder to discern exactly what united them beyond this.

Though the Republicans swept to victory in 1920, the electoral map that year painted a picture of a nation still very much divided along an all-too-familiar north–south axis. The Democrats carried almost every southern state in 1920 and African Americans were virtually locked out from voting across the region. Indeed, the 67th Congress that convened in March 1921 was hardly a mirror of the evolving nation. It contained no African Americans and only a single congresswoman: Alice Robertson of Oklahoma. An even more ominous sign of the nation's failure to embrace its growing diversity could be found with the rebirth of the Ku Klux Klan in 1915. In the decade that followed, the Klan signed up millions of enthusiastic new members across the nation. Its earlier tenets of hate and exclusion were extended well beyond African Americans, but the sense that this scourge of the Reconstruction era was back stronger than ever made it clear that the inclusion of minorities within the nation's politics was still far from secure.

The nation had grown significantly after 1865, with massive immigration, westward expansion, and overseas imperialism. Where this had seen the United States become physically united—closing the "frontier" between the East and West Coasts—again such unity had come at a cost. For many Native Americans, this could be seen through displacement and families torn apart as their children were sent to assimilationist boarding schools. Meanwhile, immigration from Europe and Asia helped populate the expanding nation but brought about a significant renaissance in nativism and xenophobia across the nation. Indicative of this were the arrests of Nicola Sacco and Bartolomeo Vanzetti in 1920. On the basis of relatively flimsy evidence, the two were convicted of murder, but many protested that the two had been convicted because they were Italians with radical political beliefs, rather than because their guilt had been proven. Finally, the annexation of overseas possessions helped highlight the growing power of the United States, but also created U.S. colonial subjects, many of whom were still not entitled to self-government or the full rights of U.S. citizenship in 1920. Native Americans, Chinese immigrants, and Filipinos all faced very different challenges, but all were treated as rather unwanted by consecutive U.S. administrations.

declare war in the future (Cooper, 2001: 118). As time went by, however, he became increasingly implacable in his defense of the treaty.

Though there was always a band of "irreconcilables" in the Senate opposed to the treaty in its entirety, there were others—the so-called "reservationists," led by Republican Henry Cabot Lodge—who called for some changes. In the weeks that followed, Wilson crisscrossed the nation trying to convince his fellow Americans of the wisdom of the treaty, *without* the reservations called for by Lodge. The continued stress of these travels stretched Wilson's already failing health to breaking point and, by October, the president was left housebound following a massive stroke that left him with partial paralysis (Macmillan, 2002: 498–499). The following month, the Senate failed to muster the majority needed to ratify the treaty and—for the first time in U.S. history—a peace treaty negotiated and signed by the U.S. president was rejected. Ultimately, it was not until the late summer of 1921 that the United States signed a peace treaty with the German government.

The home front

Though the United States was only involved in the Great War for a relatively short period, the conflict's effects on the home front were quite wide-ranging. In order to mobilize the nation rapidly, federal spending increased enormously and the nation's industries were directed toward the war effort. To help fund this, Congress passed the 1917 and 1918 War Revenue Acts, levying a number of different taxes on businesses and individuals. In addition, Treasury Secretary William McAdoo supported the sale of "Liberty bonds" to the general population—basically, a form of borrowing from the nation. The bonds, rebranded as "Victory bonds" toward the end of the war, were pushed with extensive propaganda linking the purchase of bonds to patriotism (Rockoff, 2005: 315–326). However, raising money was just part of the government's multi-tiered approach to managing the wartime economy.

In addition to fundraising, the government took great pains to control the nation's economy. The nation's war footing allowed for an almost unprecedented level of federal government intervention and interference. Much of this came in the form of price fixing and prioritizing what was being produced. These efforts were delegated to new central government agencies, led by men whose appointment did not appear merely partisan in nature: the War Industries Board (led by financier Bernard Baruch), the Food Administration (led by future Republican president, Herbert Hoover), and the Fuel Administration (led by lawyer, and son of a former Republican president, Harry Garfield). Though there were certainly efficiency benefits from centralizing control of the nation's economic resources, as Hugh Rockoff notes, there was a drop off in terms of expertise that went into the decision-making process. Though most of these agencies were short-lived, not long outlasting the war, they set important precedents for government economic interventions in the 1930s and 1940s (Rockoff, 2005: 328–338).

In foreign affairs, the Spanish–American War of 1898 had united the U.S. toward victory against a common foe, and in 1917, the nation had once again brought northerners and southerners together against overseas enemies. However, where the Spanish–American War had been broadly popular at the outset, it was not long before the cracks started to show. The decision to annex former Spanish colonies, and the far less popular Philippine–American War that followed, saw the rise of a large and diverse anti-imperialist movement, staunchly critical of the nation's course. Entry to the Great War in 1917 might not have exacerbated the North–South divide but it did serve to highlight the differing opinions of the whole nation's diverse population, many of whom had little sympathy for Britain and France. The postwar situation saw the nation once again divided over whether the United States should get more actively involved in world affairs or retreat back toward relative hemispheric isolation. Such debates would continue throughout the decades that followed.

Industrialization had brought unheard of wealth to the nation, but it remained disproportionately in the hands of a select few in the upper echelons of society. Despite the reforms of the Progressive Era, the gap between rich and poor continued to grow ever wider, and the 1920s only furthered this division. It was a decade that, in many ways, saw a return to the laissez-faire economics and pro-business governance that had characterized the earlier Gilded Age. The anti-leftist sentiment that ran across the country during the Red Scare led to increasing suspicion of unionism and working class activism. In late 1919 and early 1920, the Department of Justice organized the so-called "Palmer Raids" that aimed to root out political subversives. These led to thousands of arrests and the deportation of many foreign nationals. The momentum of a more activist, radical left had been severely impeded.

To say that the central mission of Reconstruction—to reunite a nation—had been unsuccessful, would be unfair. The fear that another formal split between the North and South might occur, now seemed consigned to the past. However, though the great rift between the Union and Confederacy had been overcome, reunion had come at a cost. Where old divisions had faded, new ones had arisen. The 1920s were to be a decade of relative prosperity and growth but many of the issues that had divided U.S. citizens remained as contentious as ever. Regionalism, race, economics, immigration, foreign policy, and party politics continued to form clear dividing lines across the nation. President Harding might have represented a new "post-war" generation, as the first president to be born after the Civil War's end, but in many ways the quest to bring the nation together remained far from complete when he took office.

The rapid mobilization of the nation led, inevitably, to a reconfiguration of employment on the home front, as hundreds of thousands of working men entered the armed forces. Following the initial U.S. declaration of war, Congress passed the Selective Service Act, allowing for a draft (conscription). As the war progressed, Congress pushed for greater numbers of draftees, extending the age range to those between 18 and 45 in early 1918. By the end of the war 2.8 million men had been inducted into the armed forces via the draft. When added to the volunteers, around 4.5 million men served in the U.S. armed forces during the war (Zieger, 2001: 61). Though the bulk of these men were in service mainly in 1918, and only for a short period before the war ended, they created a considerable labor shortage at home. As a result of these changes, jobs previously deemed only suitable for men were gradually opened to women. Some of these were in the military—often clerical roles, or jobs in communications and nursing. However, women also took on jobs in munitions factories, as truck drivers, and other such positions that had been regarded as "masculine" roles before the war. Three quarters of a million took on office jobs, while around 400,000 took on manufacturing and laboring roles. As a consequence, around half a million left domestic employment (Zieger, 2001: 142–144). Though many of these shifts in women's work were temporary, the increased pressure during wartime for equal rights for women were not. More militant leaders, such as Alice Paul, leader of the new National Women's Party, criticized the president for his inaction on suffrage and led protests outside the White House. More conservative activists, such as Carrie Chapman Catt, now head of the AWSA, rejected direct action and instead renewed calls for an amendment to the U.S. Constitution to allow for women's suffrage [*Doc. 24, p150*]. By mid-1919, Congress reluctantly backed a women's suffrage amendment that was eventually ratified in the summer of 1920.

The war brought opportunities not only for women, but also for many African Americans across the United States. Aside from the 400,000 African Americans serving in the U.S. armed forces in largely non-combatant roles, the war saw increased migration of black citizens from the segregated South to industrial jobs in the North—the beginnings of the first Great Migration. Both of these moves posed a threat to deeply held views of racial hierarchy. Wartime pressure pushed the government to reluctantly support African American workers' rights during the war but, after the fighting stopped, government backing swiftly evaporated (Zieger, 2001: 130–135). After the war, African Americans who had fought for their country returned, and many of those who had moved out of the South remained where they were. This led to new tensions in both the South and the rest of the country. In the summer of 1919, around twenty-five race riots took place. A riot in Chicago led to thirty-eight deaths in two weeks, and another in Longview, Texas, led to the implementation of martial law (Durham, 1980). African Americans might have fought for "democracy" overseas, but it led to little in the way of support for their rights when they returned.

In order to keep public opinion on side during tax rises, participation in a conflict that many had strong reservations about, and shifts in the makeup of the workforce, the government undertook a significant propaganda campaign. The Committee on Public Information (CPI) was formed under the direction of journalist George Creel to churn out propaganda and censor anything that it deemed counter to the war effort. For Alan Axelrod (2009, xi–xii), the CPI was the century's 'first, most ambitious, and most successful experiment in propaganda', creating a precedent that would prove informative to the German government of the 1930s. Aside from information control, the government also took more formal measures to stifle internal dissent. Hundreds of Germans and other "enemy" aliens were interned, and measures were enacted to restrict their rights for the duration of the conflict. More wide-ranging were the Espionage Act of 1917 and Sedition Act of 1918, which outlined formal measures to stop the dissemination of information and ideas that ran counter to the war effort. Indeed, the leader of the Socialist Party, Eugene Debs, was arrested for speaking out against the war—a move supported by the Supreme Court in its 1919 decision *U.S. v. Debs*. Debs was given a ten-year prison sentence and would go on to run for the presidency in 1920 from his prison cell (he was released on Christmas Day 1921, following a pardon from President Warren Harding).

Debs was not the only left wing figure to oppose Wilson's government. Though the largest trade union in the nation, the American Federation of Labor, had been quiet for much of the war due to a "no strike" agreement with the government, it and its more radical offshoot, the Industrial Workers of the World (known as the "Wobblies"), grew increasingly frustrated. 1919 saw not only race riots, but widespread strike action. Among the first was also one of the largest: the Seattle General Strike. In Seattle, more than 100 trade unions went on strike in support of ship workers, leading to headlines across the country—some called it the start of a revolution (Friedheim, 2018: vii–viii). Such action, when combined with the ongoing civil war in Russia that pitted the Communist Bolsheviks of Vladimir Lenin against an alliance of non-Bolshevik forces, including an American Expeditionary Force, led many to fear the spread of Communism at home. That summer, when bombs were posted to high profile officials, anti-Communist hysteria reached a peak in what became known as the first "Red Scare". The government reaction saw the creation of a task force, under the auspices of the Bureau of Investigation (precursor to the FBI), to hunt out "subversives". Adding further to a growing sense of unrest, in September, much of Boston's Police Force went on strike, leading to chaos in the city, only ended by the use of armed force. Peacetime, it appeared to many, seemed more volatile than wartime.

By the end of 1919, the United States looked more fragmented than it had for years. Women, African Americans, and trade unionists were protesting against what they saw as injustices in the system. The nation had been seized with anti-Communist hysteria and race rioting, and meanwhile

President Wilson had been preoccupied with his losing battle to secure the treaty that represented (part of) his vision for a post-war world. Wilson's debilitating stroke that October seemed to represent the symbolic end of his administration—under siege from all sides, the president had been pushed beyond his limits. His wife, Edith, acted as something of a caretaker president, relaying messages to the cabinet and Congress from her housebound husband. Meanwhile, the Republicans, who had made solid gains in the 1918 midterms, looked set for a landslide victory in 1920. Though the Great War had been a success in military terms, and temporarily united most of a reluctant nation behind the war effort, its aftermath showed how fragile such unity had been.

11 Conclusion

The election of 1920 and the end of an era

As 1920 dawned, President Wilson was shattered: personally and politically. The president never fully recovered from his devastating stroke and his presidency never really recuperated after the defeat of the Versailles treaty. In January, the United States was conspicuous by its absence at the inaugural meeting of the League of Nations—a symbolic end to Wilson's internationalist post-war ambitions. That same month, the Eighteenth Amendment came into effect, bringing about the nationwide prohibition of the manufacture, transportation, and sale of alcoholic beverages. Prohibition had long been an aim of a wing of a progressive movement that felt that alcohol was the underlying cause of immorality and social ills. Its realization in 1920, along with the ratification of the Nineteenth Amendment that summer extending the franchise to women across the nation, brought about another symbolic conclusion. These two constitutional amendments brought an effective end to the raft of progressive reforms that had characterized the previous two decades.

The Republican Party, now more fully recovered from its disastrous splintering of 1912, appeared resurgent. Choosing a candidate to win back the White House, however, proved difficult. The party convention was unable to select a favorite until a dark horse surged to the fore following a meeting of party bosses in a famously "smoke-filled" room. The unlikely nominee was Warren G. Harding, a character quite unlike the energetic and proactive Theodore Roosevelt. Harding, a former newspaper editor from Ohio, owed his political career to party bosses and was happy to fall in line with their wishes. He rejected Wilsonian activism and reform both at home and overseas. Instead, Harding promised a return to a far more conservative "normalcy"—a term so vague as to have mass appeal. His running mate was Calvin Coolidge, the quiet governor of Massachusetts who had first come to national attention when he quashed the Boston Police Strike of 1919. To vote Republican in 1920 was to opt for a return to the sort of conservativism last seen during the McKinley administration.

The Democrats, aware that winning that November was a long shot, also opted for a former newspaper editor from Ohio, James Cox. Unlike Harding, however, Cox was saddled with the inheritance of growing public and the cessation of such attacks looked unlikely to survive if the war continued for any great length of time (Doenecke, 2011: 77–79).

Aside from the threat to U.S. lives in the Atlantic, there were significant domestic political factors guiding Wilson's policy of neutrality. Firstly, U.S. businesses had made it clear they did not want the conflict to interfere with trade and, of course, there was an excellent opportunity for the U.S. to benefit while its rivals were busy. However, such a policy was not without its dangers, as increasing trade during a foreign war—particularly with Britain—put inevitable pressure on Germany's reluctant decision to cease attacks on non-military Atlantic shipping (Floyd, 2013: 3–5). Added to these economic considerations were the deep-seated divisions among the American populace regarding the war's combatants, a factor Wilson had acknowledged in his August 1914 declaration of neutrality. Many Irish American voters, who had supported Wilson in 1912, strongly opposed joining a war to support the British whom they regarded as denying the right of Ireland to self-government. In addition, many German Americans and others from the Austro–Hungarian and Ottoman empires were reluctant to support action that might see them take up arms against the countries of their ancestors. To join the Great War in the election year of 1916 would have been, to put it mildly, electorally difficult.

Many First World War historians have presented Wilson as 'instinctively sympathetic to Britain on cultural grounds', and have regarded his actions as tending, marginally, toward the Allied nations (Sheffield, 2002: 65). M. Ryan Floyd's recent work explores in detail what he regards as Wilson's drift, by late 1915, away from neutrality in all but name. For Floyd, the failure of repeated diplomatic overtures, combined with the various U-boat infractions in the Atlantic, saw Wilson increasingly come to believe that Germany was a 'militaristic state'. The British, for their part, did all they could to support such a shift in direction, making tactically timed concessions to the U.S. while becoming increasingly bound to them economically (Floyd, 2013: 5–6). Yet, despite a growing shift toward the Allied cause within the Wilson administration, when he campaigned for re-election in 1916, his party used the slogan "He kept us out of war!" So clear was the anti-war sentiment among the American people that the Republican Party's platform in June 1916 proclaimed its commitment to peace and neutrality as well. Though progressivism and domestic affairs certainly played their part in the election that November, it was clear that a vote for Wilson was still widely regarded as a vote for continued neutrality, and his narrow victory gave him a mandate to continue along that path.

The end of neutrality and peace without victory

Despite being heralded as the figure who kept the U.S. out of the Great War, the election of 1916 perversely ensured that Wilson would also be the one to take the United States into the conflict. In January of 1917, after huge losses on the Somme the previous year, political and military leaders in Germany decided to take a gamble and resume unrestricted submarine warfare in the Atlantic. German officials were fully aware—due to Wilson's strong words of 1915—that such an action would almost certainly require the U.S. to declare war upon the German Empire. However, they reasoned that if sufficient progress could be made before the United States was able to mobilize, it might yet be worth it to deny Britain of its vital food supplies from North America (Sheffield, 2002: 67).

In February, Wilson reacted to Germany's gamble by breaking off diplomatic relations. Soon afterward, German U-boats stepped up their campaign and sank a series of U.S. vessels during February and March that led to increased calls for war from within the United States. This pressure was further exacerbated by a telegram intercepted by the British and passed on to the United States. German Foreign Minister Arthur Zimmerman had sent the telegram to Mexico, requesting a formal alliance (if the U.S. were to join the Great War on the Allied side). In return, Germany would help Mexico reclaim territories lost to the U.S. in the Mexican–American War. The Zimmerman telegram hit headlines in March 1917 and redoubled calls for a response. Meanwhile, in Russia, the autocratic Tsar Nicholas II was toppled and a new provisional government was formed. The end of the tsarist regime made an alliance of sorts with Russia appear more acceptable from a U.S. standpoint. Wilson met with his cabinet on 20 March, and they agreed that the next logical step must be taken. The following day, the president called for a special session of Congress (Kennedy, 1980/2004: 10). Wilson explained his position as that of a man who had done all he could to avoid war and was now forced into it by German actions [*Doc. 23, p148*]. On 4 April, the Senate voted for a declaration of war by eighty-two votes to six, and on 6 April, the House followed suit by a margin of 373 to 50 (Stevenson, 2017: 64). The president who had kept the U.S. out of war now led them into it.

Despite the U.S. declaration of war against Germany, Wilson was determined that his nation should remain as separate as possible from its new "allies". The president defined the U.S. as an "associate" power, rather than a fully-fledged "ally" and sought to keep both direct U.S. military involvement—and his nation's war aims—firmly under his direction (Woodward, 1993: 42–43). Militarily, the United States was forced to mobilize rapidly and the impact of the U.S. Army would not truly be felt for more than a year. Prior to this, it would be fair to say that the primary U.S. influences on the Allied war effort in Europe were via financial support and—perhaps more decisively—a much needed boost to Allied morale. The U.S. Navy soon helped supplement British naval forces in the Atlantic and John Pershing was assigned to head the Army's American Expeditionary Force (AEF). The AEF saw its first small-scale action at Cantigny in Northern France on 28 May 1918, but thereafter grew rapidly so that there were thirty-nine U.S. divisions in Europe by the end of September (Sheffield, 2002: 235). Though it is easy to overemphasize the significance of the AEF in the victory, it was doubtless a contributing factor to coalition success.

Wilson made clear before the U.S. joined the war that he believed in "peace without victory," fearing a punitive peace would only lead to future turmoil. The president elaborated upon this stance when he announced his "Fourteen Points" in January 1918. They outlined a path to future global stability that rejected 'conquest and aggrandizement' or 'secret covenants'. He believed that his vision represented 'the only possible plan' for a lasting world peace (Wilson, 1918). Wilson's plan was, however, not wholly agreeable to Britain and France. This was especially the case when it came to Wilson's talk of national 'self-determination', which saw him hailed by nationalists across Asia and Africa as 'the prophet of a new era in world affairs, one in which justice, rather than power, would be the central principle of international relations' (Manela, 2009: 3). Added to this anti-colonial tone, the idea of freedom of the seas affronted Britain's long-held sense of naval security, and the idea of peace without victory failed to win over a French nation ravaged by years of warfare on their own soil. Wilson's rhetoric was idealistic but, for many, seemed far from realistic.

When a general armistice was finally agreed on 11 November 1918, the administration's attention turned to how Wilson's vision of a post-war world might best be accomplished. Wilson travelled to Paris with a team of handpicked—and largely sympathetic—colleagues for a peace conference at the Palace of Versailles. He went on to spend an unprecedented amount of time outside of the United States for a sitting president. At the center of Wilson's solution to maintaining post-war peace was the idea of "collective security". He felt this would best be secured through the creation of an international body: the League of Nations. Over the course of the peace conference, however, Wilson's high-minded idealism soon gave way to a variety of compromises at the behest of French leader Georges Clemenceau and British Prime Minister David Lloyd George. The resulting Treaty of Versailles (1919) was far more punitive than Wilson's team desired. Yet, he felt that the treaty, and most importantly the League of Nations, were worth the compromises to achieve his wider goals.

When Wilson returned home he was well aware that a formidable challenge still lay ahead in gaining Senate ratification of the treaty—something that would require a two-thirds majority. Opposition in the United States came from a range of sources. Added to isolationists already unhappy with the extent of U.S. international commitments, there were those who were disappointed with the compromises Wilson had made on his professed ideals. For many in the middle, the key stumbling block appeared to be the League of Nations itself, and particularly Article X of the League Covenant, which appeared to commit member nations to come to the military aid of other members when under attack. Wilson defended the article as the only thing that would make the League more than a 'debating society', but played down the idea that it would take away the power of the U.S. Congress to

Part II

Documents

Document 1

ABRAHAM LINCOLN – "THE GETTYSBURG ADDRESS," 19 NOVEMBER 1863

A speech given at the dedication of the Soldiers' National Cemetery at Gettysburg, Pennsylvania, where the most costly battle of the Civil War had been fought that July.

Fourscore and seven years ago our fathers brought forth on this continent, a new nation, conceived in liberty, and dedicated to the proposition that all men are created equal. Now we are engaged in a great civil war, testing whether that nation, or any nation so conceived and so dedicated, can long endure. We are met on a great battle field of that war. We have come to dedicate a portion of that field, as a final resting-place for those who here gave their lives that that nation might live. It is altogether fitting and proper that we should do this. But in a larger sense we cannot dedicate—we cannot consecrate—we cannot hallow—this ground. The brave men, living and dead who struggled here have consecrated it far above our poor power to add or detract. The world will little note nor long remember what we say here, but it can never forget what they did here. It is for us, the living, rather, to be dedicated here to the unfinished work which they who fought here have thus far so nobly advanced. It is rather for us to be here dedicated to the great task remaining before us—that from these honored dead we take increased devotion to that cause for which they here gave the last full measure of devotion; that we here highly resolve that these dead shall not have died in vain; that this nation, under God, shall have a new birth of freedom; and that government of the people, by the people, for the people, shall not perish from the earth.

Source: Luther Emerson Robinson, *Lincoln's Masterpieces* (New York: Knickerbocker Press, c.1923): 4.

Document 2

FREDERICK DOUGLASS – "WHAT THE BLACK MAN WANTS," APRIL 1865

Excerpt from a speech delivered before the Annual Meeting of the Massachusetts Anti-Slavery Society in Boston. At this point Douglass is explaining why African Americans need the vote.

[...] It may be asked, "Why do you want it? Some men have got along very well without it. Women have not this right." Shall we justify one wrong by another? That is the sufficient answer. Shall we at this moment justify the deprivation of the negro of the right to vote, because some one else is deprived of that privilege? I hold that women, as well as men, have the right to vote (applause), and my heart and my voice go with the movement to extend suffrage to woman; but that question rests upon another basis than that on which our right rests. We may be asked, I say, why we want it. I will tell you why we want it. We want it because it is our *right*, first of all. (Applause) No class of men can, without insulting their own nature, be content with any deprivation of their rights. We want it, again, as a means for educating our race. Men are so constituted that they derive their conviction of their own possibilities largely from the estimate formed of them by others. If nothing is expected of a people, that people will find it difficult to contradict that expectation. By depriving us of suffrage, you affirm our incapacity to form an intelligent judgment respecting public men and public measures; you declare before the world that we are unfit to exercise the elective franchise, and by this means lead us to undervalue ourselves, to put a low estimate upon ourselves, and to feel that we have no possibilities like other men. Again, I want the elective franchise, for one, as a colored man, because ours is a peculiar government, based upon a peculiar idea, and that idea is universal suffrage. If I were in a monarchical government, or an autocratic or aristocratic government, where the few bore rule and the many were subject, there would be no special stigma resting upon me, because I did not exercise the elective franchise. It would do me no great violence. Mingling with the mass, I should partake of the strength of the mass; I should be supported by the mass, and I should have the same incentives to endeavor with the mass of my fellow-men; it would be no particular burden, no particular deprivation; but here, where universal suffrage is the rule, where that is the fundamental idea of the Government, to rule us out is to make us an exception, to brand us with the stigma of inferiority, and to invite to our heads the missiles of those about us; therefore, I want the franchise for the black man. [...]

Source: *The Equality of All Men Before the Law, Claimed and Defended in Speeches by Hon. William D. Kelley, Wendell Phillips, and Frederick Douglass and Letters from Elizur Wright and Wm. Heighton* (Boston: Press of Geo. C. Rand & Avery, 1865): 37.

Document 3

FOURTEENTH AMENDMENT TO THE UNITED STATES CONSTITUTION, PASSED BY CONGRESS 13 JUNE 1866 AND RATIFIED 9 JULY 1868

Section 1.

All persons born or naturalized in the United States, and subject to the jurisdiction thereof, are citizens of the United States and of the State wherein they reside. No State shall make or enforce any law which shall abridge the privileges or immunities of citizens of the United States; nor shall any State deprive any person of life, liberty, or property, without due process of law; nor deny to any person within its jurisdiction the equal protection of the laws.

Section 2.

Representatives shall be apportioned among the several States according to their respective numbers, counting the whole number of persons in each State, excluding Indians not taxed. But when the right to vote at any election for the choice of electors for President and Vice-President of the United States, Representatives in Congress, the Executive and Judicial officers of a State, or the members of the Legislature thereof, is denied to any of the male inhabitants of such State, being twenty-one years of age, and citizens of the United States, or in any way abridged, except for participation in rebellion, or other crime, the basis of representation therein shall be reduced in the proportion which the number of such male citizens shall bear to the whole number of male citizens twenty-one years of age in such State.

Section 3.

No person shall be a Senator or Representative in Congress, or elector of President and Vice-President, or hold any office, civil or military, under the United States, or under any State, who, having previously taken an oath, as a member of Congress, or as an officer of the United States, or as a member of any State legislature, or as an executive or judicial officer of any State, to support the Constitution of the United States, shall have engaged in insurrection or rebellion against the same, or given aid or comfort to the enemies thereof. But Congress may by a vote of two-thirds of each House, remove such disability.

Section 4.

The validity of the public debt of the United States, authorized by law, including debts incurred for payment of pensions and bounties for services in suppressing insurrection or rebellion, shall not be questioned. But neither the United States nor any State shall assume or pay any debt or obligation incurred in aid of insurrection or rebellion against the United States, or any claim for the loss or emancipation of any slave; but all such debts, obligations and claims shall be held illegal and void.

Section 5.

The Congress shall have the power to enforce, by appropriate legislation, the provisions of this article.

Source: U.S. National Archives and Records Administration, *Our Documents*, www.ourdocuments.gov/doc.php?flash=false&doc=43&page=transcript (accessed 14 December 2019).

Document 4

ANDREW JOHNSON – VETO MESSAGE TO THE HOUSE OF REPRESENTATIVES, 2 MARCH 1867

Excerpt from the president's veto message, explaining his objections to the 1867 Reconstruction Bill

[…] It is plain that the authority here given to the military officer amounts to absolute despotism. But to make it still more unendurable, the bill provides that it may be delegated to as many subordinates as he chooses to appoint, for it declares that he shall "punish or cause to be punished." Such a power has not been wielded by any monarch in England for more than five hundred years. In all that time no people who speak the English language have borne such servitude. It reduces the whole population of the ten States—all persons, of every color, sex, and condition, and every stranger within their limits—to the most abject and degrading slavery. No master ever had a control so absolute over the slaves as this bill gives to the military officers over both white and colored persons.

It may be answered to this that the officers of the Army are too magnanimous, just, and humane to oppress and trample upon a subjugated people. I do not doubt that army officers are as well entitled to this kind of confidence as any other class of men. But the history of the world has been written in vain if it does not teach us that unrestrained authority can never be safely trusted in human hands. It is almost sure to be more or less abused under any circumstances, and it has always resulted in gross tyranny where the rulers who exercise it are strangers to their subjects and come among them as the representatives of a distant power, and more especially when the power that sends them is unfriendly. Governments closely resembling that here proposed have been fairly tried in Hungary and Poland, and the suffering endured by those people roused the sympathies of the entire world. It was tried in Ireland, and, though tempered at first by principles of English law, it gave birth to cruelties so atrocious that they are never recounted without just indignation. The French Convention armed its deputies with this power and sent them to the southern departments of the Republic. The massacres, murders, and other atrocities which they committed show what the passions of the ablest men in the most civilized society will tempt them to do when wholly unrestrained by law. [...]

Source: *A Compilation of the Messages and Papers of the Presidents*, Vol. 9 (New York: Bureau of National Literature, 1913): 3700.

Document 5

"AN ACT TO CONFER CIVIL RIGHTS ON FREEDMEN, AND FOR OTHER PURPOSES," 1865

The first section of several of the so-called "black codes" enacted in Mississippi and approved on 25 November 1865.

Section 1. *Be it enacted by the legislature of the State of Mississippi,* That all freedmen, free negroes and mulattoes may sue and be sued, implead and be impleaded, in all the courts of law and equity of this State, and may acquire personal property, and choses in action, by descent or purchase, and may dispose of the same in the same manner and to the same extent that white persons may: *Provided,* That the provisions of this section shall not be so construed as to allow any freedman, free negro or mulatto to rent or lease lands or tenements except in incorporated cities or towns, in which places the corporate authorities shall control the same.

[...] Sec. 3. * * * all freedmen, free negroes or mulattoes who do now and have herebefore lived and cohabited together as husband and wife shall be taken and held in law as legally married, and the issue shall be taken and held as legitimate for all purposes; and it shall not be lawful for any freedman, free negro or mulatto to intermarry with any white person; nor for any white person to intermarry with any freedman, free negro or mulatto; and any person who shall so intermarry shall be deemed guilty of felony, and on conviction thereof shall be confined in the State penitentiary for life; and those shall be deemed freedmen, free negroes and mulattoes who are of pure negro blood, and those descended from a negro to the third generation, inclusive, though one ancestor in each generation may have been a white person.

[...] Sec. 6. * * * all contracts for labor made with freedmen, free negroes and mulattoes for a longer period than one month shall be in writing, and a duplicate, attested and read to said freedman, free negro or mulatto by a beat, city or county officer, or two disinterested white persons of the county in which the labor is to performed, of which each party shall have one; and said contracts shall be taken and held as entire contracts, and if the laborer shall quit the service of the employer before the expiration of his term of service, without good cause, he shall forfeit his wages for that year up to the time of quitting.

Sec. 7. * * * every civil officer shall, and every person may, arrest and carry back to his or her legal employer any freedman, free negro, or mulatto who shall have quit the service of his or her employer before the expiration of his or her term of service without good cause; and said officer and person shall be entitled to receive for arresting and carrying back every deserting employe [sic] aforesaid the sum of five dollars, and ten cents per mile from the place of arrest to the place of delivery; and the same shall be paid by the employer, and held as a set-off for so much against the wages of the deserting employe [sic].

[…] Sec. 9. * * * if any person shall persuade or attempt to persuade, entice, or cause any freedman, free negro or mulatto to desert from the legal employment of any person before the expiration of his or her term of service, or shall knowingly employ any such deserting freedman, free negro or mulatto, or shall knowingly give or sell to any such deserting freedman, free negro or mulatto, any food, raiment, or other thing, he or she shall be guilty of a misdemeanor. […]

Source: Walter L. Fleming, ed., *West Virginia University Documents Relating to Reconstruction*: *No. 8, Laws Relating to Freedmen, 1865–6* (Morgantown, WV: West Virginia University, 1904): 13–15.

Document 6

TOM WATSON – "THE NEGRO QUESTION IN THE SOUTH," 1892

Excerpts from Tom Watson's thoughts on the need for racial solidarity for the future success of the Populist Party. Watson later repudiated this stance and embraced white supremacy.

[…] Why should the colored man always be taught that the white man of his neighborhood hates him, while a Northern man, who taxes every rag on his back, loves him? Why should not my tenant come to regard me as his friend rather than the manufacturer who plunders us both? Why should we perpetuate a policy which drives the black man into the arms of the Northern politician?

Why should we always allow Northern and Eastern Democrats to enslave us forever by threats of the Force Bill?

Let us draw the supposed teeth of this fabled dragon by founding our new policy upon justice—upon the simple but profound truth that, if the voice of passion can be hushed, the self-interest of both races will drive them to act in concert. There never was a day during the last twenty years when the South could not have flung the money power into the dust by patiently teaching the Negro that we could not be wretched under any system which would not afflict him likewise; that we could not prosper under any law which would not also bring its blessings to him.

To the emasculated individual who cries "Negro supremacy!" there is little to be said. His cowardice shows him to be a degeneration from the race which has never yet feared any other race. Existing under such conditions as they now do in this country, there is no earthly chance for Negro domination, unless we are ready to admit that the colored man is our superior in will power, courage, and intellect.

Not being prepared to make any such admission in favor of any race the sun ever shone on, I have no words which can portray my contempt for the white men, Anglo-Saxons, who can knock their knees together, and through their chattering teeth and pale lips admit that they are afraid the Negroes will "dominate us."

The question of social equality does not enter into the calculation at all. That is a thing each citizen decides for himself. No statute ever yet drew the latch of the humblest home—or ever will. Each citizen regulates his own visiting list—and always will.

The conclusion, then, seems to me to be this: the crushing burdens which now oppress both races in the South will cause each to make an effort to cast them off. They will see a similarity of cause and a similarity of remedy. They will recognize that each should help the other in the work of repealing bad laws and enacting good ones. They will become political allies, and neither can injure the other without weakening both. It will be to the interest of both that each should have justice. And on these broad lines of mutual interest, mutual forbearance, and mutual support the present will be made the stepping-stone to future peace and prosperity. [...]

Source: B. O. Flower, ed., *The Arena*, Vol. 6 (Boston: The Arena Publishing Co., 1892): 549–550.

Document 7

BOOKER T. WASHINGTON – "ATLANTA COMPROMISE" SPEECH, 18 SEPTEMBER 1895

Excerpt from a speech given at an exposition in Atlanta, Georgia.

[...] To those of the white race who look to the incoming of those of foreign birth and strange tongue and habits for the prosperity of the South, were I permitted I would repeat what I say to my own race, 'Cast down your bucket where you are.' Cast it down among the 8,000,000 Negroes whose habits you know, whose fidelity and love you have tested in days when to have proved treacherous meant the ruin of your firesides. Cast down your bucket among these people who have, without strikes and labor wars, tilled your fields, cleared your forests, builded [sic] your railroads and cities, and brought forth treasures from the bowels of the earth, and helped make possible this magnificent representation of the progress of the South. Casting down your bucket among my people, helping and encouraging them as you are doing on these grounds, and, with education of head, hand and heart, you will find that they will buy your surplus land, make blossom the waste places in your fields, and run your factories. While doing this, you can be sure in the future, as in the past, that you and your families will be surrounded by the most patient, faithful, law-abiding, and unresentful people that the world has seen. As we have proved our loyalty to you in the past, in nursing your children, watching by the sick bed of your mothers and fathers, and often following them with tear-dimmed eyes to their graves, so in the future, in our humble way, we shall stand by you with a devotion that no foreigner can approach, ready to lay down our lives, if need be, in defense of yours, interlacing our industrial, commercial, civil, and religious life with yours in a way that shall make the interests of both races one. In all things that are purely social we can be as separate as the fingers, yet one as the hand in all things essential to mutual progress. [...]

Source: Booker T. Washington, *The Story of My Life and Work* (Toronto: J.L. Nichols & Co., 1900): 167–168.

Document 8

SITTING BULL – SPEECH TO A U.S. CONGRESSIONAL COMMISSION, 1883

Excerpts from Sitting Bull's speech relating to U.S. promises.

[...] If a man loses anything, and goes back and looks carefully for it he will find it, and that is what the Indians are doing now when they ask you to give them the things that were promised them in the past; and I do not consider that they should be treated like beasts, and that is the reason I have grown up with the feelings I have. Whatever you wanted of me I have obeyed, and I have come when you called me. The Great Father [U.S. president] sent me word that whatever he had against me in the past has been forgiven and thrown aside, and he would have nothing against me in the future, and I accepted his promises and came in; and he told me not to step aside from the white man's path, and I told him I would not, and I am doing my best to travel in that path ....

When we sold the Black Hills we got a very small price for it, and not what we thought we ought to have received. I used to think that the size of the payments would remain the same all the time, but they are growing smaller all the time. I want you to tell the Great Father everything I have said, and that we want some benefit from the promises he has made us; and I don't think I should be tormented with anything about giving up any part of my land until those promises are fulfilled—I would rather wait until that time, when I will be ready to transact any business he may desire ....

Our reservation is not as large as we want it to be, and I suppose the Great Father owes us money now for land he has taken from us in the past. You white men advise us to follow your ways, and therefore I talk as I do. When you have a piece of land, and anything trespasses on it, you catch it and keep it until you get damages, and I am doing the same thing now; and I want you to tell all this to the Great Father for me. I am looking into the future for the benefit of my children, and that is what I mean, when I say I want my country taken care of for me. My children will grow up here, and I am looking ahead for their benefit, and for the benefit of my children's children, too; and even beyond that again. I sit here and look around me now, and I see my people starving, and I want the Great Father to make an increase in the amount of food that is allowed us now, so that they may be able to live. [...]

Source: Warren K. Moorehead, *The American Indian in the United States, Period 1850–1914* (Andover, MA: The Andover Press, 1914): 196–197.

Document 9

FREDERICK JACKSON TURNER – "THE SIGNIFICANCE OF THE FRONTIER IN AMERICAN HISTORY," 1893

Short extract from a paper originally read to the American Historical Association in July 1893.

[...] The American frontier is sharply distinguished from the European frontier—a fortified boundary line running through dense populations. The most significant thing about the American frontier is, that it lies at the hither edge of free land. In the census reports it is treated as the margin of that settlement which has a density of two or more to the square mile. The term is an elastic one, and for our purposes does not need sharp definition. We shall consider the whole frontier belt, including the Indian country and the outer margin of the "settled area" of the census reports. This paper will make no attempt to treat the subject exhaustively; its aim is simply to call attention to the frontier as a fertile field for investigation, and to suggest some of the problems which arise in connection with it.

In the settlement of America we have to observe how European life entered the continent, and how America modified and developed that life and reacted on Europe. Our early history is the study of European germs developing in an American environment. Too exclusive attention has been paid by institutional students to the Germanic origins, too little to the American factors. The frontier is the line of most rapid and effective Americanization. The wilderness masters the colonist. It finds him a European in dress, industries, tools, modes of travel, and thought. It takes him from the railroad car and puts him in the birch canoe. It strips off the garments of civilization and arrays him in the hunting shirt and the moccasin. It puts him in the log cabin of the Cherokee and Iroquois and runs an Indian palisade around him. Before long he has gone to planting Indian corn and plowing with a sharp stick; he shouts the war cry and takes the scalp in orthodox Indian fashion. In short, at the frontier the environment is at first too strong for the man. He must accept the conditions which it furnishes, or perish, and so he fits himself into the Indian clearings and follows the Indian trails. Little by little he transforms the wilderness, but the outcome is not the old Europe, not simply the development of Germanic germs, any more than the first phenomenon was a case of reversion to the Germanic mark. The fact is, that here is a new product that is American. At first, the frontier was the Atlantic coast. It was the frontier of Europe in a very real sense. Moving westward, the frontier became more and more American. As successive terminal moraines result from successive glaciations, so each frontier leaves its traces behind it, and when it becomes a settled area the region still partakes of the frontier characteristics. Thus the advance of the frontier has meant a steady movement away from the influence of Europe, a steady growth of independence on American lines. And to study this advance, the men who grew up under these conditions, and the political, economic, and social results of it, is to study the really American part of our history. [...]

Source: Frederick Jackson Turner, *The Frontier in American History* (New York: Henry Holt & Co., 1920): 3–4.

Document 10

RUTHERFORD B. HAYES – PRESIDENTIAL INAUGURAL ADDRESS, 5 MARCH 1877

Short excerpts from near the beginning and the end of the president's address.

[...] The permanent pacification of the country upon such principles and by such measures as will secure the complete protection of all its citizens in the free enjoyment of all their constitutional rights is now the one subject, in our public affairs, which all thoughtful and patriotic citizens regard as of supreme importance.

Many of the calamitous efforts of the tremendous revolution which has passed over the Southern States still remain. The immeasurable benefits which will surely follow, sooner or later, the hearty and generous acceptance of the legitimate results of that revolution, have not yet been realized. Difficult and embarrassing questions meet us at the threshold of this subject. The people of those States are still impoverished, and the inestimable blessing of wise, honest, and peaceful self-government is not fully enjoyed. Whatever difference of opinion may exist as to the cause of this condition of things, the fact is clear, that, in the progress of events, the time has come when such government is the imperative necessity required by all the varied interests, public and private, of those States. But it must not be forgotten that only a local government which recognizes and maintains inviolate the rights of all is a true self-government.

With respect to the two distinct races whose peculiar relations to each other have brought upon us the deplorable complications and perplexities which exist in those States, it must be a government which guards the interests of both races carefully and equally. It must be a government which submits loyally and heartily to the Constitution and the laws—the laws of the nation and the laws of the States themselves—accepting and obeying faithfully the whole Constitution as it is.

[...] Looking for the guidance of that Divine Hand by which the destinies of nations and individuals are shaped, I call upon you, Senators, Representatives, Judges, fellow citizens, here and everywhere, to unite with me in an earnest effort to secure to our country the blessings, not only of material prosperity, but of justice, peace, and union—a Union depending not upon the constraint of force, but upon the loving devotion of a free people; "and that all things may be so ordered and settled upon the best and surest foundations that peace and happiness, truth and justice, religion and piety, may be established among us for all generations."

Source: Charles Richard Williams, *The Life of Rutherford Birchard Hayes: Nineteenth President of the United States*, Vol. 2 (Boston: Houghton Mifflin, 1914): 7, 11.

Document 11

"TO REPUBLICANS AND INDEPENDENT VOTERS," 1884

An excerpt from an appeal to voters to boycott the candidacy of James G. Blaine for the presidency.

The nomination of James G. Blaine for the presidency by the Republican National Convention of 1884, has precipitated a question of great difficulty and supreme moment upon the American people. By this action the voter's attention is forced away from consideration of party principles and policies to the scrutiny of party candidates and the duties of citizenship. It is all the more deplorable and dangerous because Mr. Blaine's nomination was made with all the outward forms and circumstance of popular party choice. But those who were on the spot know how fictitious is the claim that it was the irresistible demand of the great body of republicans of the northwest. They are not oblivious to the necessity of honor, integrity and a pure record in a presidential candidate, however noisy and bawling politicians may misrepresent them ....

No unknown man was nominated. His record is notorious. Its "magnetic brilliancy" cannot hide its utter lack of principle, unselfish purpose or public good accomplished.

As a member of Congress, his voice was never raised, his vote never cast, for a measure to protect the public domain from the raids of land grabbers and corporate plunderers.

As a speaker of the House of Representatives, he did not scruple to prostitute a judicial decision to personal gain.

As United States Senator, in the language of Senator Edmunds, "he jumped up, musket in hand, from behind the breastworks of Jay Gould's lobby to fire into the backs" of those Senators who were endeavoring to make the Union Pacific Railway Company keep its contract with the government. [...]

Source: "To Republicans and Independent Voters" (Chicago: Central Committee of Republicans and Independents, 1884): 1–2.

Document 12

POPULIST PARTY PLATFORM, 1892

An excerpt from the platform set out at the party convention on 4 July 1892 in Omaha, Nebraska.

[...] While our sympathies as a party of reform are naturally upon the side of every proposition on which will tend to make men intelligent, virtuous and temperate, we nevertheless regard these questions—important as they are—as secondary to the great issues now pressing for solution, and upon which not only our industrial prosperity, but the very existence of free institutions depend, and we ask all men to first help us to determine whether we are to have a Republic to administer, before we differ as to the conditions upon which it is to be administered, believing that the forces of reform this day organized will never cease to move forward until every wrong is righted and equal rights and privileges established for all the men and women of this country; we declare, therefore

[...] First. That the union of the labor forces of the United States this day consummated shall be permanent and perpetual; may its spirit enter into all hearts for the salvation of the Republic and the uplifting of mankind.

Second. Wealth belongs to him who creates it, and every dollar taken from industry without an equivalent is robbery. "If any man will not work neither shall he eat." The interests of rural and civil labor are the same; their enemies are identical.

Third. We believe that the time has come when the railroad corporations will either own the people or the people must own the railroads, and should the government enter upon the work of owning and managing all railroads, we should favor an amendment to the Constitution by which all persons engaged in the Government service shall be placed under a civil service regulation of the most rigid character, so as to prevent the increase of the power of the national administration by the use of such Government employes [sic] ....

We demand a national currency, safe, sound and flexible, issued by the General Government only, a full legal tender for all debts, public and private and that without the use of banking corporations, a just, equitable and efficient means of distribution direct to the people at a tax not to exceed 2 per cent per annum, to be provided as set forth in the subtreasury plan of the farmers' alliance, or a better system; also by payments in discharge of its obligations for public improvements.

We demand free and unlimited coinage of silver and gold at the present legal ratio of l6 to 1.

We demand that the amount of circulating medium be speedily increased to not less than $50 per capita.

We demand a graduated income tax.

We believe that the money of the country should be kept, as much as possible, in the hands of the people, and hence we demand that all State and National revenues shall be limited to the necessary expenses of the Government, economically and honestly administered. [...]

Source: Vincent Cuthbert, *The Platform Text-Book; Containing the Declaration of Independence, the Constitution of the United States, and All the Platforms of All the Parties* (Omaha, NE: Vincent Pub. Co, 1900): 133–134.

Document 13

ANDREW CARNEGIE – "WEALTH," 1889

An excerpt from an essay that originally appeared in the North American Review.

[...] The problem of our age is the proper administration of wealth, so that the ties of brotherhood may still bind together the rich and poor in harmonious relationship. The conditions of human life have not only been changed, but revolutionized, within the past few hundred years. In former days there was little difference between the dwelling, dress, food, and environment of the chief and those of his retainers. The Indians are to-day where civilized man then was. When visiting the Sioux, I was led to the wigwam of the chief. It was just like the others in external appearance, and even within the difference was trifling between it and those of the poorest of his braves. The contrast between the palace of the millionaire and the cottage of the laborer with us to-day measures the change which has come with civilization.

This change, however, is not to be deplored, but welcomed as highly beneficial. It is well, nay, essential for the progress of the race, that the houses of some should be homes for all that is highest and best in literature and the arts, and for all the refinements of civilization, rather than that none should be so. Much better this great irregularity than universal squalor. Without wealth there can be no Mæcenas. The "good old times" were not good old times. Neither master nor servant was as well situated then as to-day. A relapse to old conditions would be disastrous to both—not the least so to him who serves—and would sweep away civilization with it. But whether the change be for good or ill, it is upon us, beyond our power to alter, and therefore to be accepted and made the best of. It is a waste of time to criticize the inevitable ....

There are but three modes in which surplus wealth can be disposed of. It can be left to the families of the decedents; or it can be bequeathed for public purposes; or, finally, it can be administered during their lives by its possessors. Under the first and second modes most of the wealth of the world that has reached the few has hitherto been applied. [Carnegie then proceeds to outline the drawbacks of the first two methods, before addressing the third] ....

There remains, then, only one mode of using great fortunes; but in this we have the true antidote for the temporary unequal distribution of wealth, the reconciliation of the rich and the poor—a reign of harmony—another ideal, differing, indeed, from that of the Communist in requiring only the further evolution of existing conditions, not the total overthrow of our civilization. It is founded upon the present most intense individualism, and the race is prepared to put it in practice by degrees whenever it pleases. Under its sway we shall have an ideal state, in which the surplus wealth of the few will become, in the best sense, the property of the many, because administered for the common good, and this wealth, passing through the hands of the few, can be made a much more potent force for the elevation of our race than if it had been distributed in small sums to the people themselves. Even the poorest can be made to see this, and to agree that great sums gathered by some of their fellow-citizens and spent for public purposes, from which the masses reap the principal benefit, are more valuable to them than if scattered among them through the course of many years in trifling amounts. [...]

Source: Andrew Carnegie, "Wealth," *North American Review*, Vol. 148, no. 391 (June 1889): 653–654, 657, 660.

Document 14

SAMUEL GOMPERS – TESTIMONY BEFORE THE SENATE COMMITTEE ON EDUCATION AND LABOR, 1883

This excerpt relates to testimony on the eight-hour working day.

[...] That labor deserves a reduction of the hours of toil I believe hardly any one will dispute, unless when he is on "the other side of the house" and labor is seeking to enforce such a reduction against his interest, as he thinks. The general reduction of hours of labor to eight per day would reach further than any other reformatory measure; it would be of more lasting benefit; it would create a greater spirit in the working man; it would make him a better citizen, a better father, a better husband, a better man in general. The "voting cattle," so called, those whose votes are purchased on election day, are drawn from that class of our people whose life is one continuous round of toil. They cannot be drawn from workingmen who work only eight hours. A man who works but eight hours a day possesses more independence both economically and politically. It is the man who works like his machine and never knows when to stop, until in his case perpetual motion is almost arrived at – *he* is the man whose vote you can buy. The man who works longest is the first to be thrown out on the side-walk, because his recreation is generally drink.

Source: University of Maryland, *Samuel Gompers Project*, www.gompers.umd.edu/Shorter%20hours%20sg%201883.htm (accessed 14 December 2019).

Document 15

THEODORE ROOSEVELT – "COROLLARY TO THE MONROE DOCTRINE," 1904

Excerpt from President Roosevelt's message to Congress, delivered on 6 December 1904.

[…] It is not true that the United States feels any land hunger or entertains any projects as regards the other nations of the Western Hemisphere save such as are for their welfare. All that this country desires is to see the neighboring countries stable, orderly, and prosperous. Any country whose people conduct themselves well can count upon our hearty friendship. If a nation shows that it knows how to act with reasonable efficiency and decency in social and political matters, if it keeps order and pays its obligations, it need fear no interference from the United States. Chronic wrongdoing, or an impotence which results in a general loosening of the ties of civilized society, may in America, as elsewhere, ultimately require intervention by some civilized nation, and in the Western Hemisphere the adherence of the United States to the Monroe Doctrine may force the United States, however reluctantly, in flagrant cases of such wrongdoing or impotence, to the exercise of an international police power. If every country washed by the Caribbean Sea would show the progress in stable and just civilization which with the aid of the Platt Amendment Cuba has shown since our troops left the island, and which so many of the republics in both Americas are constantly and brilliantly showing, all question of interference by this Nation with their affairs would be at an end. Our interests and those of our southern neighbors are in reality identical. They have great natural riches, and if within their borders the reign of law and justice obtains, prosperity is sure to come to them. While they thus obey the primary laws of civilized society they may rest assured that they will be treated by us in a spirit of cordial and helpful sympathy. We would interfere with them only in the last resort, and then only if it became evident that their inability or unwillingness to do justice at home and abroad had violated the rights of the United States or had invited foreign aggression to the detriment of the entire body of American nations. It is a mere truism to say that every nation, whether in America or anywhere else, which desires to maintain its freedom, its independence, must ultimately realize that the right of such independence can not be separated from the responsibility of making good use of it. [...]

Source: U.S. National Archives and Records Administration, *Our Documents*, www.ourdocuments.gov/doc.php?flash=false&doc=56&page=transcript (accessed 14 December 2019).

Document 16

JOHN HAY – THE FIRST "OPEN DOOR" NOTE, 1899

Excerpt from Secretary of State Hay's message to Andrew D. White, the U.S. Minister to Germany, on 6 September 1899. "Open Door" notes were also sent to Russia, the United Kingdom, France, Italy and Japan.

[...] Earnestly desirous to remove any cause of irritation and to insure at the same time to the commerce of all nations in China the undoubted benefits which should accrue from a formal recognition by the various powers claiming "spheres of interest" that they shall enjoy perfect equality of treatment for their commerce and navigation within such "spheres," the Government of the United States would be pleased to see His German Majesty's Government give formal assurances, and lend its cooperation in securing like assurances from the other interested powers, that each within its respective sphere of whatever influence—

First. Will in no way interfere with any treaty port or any vested interest within any so-called "sphere of interest" or leased territory it may have in China.

Second. That the Chinese treaty tariff of the time being shall apply to all merchandise landed or shipped to all such ports as are within said "sphere of interest" (unless they be "free ports"), no matter to what nationality it may belong, and that duties so leviable shall be collected by the Chinese Government.

Third. That it will levy no higher harbor dues on vessels of another nationality frequenting any port in such "sphere" than shall be levied on vessels of its own nationality, and no higher railroad charges over lines built, controlled, or operated within its "sphere" on merchandise belonging to citizens or subjects of other nationalities transported through such "sphere" than shall be levied on similar merchandise belonging to its own nationals transported over equal distances. [...]

Source: *Notes on the Policies of the "Open Door" (or Principle of Equality of Opportunity) and of the Preservation of the Territorial and Political Integrity of the Chinese Empire, with References to the Papers on these Subjects, and Including Copies of the Principal Declarations Made and Received by the Government of the United States* (Washington: Department of State, 1908): 22.

Document 17

THE PHILIPPINE DECLARATION OF INDEPENDENCE, 1898

Excerpts from the declaration, written in June 1898 by Ambrosio Rianzares Bautista in support of a new Filipino-run government for the Philippine Islands. This is a translation from the Spanish original made by Sulpicio Guevara.

[...] **We** recognize, approve, and ratify, with all the orders emanating from the same, the Dictatorship established by Don Emilio Aguinaldo whom we revere as the Supreme Head of this Nation, which today begins to have a life of its own, in the conviction that he has been the instrument chosen by God, in spite of his humble origin, to effectuate the redemption of this unfortunate country as foretold by Dr. Don José Rizal in his magnificent verses which he composed in his prison cell prior to his execution, liberating it from the Yoke of Spanish domination, ...

Moreover, we confer upon our famous Dictator Don Emilio Aguinaldo all the powers necessary to enable him to discharge the duties of Government, including the prerogatives of granting pardon and amnesty,

And, lastly, it was resolved unanimously that this Nation, already free and independent as of this day, must use the same flag which up to now is being used, whose design and colors are found described in the attached drawing, the white triangle signifying the distinctive emblem of the famous Society of the "Katipunan" which by means of its blood compact inspired the masses to rise in revolution; the three stars, signifying the three principal Islands of this Archipelago-Luzon, Mindanao, and Panay where this revolutionary movement started; the sun representing the gigantic steps made by the sons of the country along the path of Progress and Civilization; the eight rays, signifying the eight provinces-Manila, Cavite, Bulacan, Pampanga, Nueva Ecija, Bataan, Laguna, and Batangas - which declared themselves in a state of war as soon as the first revolt was initiated; and the colors of Blue, Red, and White, commemorating the flag of the United States of North America, as a manifestation of our profound gratitude towards this Great Nation for its disinterested protection which it lent us and continues lending us. [...]

Source: Wikisource, https://en.wikisource.org/wiki/Philippine_Declaration_of_Independence (accessed 14 December 2019).

Document 18

THOMAS DIXON – *THE LEOPARD'S SPOTS*, 1902

Excerpt from Dixon's novel about the Reconstruction era, subtitled "A Romance of the White Man's Burden, 1865–1900". In this extract the

Reverend Durham explains to Charlie Gaston (the governor-elect of North Carolina) the dangers of making any concessions to African Americans.

[…] When this telegram [relating to a secret wedding] came he was in his office hard at work on his inaugural address, outlining the policy of his administration. He was in a heated argument with the Preacher about the article on education, which followed his recommendation of the disfranchisement of the Negro.

He had advised large appropriations for the industrial training of negroes along the lines of the new movement of their more sober leaders.

"It's a mistake," argued the Preacher, "if the Negro is made master of the industries of the South he will become the master of the South. Sooner than allow him to take the bread from their mouths, the white men will kill him here, as they do North, when the struggle for bread becomes as tragic. The Negro must ultimately leave this continent. You might as well begin to prepare for it."

"But we propose to train him principally in Agriculture. We need millions of good farmers," persisted Gaston.

"So much the worse, I tell you," replied the Preacher. "Make the Negro a scientific and successful farmer, and let him plant his feet deep in your soil, and it will mean a race war."

"It seems to me impracticable ever to move him."

"Why?" asked the Preacher. "Those over certain ages can be left to end their days here. The Negro has cost us already the loss of $7,000,000,000, a war that killed a half million men, the debauchery of our suffrage, the corruption of our life, and threatens the future with anarchy. Lincoln was right when he said, 'There is a physical difference between the white and the black races, which I believe will forever forbid them living together on terms of social and political equality.'

"Even you are still labouring under the delusions of 'Reconstruction.' The Ethiopian can not change his skin, or the leopard his spots. Those who think it possible will always tell you that the place to work this miracle is in the South. Exactly. If a man really believes in equality, let him prove it by giving his daughter to a negro in marriage. That is the test. When she sinks with her mulatto children into the black abyss of a Negroid life, then ask him! Your scheme of education is humbug. You don't believe that any amount of education can fit a negro to rule an Anglo-Saxon, or to marry his daughter. Then don't be a hypocrite."

"But can we afford to stop his education?"

"The more you educate, the more impossible you make his position in a democracy. Education! Can you change the colour of his skin, the kink of his hair, the bulge of his lips, the spread of his nose, or the beat of his heart, with a spelling book? The Negro is the human donkey. You can train him, but you can't make of him a horse. Mate him with a horse, you lose the horse, and get a larger donkey called a mule, incapable of preserving his species. What is called our race prejudice is simply God's first law of nature—the instinct of self preservation." [...]

Source: Thomas Dixon, Jr., *The Leopard's Spots: A Romance of the White Man's Burden, 1865–1900* (New York: Doubleday, Page & Co., 1902; Project Gutenberg, 2017), chap. 17, www.gutenberg.org/ebooks/54765 (accessed 14 December 2019).

Document 19

REPORTS OF THE DILLINGHAM IMMIGRATION COMMISSION, 1910

Excerpt from the committee's conclusions and recommendations.

[...] The old and the new immigration differ in many essentials. The former was, from the beginning, largely a movement of settlers who came from the most enlightened sections of Europe for the purpose of making themselves homes in the New World. They entered practically every line of activity in nearly every part of the country. Coming during a period of agricultural development, many of them entered agricultural pursuits, sometimes as independent farmers, but more often as farm laborers, who, nevertheless, as a rule soon became landowners. They formed an important part of the great movement toward the West during the last century, and as pioneers were most potent factors in the development of the territory between the Allegheny Mountains and the Pacific coast. They mingled freely with the native [born] Americans and were quickly assimilated, although a large proportion of them, particularly in later years, belonged to non-English-speaking races. This natural bar to assimilation, however, was soon overcome by them, while the racial identity of their children was almost entirely forgotten.

On the other hand, the new immigration has been largely a movement of unskilled labouring men who have come, in large part temporarily, from the less progressive and advanced countries of Europe in response to the call for industrial workers in the eastern and middle western States. They have almost entirely avoided agricultural pursuits, and in cities and industrial communities have congregated together in sections apart from native [born] Americans and the older immigrants to such an extent that assimilation has been slow as compared to that of the earlier non-English-speaking races.

The new immigration as a class is far less intelligent than the old, approximately one-third of all those over 14 years of age being illiterate when admitted. Racially they are for the most part essentially unlike the British, German, and other peoples who came during the period prior to 1880, and generally speaking they are actuated in coming by different ideals, for the old immigration came to be a part of the country, while the new, in a large measure, comes with the intention of profiting, in a pecuniary way, by the superior advantages of the New World and then returning to the old country. [...]

Source: The [Dillingham] Immigration Commission, *Brief Statement of the Conclusions and Recommendations of the Immigration Commission with Views of the Minority* (Washington: Government Printing Office, 1910): 8–9.

Document 20

W. E. B. DU BOIS – "THE TALENTED TENTH," 1903

Excerpt from the start of Du Bois' famous essay, outlining why the "talented tenth" are so important.

The Negro race, like all races, is going to be saved by its exceptional men. The problem of education, then, among Negroes must first of all deal with the Talented Tenth; it is the problem of developing the Best of this race that they may guide the Mass away from the contamination and death of the Worst, in their own and other races. Now the training of men is a difficult and intricate task. Its technique is a matter for educational experts, but its object is for the vision of seers. If we make money the object of man-training, we shall develop money-makers but not necessarily men; if we make technical skill the object of education, we may possess artisans but not, in nature, men. Men we shall have only as we make manhood the object of the work of the schools—intelligence, broad sympathy, knowledge of the world that was and is, and of the relation of men to it—this is the curriculum of that Higher Education which must underlie true life. On this foundation we may build bread winning, skill of hand and quickness of brain, with never a fear lest the child and man mistake the means of living for the object of life.

If this be true—and who can deny it—three tasks lay before me; first to show from the past that the Talented Tenth as they have risen among American Negroes have been worthy of leadership; secondly, to show how these men may be educated and developed; and thirdly, to show their relation to the Negro problem.

You misjudge us because you do not know us. From the very first it has been the educated and intelligent of the Negro people that have led and elevated the mass, and the sole obstacles that nullified and retarded their efforts were slavery and race prejudice; for what is slavery but the legalized survival of the unfit and the nullification of the work of natural internal leadership? Negro leadership, therefore, sought from the first to rid the race of this awful incubus that it might make way for natural selection and the survival of the fittest. [...]

Source: *The Negro Problem: A Series of Articles by Representative American Negroes of To-day* (New York: James Pott & Co., 1903): 33–35.

Document 21

WILLIAM JENNINGS BRYAN – "CROSS OF GOLD" SPEECH, 1896

Excerpt from Bryan's speech to the Democratic Party Convention of 1896 in Chicago, which focused on the issue of bimetallism.

[...] The sympathies of the Democratic party, as described by the platform, are on the side of the struggling masses, who have ever been the foundation of the Democratic party. [Applause.] There are two ideas of Government. There are those who believe that if you just legislate to make the well-to-do prosperous that their prosperity will leak through on those below. The Democratic idea has been that if you legislate to make the masses prosperous their prosperity will find its way up and through every class and rest upon it. [Applause.]

You come to us and tell us that the great cities are in favor of the gold standard. I tell you that the great cities rest upon these broad and fertile prairies. Burn down your cities and leave our farms, and your cities will spring up again as if by magic. But destroy our farms and the grass will grow in the streets of every city in the country. [Applause.] My friends, we shall declare that this nation is able to legislate for its own people on every question without waiting for the aid or consent of any other nation on earth. [Applause.] Upon that issue we expect to carry every single State in this Union. [Applause.]

I shall not slander the fair State of Massachusetts, nor the State of New York, by saying that when its citizens are confronted with the proposition, is this nation able to attend to its own business—I will not slander either one by saying that the people of those States will declare our helpless impotency as a nation to attend to our own business.

It is the issue of 1776 over again. Our ancestors, when but 3,000,000, had the courage to declare their political independence of every other nation upon earth. Shall we, their descendants, when we have grown to 70,000,000 million, declare that we are less independent than our forefathers? No, my friends, it will never be the judgment of this people.

Therefore, we care not upon what lines the battle is fought. If they say bimetallism is good, but we cannot have it till some nation helps us, we reply that, instead of having a gold standard because England has, we shall restore bimetallism and then let England have bimetallism because the United States has. [Applause.] If they dare to come out and in the open and defend the gold standard as a good thing, we shall fight them to the uttermost, having behind us the producing masses of the nation and the world. Having behind us the commercial interests, and the laboring interests, and all the toiling masses, we shall answer their demands for a gold standard by saying to them, you shall not press down upon the brow of labor this crown of thorns. You shall not crucify mankind upon a cross of gold.

Source: "Speech that Made Bryan," *The Sun* [New York], 11 July 1896: 3.

Document 22

THEODORE ROOSEVELT – "THE MAN WITH THE MUCK-RAKE," 1906

Excerpt from a speech Roosevelt gave in Washington D.C. on 14 April 1906, during the laying of the cornerstone of a government office building.

[...] In "Pilgrim's Progress" the Man with the Muck Rake is set forth as the example of him whose vision is fixed on carnal instead of on spiritual things. Yet he also typifies the man who in this life consistently refuses to see aught that is lofty, and fixes his eyes with solemn intentness only on that which is vile and debasing. Now, it is very necessary that we should not flinch from seeing what is vile and debasing. There is filth on the floor, and it must be scraped up with the muck-rake; and there are times and places where this service is the most needed of all the services that can be performed. But the man who never does anything else, who never thinks or speaks or writes, save of his feats with the muck-rake, speedily becomes, not a help to society, not an incitement to good, but one of the most potent forces for evil.

There are in the body politic, economic and social, many and grave evils, and there is urgent necessity for the sternest war upon them. There should be relentless exposure of and attack upon every evil man whether politician or business man, every evil practice, whether in politics, in business, or in social life. I hail as a benefactor every writer or speaker, every man who, on the platform, or in book, magazine, or newspaper, with merciless severity makes such attack, provided always that he in his turn remembers that the attack is of use only if it is absolutely truthful. The liar is no whit better than the thief, and if his mendacity takes the form of slander, he may be worse than most thieves. It puts a premium upon knavery untruthfully to attack an honest man, or even with hysterical exaggeration to assail a bad man with untruth. An epidemic of indiscriminate assault upon character does no good, but very great harm. The soul of every scoundrel is gladdened whenever an honest man is assailed, or even when a scoundrel is untruthfully assailed. [...]

Source: Theodore Roosevelt, *Presidential Addresses and State Papers, April 14, 1906, to January 14, 1907*, Vol. 5 (New York: The Review of Reviews Co., 1910): 713–714.

Document 23

WOODROW WILSON – ADDRESS TO CONGRESS LEADING TO A WAR AGAINST GERMANY, 1917

Excerpt from Wilson's address to a special joint session of Congress on 2 April 1917, encouraging them to vote in favor of a declaration of war against Germany.

[...] Property can be paid for; the lives of peaceful and innocent people cannot be. The present German submarine warfare against commerce is a warfare against mankind.

It is a war against all nations. American ships have been sunk, American lives taken, in ways which it has stirred us very deeply to learn of, but the ships and people of other neutral and friendly nations have been sunk and overwhelmed in the waters in the same way. There has been no discrimination. The challenge is to all mankind. Each nation must decide for itself how it will meet it. The choice we make for ourselves must be made with a moderation of counsel and a temperateness of judgment befitting our character and our motives as a nation. We must put excited feeling away. Our motive will not be revenge or the victorious assertion of the physical might of the nation, but only the vindication of right, of human right, of which we are only a single champion.

When I addressed the Congress on the twenty-sixth of February last I thought that it would suffice to assert our neutral rights with arms, our right to use the seas against unlawful interference, our right to keep our people safe against unlawful violence. But armed neutrality, it now appears, is impracticable. Because submarines are in effect outlaws when used as the German submarines have been used against merchant shipping, it is impossible to defend ships against their attacks as the law of nations has assumed that merchantmen would defend themselves against privateers or cruisers, visible craft giving chase upon the open sea. It is common prudence in such circumstances, grim necessity indeed, to endeavor to destroy them before they have shown their own intention. They must be dealt with upon sight, if dealt with at all. The German Government denies the right of neutrals to use arms at all within the areas of the sea which it has proscribed, even in the defense of rights which no modern publicist has ever before questioned their right to defend. The intimation is conveyed that the armed guards which we have placed on our merchant ships will be treated as beyond the pale of law and subject to be dealt with as pirates would be. Armed neutrality is ineffectual enough at best; in such circumstances and in the face of such pretensions it is worse than ineffectual: it is likely only to produce what it was meant to prevent; it is practically certain to draw us into the war without either the rights or the effectiveness of belligerents. There is one choice we cannot make, we are incapable of making: we will not choose the path of submission and suffer the most sacred rights of our Nation and our people to be ignored or violated. The wrongs against which we now array ourselves are no common wrongs; they cut to the very roots of human life. [...]

Source: U.S. National Archives and Records Administration, *Our Documents*, www.ourdocuments.gov/doc.php?flash=false&doc=61&page=transcript (accessed 14 December 2019).

Document 24

CARRIE CHAPMAN CATT – *WOMAN SUFFRAGE BY FEDERAL CONSTITUTIONAL AMENDMENT*, 1917

Below is the introduction to a volume on women's suffrage published by the National Woman Suffrage Publishing Company in 1917.

No effort is made in the following pages to present an argument for woman suffrage. No careful observer of the modern trend of human affairs, doubts that "governments of the people" are destined to replace the monarchies of the world. No listener will fail to hear the rumble of the rising tide of democracy. No watcher of events will deny that the women of all civilized lands will be enfranchised eventually as part of the people entitled to give consent and no American possessed of political foresight doubts woman suffrage in our land as a coming fact.

The discussion herein is strictly confined to the reasons why an amendment to the Federal Constitution is the most appropriate method of dealing with the question. This proposed amendment was introduced into Congress in 1878 at the request of the National Woman Suffrage Association. Since 1882 the Senate Committee has reported it with a favorable majority every year except in 1890 and 1896. Twice only has it gone to vote in the Senate. The first time was on January 25, 1887; the second, March 19, 1914. In the House it has been reported from Committee seven times, twice by a favorable majority, three times by an adverse majority and twice without recommendation. The House has allowed the measure to come to vote but once, in 1915. Yet while women of the nation in large and increasing numbers have stood at doors of Congress waiting and hoping, praying and appealing for the democratic right to have their opinions counted in affairs of their government, millions of men have entered through our gates and automatically have passed into voting citizenship without cost of money, time or service, aye, without knowing what it meant or asking for the privilege. Among the enfranchised there are vast groups of totally illiterate, and others of gross ignorance, groups of men of all nations of Europe, uneducated Indians and Negroes. Among the unenfranchised are owners of millions of dollars worth of property, college presidents and college graduates, thousands of teachers in universities, colleges and public schools, physicians, lawyers, dentists, journalists, heads of businesses, representatives of every trade and occupation and thousands of the nation's homekeepers. The former group secured its vote without the asking; the latter appeals in vain to Congress for the removal of the stigma this inexplicable contrast puts upon their sex. It is hoped this little book may gain attention where other means have failed.

Source: Carrie Chapman Catt, *Woman Suffrage by Federal Constitutional Amendment* (New York: National Woman Suffrage Publishing Co., 1917): i–iii.

Glossary

Bimetallism In the context of this period, the use of both gold and silver as a basis for U.S. currency.

Bourbon Democrats Critical nickname for economically conservative Democrats, many of whom supported the policies of President Grover Cleveland. In the South, Bourbon Democrats were also closely associated with white supremacist "Redemption".

Dollar Diplomacy A term most often associated with the foreign policy of the William Howard Taft administration. It refers to the use of economic investment to extend U.S. influence overseas.

Electoral College A group of individuals selected to represent the presidential votes of the various U.S. states in presidential elections. Each state is apportioned Electoral College votes based on the number of U.S. senators they return (two for each state) added to the number of U.S. representatives they return (varying based upon their population). A president needs to win an absolute majority in the Electoral College to be sure of election to the presidency. This can, on occasion, result in the election of a president who wins fewer popular votes than another candidate in the race (in this period, see both 1876 and 1888 for examples). Even more often, it means presidents can be elected without winning an absolute majority of the popular vote even if they better their nearest rival.

Front-porch campaign An election campaign where a candidate primarily remains at home and allows journalists and voters to come to them, rather than touring the nation to gain attention and canvass votes.

Frontier Thesis An idea expounded by the historian Frederick Jackson Turner, in which the conquest of the nation's western "frontier" had been fundamental in shaping the distinct identity of U.S. citizens and the nation as a whole.

Fusion A method used in elections where two or more parties "fuse" their electorates by running the same candidate on differing party tickets. William Jennings Bryan was effectively a "fusion candidate" for the presidency in 1896, running as the candidate for both the Democratic Party and Populist Party.

Gilded Age A broad term that refers to the post-Reconstruction period, characterized by rapid industrial growth and laissez-faire government.

Gold Standard In contrast to "bimetallism," adherence to a "gold standard" means a nation's currency is based solely on its value in relation to gold.

"Grand Old Party" (G.O.P.) A common nickname for the Republican Party.

Great Migration A period of large-scale migration of African Americans from the South that is often said to have started during the Great War period.

Half-breeds A faction of the Republican Party led by James G. Blaine that supposedly opposed the spoils system that they linked to their rival Stalwart faction.

Ku Klux Klan (KKK) The name for two white supremacist terror organizations. The first was founded in 1866 and rose to prominence during the Reconstruction Era in the South before being effectively suppressed by the end of the 1870s. The second incarnation of the Klan, established in 1915, was a larger and more nationally active racist and nativist organization that rose to prominence in the 1920s.

Laissez-faire A term denoting a "hands off" approach to affairs. In the Gilded Age, it is often used to denote low levels of government intervention and/or regulation of big businesses.

Large Policy A policy advocated by Theodore Roosevelt and Henry Cabot Lodge, which sought to project U.S. power through a large military—and particularly a naval—presence beyond the bounds of the contiguous states, as well as territorial acquisitions overseas. It is usually linked to the Spanish–American War period and the writings of naval strategist Alfred Thayer Mahan.

Manifest Destiny A phrase generally attributed to newspaper editor John L. Sullivan in 1845, which referred to a divinely mandated destiny for the United States to expand its borders and its form of government across the North American continent.

Monroe Doctrine Set out by President James Monroe in 1823, it outlined the commitment of the United States to oppose any future European imperial intervention or territorial annexation in the Western Hemisphere.

Muckrakers A term used by Theodore Roosevelt in 1906 to critique what he saw as "excessive" investigative journalists who played a major role in highlighting social and industrial wrongdoing in the Progressive Era. It related to a character in John Bunyan's *The Pilgrim's Progress* (1678) and was adopted by both critics and advocates of such journalism.

Mugwump Nickname for Republicans who left the party following the nomination of James G. Blaine as their presidential candidate in 1884. Most Mugwumps joined the Democrats, preferring their candidate that year, Grover Cleveland.

National Association for the Advancement of Colored People (NAACP) A civil rights organization formed in 1909 to campaign and provide legal support for African American civil rights.

Nativism A general term relating to xenophobic or anti-immigration sentiment. Nativists claim to support the rights and interests of "native-born" U.S. citizens which they feel are threatened by immigrants (not to be confused with Native Americans).

Populism In the 1890s, the term referred to a broad, mainly agrarian, movement advocating a variety of economic and social reforms, including greater regulation of big businesses and a commitment to bimetallism.

Progressivism In the period c.1890–1920, the term referred to a range of social reform movements aimed at combatting the perceived ills of the industrial society that had grown so rapidly during the Gilded Age.

Reconstruction Usually refers to the period (c.1865–1876) that followed the American Civil War, when various methods were used to reunify the nation and assert African American civil rights after the abolition of slavery.

Redemption A period that followed Reconstruction in southern politics. Redeemers sought to undo many of the reforms of the Reconstruction Era and reassert white supremacism in the South. Many Bourbon Democrats in the South were Redeemers.

Robber Baron A pejorative term referring to the major businessmen and financiers of the Gilded Age.

Solid South A term used to describe the firm hold the Democratic Party held over many southern states after the period of "Redemption," which lasted well past the period covered here.

Spoils System A political arrangement whereby support and loyalty to a political candidate or party is rewarded with political offices or favors (the "spoils") if that candidate or party is successful. In the Gilded Age, this term was mostly linked to the distribution of government jobs in the civil service.

Stalwarts A faction of the Republican Party, effectively led by New York Senator Roscoe Conkling, which favored the spoils system and supported President Grant for a third presidential term in 1876. It stood in opposition to the "Half-breed" faction.

Tammany Hall Established in 1789, it became the main organizing body of the Democratic Party in New York City. It was strongly linked to political corruption during the mid-nineteenth century.

Tariff An import/export tax on goods entering/leaving a nation.

Trade reciprocity An agreement between nations to agree to lower specific tariffs that otherwise exist between them.

Trust A combination of different businesses that creates a larger, more powerful entity. When a trust (or a single company) becomes so large as to gain effective control over an entire industry or service, it is called a monopoly.

Guide to further reading

As this book covers a significant part of U.S. history and a number of important historical themes, it is impossible to do justice to the historiography in a short section such as this. For this reason, the book contains as many references as possible to key texts in the field and contains quite a large bibliography for readers to explore. However, for those wishing to embark upon further reading along the lines of the main themes broached in the chapters here, this section provides a concise overview of some particularly useful works that serve as great platforms from which to explore the rich world of American history between 1865 and 1920.

There are several online databases that provide excellent starting points for those wishing to explore primary sources from this era, beyond the selection covered in this volume. For newspaper articles, the Library of Congress' *Chronicling America* site (https://chroniclingamerica.loc.gov) is an exceptional database of historical American newspapers. The U.S. National Archives' *Our Documents* site (www.ourdocuments.gov), and the Library of Congress' *Digital Collections* site (https://loc.gov/collections) provide access to a wealth of key documents, maps and images from across this period. Finally, several U.S. universities have transcribed various historical speeches and documents that are readily accessible to those seeking further primary materials. The University of California, Santa Barbara's *The American Presidency Project* (www.presidency.ucsb.edu), and the "Many Pasts" section of George Mason University's *History Matters* site (http://historymatters.gmu.edu/browse/manypasts) are among the best of these. Finally, a printed collection of documents of great value to a researcher can be found with Link and Link's *The Gilded Age and Progressive Era* (2012).

Before moving on to key books, it is worth noting a few key academic journals that provide a particular focus on this era, though they usually require a subscription fee unless your institution subscribes. Journal articles and book reviews are a great way to see the direction of the most cutting-edge scholarship available in the field. *Civil War History* covers more than perhaps its name suggests, exploring issues across the mid-century period up to and beyond the Reconstruction era. The *Journal of the Gilded Age and Progressive Era* publishes academic articles and book reviews of key works across all of the thematic areas covered in this book. Similarly, *Nineteenth Century American History*, though covering the entire long nineteenth century, offers a great window into the period focused upon here. Of course, there are numerous other excellent journals that deal with U.S. history on a far broader chronological basis, or thematically on issues such as labor history or diplomatic history, that are also invaluable and well worth searching through.

Though this book does not cover the Civil War itself, if one were looking for an in-depth volume that provides a great introduction to the period, James McPherson's *Battle Cry of Freedom* (1988) remains perhaps the most popular choice. For a valuable collection of essays that go into depth on a variety of different topics, see Grant and Reid's *Themes of the American Civil War* (2010). Added to this, of course, is Reid Mitchell's Seminar Studies book, *The American Civil War* (2001/2013), which—like all volumes in this series—offers not only an introduction to the period, but the benefit of additional primary source materials as well. Finally, a vivid consideration of Abraham Lincoln's administration can be found in Doris Kearns Goodwin's Pulitzer Prize-winning *Team of Rivals* (2005).

Moving on the Reconstruction, W. E. B. Du Bois' *Black Reconstruction in America* (1935/1998) remains a valuable early volume that stood as a powerful corrective to the white supremacist Dunning School's highly critical interpretation of Republican Reconstruction. Eric Foner's lengthy volume, *Reconstruction* (Foner, 1988/2002), is still the definitive work on the period and Foner's more recent book, *The Second Founding* (2019), explores the importance of the Civil War and Reconstruction-era amendments to the U.S. Constitution in even greater depth. Beyond Foner's work, there are many excellent books that chart Reconstruction onward toward the start of the twentieth century. C. Vann Woodward's *The Strange Career of Jim Crow* (Woodward, 1955/2002), which explores the steady unraveling of Reconstruction-era racial reforms, is the classic text for those studying the history of the post-war South. Michael Perman's *The Road to Redemption* (1984) and *Struggle for Mastery* (2001) follow the course of southern politics and disenfranchisement through to the end of the century. In addition to these works, Edward Ayres' *The Promise of the New South* (1992/2007), Heather Cox Richardson's *The Death of Reconstruction* (2004) and, most recently, Henry Louis Gates Jr.'s *Stony the Road* (2019), all offer further academic depth and complexity to the tale that is the "long" history of Reconstruction, particularly regarding race relations.

When it comes to the West, very readable and important overviews of the region, and of Native American history in particular, can be found in Dee Brown's *Bury My Heart at Wounded Knee* (1970/1991) and *The American West* (1995). However, perhaps the best overall coverage can be located in Richard White's opus, *It's Your Misfortune and None of My Own* (1991). Billington and Ridge's *American Expansion* (2001) provides a clear history of the frontier, while Arnoldo De Léon's *Racial Frontier* (2002) considers the often overlooked minority ethnic groups of the West. Also, for the important role of the environment in U.S. history, see William Cronon's *Nature's Metropolis* (1991) and Carolyn Merchant's *American Environmental History* (2007).

In terms of overviews of Gilded Age America, Sean Cashman's *America in the Gilded Age* (1993), Jack Beatty's *Age of Betrayal* (2007), Jackson Lears' *Rebirth of a Nation* (2010), and Leon Fink's *The Long Gilded Age* (2015) offer excellent and accessible coverage of the period. However, the most comprehensive volume is Richard White's masterful *The Republic for Which it Stands* (2017), covering the period 1865–1896 as part of the Oxford History of the United States series. For the politics of this era, the University of Kansas Press' American Presidency Series provides an excellent set of scholarly biographies of the lesser-known presidents, though some are now a little dated. Ulysses Grant, however, stands out among his Gilded Age peers as the subject of far wider attention. Whereas Ron Chernow's latest epic *Grant* (2017) is a very valuable addition to existing biographies of Grant, Charles Calhoun's *The Presidency of Ulysses S. Grant* (2017) gives greater focus to his time in the Executive Mansion. Finally, Charles Postel's *The Populist Vision* (2007) is the leading re-evaluation of the populist movement and helps get to grips with one of the more complex and misunderstood political phenomena of the era.

Aside from the volumes mentioned already, there are a number of outstanding works on industry, labor, and capitalism in the Gilded Age that offer valuable depth to the analysis of these specific aspects of the period. Alan Trachenberg's *The Incorporation of America* (1982) and Page Smith's *The Rise of Industrial America* (1984) provide detailed accounts of the origins of corporate and industrial America while, more recently, Richard Franklin Bensel's *The Political Economy of American Industrialization* (2000) and Robert Gordon's *The Rise and Fall of American Growth* (2017) offer in-depth explorations of the industrial economy. Albro Martin's *Railroads Triumphant* (1992) and Richard White's *Railroaded* (2011) provide valuable studies of one of the most significant drivers of economic and industrial change in the second half of the nineteenth century. For the history of labor unionism, Julie Greene's *Pure and Simple Politics* (2004) provides an excellent study of the American Federation of Labor, while Leon Fink's *Workingmen's Democracy* (1985) and Robert Weir's *Beyond Labor's Veil* (1996) focus on the Knights of Labor. Many comprehensive biographies of individual robber barons exist, such as David Nassaw's *Andrew Carnegie* (2007) and Ron Chernow's tomes on J. D. Rockefeller (1998) and J. P. Morgan (1990). However, Susie Pak's *Gentlemen Bankers* (2013) provides a great new addition to this otherwise quite biographical field, by further exploring the social milieu in which the House of Morgan arose. Finally, H. W. Brands' *American Colossus* (2010) provides a detailed and fascinating review of the rise of modern capitalism in the U.S. from the Civil War to 1900.

For U.S. expansion, Paul Frymer's *Building an American Empire* (2017) provides an excellent, in-depth overview of continental expansion, while Adam Burns' *American Imperialism* (2017) and A. G. Hopkins' *American Empire* (2018) consider—in different ways—U.S. imperial expansion beyond North America as well. On foreign policy, there are numerous books that overview the period focused upon here as part of wider U.S. foreign relations history—perhaps the best of these being the excellent, and since updated, *The American Age* (1989) by Walter LaFeber. The Spanish-American War garners far more coverage than most other foreign policy in the late nineteenth century. A valuable overview of the historiography of the conflict can be found in Louis Pérez's *The War of 1898* (1998), while a very readable and engaging account of the war and its era can be found in John Van Atta's *Charging up San Juan Hill* (2018). When it comes to the Philippine-American War, the leading work is probably Brian McAllister Linn's *The Philippine War* (2000), and for an impressive consideration of gender politics in both the Spanish–American and Philippine–American wars see Kristin Hoganson's *Fighting for American Manhood* (1998). For up-to-date coverage of the anti-imperialist movement see Michael P. Cullinane's *Liberty and American Anti-Imperialism* (2012).

For excellent thematic coverage of immigration in U.S. history, see Roger Daniels' *Coming to America* (1991) and the more targeted volume by Katherine Benton-Cohen exploring the work of the Dillingham Commission, *Inventing the Immigration Problem* (2018). To complement these works, it is well worth consulting John Higham's timeless *Strangers in the Land* (1955/2002), which explores the growth and development of nativism, along with the more recent work of Peter Shrag, *Not Fit for Our Society* (2010). The role of race in U.S. domestic and foreign policy in this period is explored usefully in several excellent volumes including Gail Bederman's *Manliness and Civilization* (1996), Michael Krenn's *The Color of Empire* (2006), and Robert Sussman's *The Myth of Race* (2014). For African American activism at the turn of the century, see Susan Carle's *Defining the Struggle* (2013), as well David Levering Lewis' study of W. E. B. Du Bois, *Biography of a Race* (1993) and Robert Norrell's recent re-evaluation of Booker T. Washington, *Up From History* (2009).

For an introduction to progressivism, there is already a focused Seminar Studies text by Lewis Gould, *America in the Progressive Era* (2001/2013). Beyond this, Maureen Flanagan's *America Reformed* (2007) offers a scholarly yet slender and accessible volume, alongside more in-depth studies such as Michael McGerr's *A Fierce Discontent* (2003) and David Traxel's *Crusader Nation* (2006). For the key figures of the era, Michael Kazin's *A Godly Hero* (2007) gives a fascinating survey of William Jennings Bryan's life, Jeffrey Rosen brings fresh perspective to the career of Louis Brandeis in *American Prophet* (2016), and Louise Knight's *Citizen* (2005) provides an engaging overview of Jane Addams' life to the turn of the century. Edmund Morris' trilogy of works on Theodore Roosevelt (1979, 2001, 2010), provide a captivating, as well as detailed, study of his life. However, for a single volume work on T. R., among the best is Kathleen Dalton's *A Strenuous Life* (2002). Taft's presidency, meanwhile, has been reviewed recently in Jonathan Lurie's well-rounded *Travails of a Progressive Conservative* (2012), while both Taft and Roosevelt are given coverage, alongside the press of the era, in Doris Kearns Goodwin's *The Bully Pulpit* (2013).

Finally, when it comes to Woodrow Wilson and the era of the Great War, John Milton Cooper's biography is a masterful introduction to the president's life (2009). However, if seeking more focus on his foreign policy, see also Lloyd Ambrosius' *Wilsonian Statecraft* (1991), Kendrick Clements' *Woodrow Wilson: World Statesman* (1999), and Erez Manela's excellent *The Wilsonian Moment* (2009). For the wartime United States, David Kennedy's *Over Here* (1980/2004) and Robert Zeiger's *America's Great War* (2001) offer comprehensive coverage, while Michael Kazin's *War Against War* (2017) provides greater focus upon opposition to the war on the home front. Finally, for an in-depth exploration of the fight for women's rights in the United States, see Corrine McConnaughty's *The Woman Suffrage Movement in America* (2015).

References

Further primary sources

Arthur, C. (1882) 'Veto of the Chinese Exclusion Bill, 4 April', *Miller Center*, University of Virginia. Available at: https://millercenter.org/the-presidency/presidential-speeches/april-4-1882-veto-chinese-exclusion-act [accessed 12 June 2019].

Chinese Exclusion Act. (1882) *Our Documents*, Available at: www.ourdocuments.gov/doc.php?flash=true&doc=47 [accessed 12 June 2019].

Democratic Party Platform. (1896) *American Presidency Project*. Available at: www.presidency.ucsb.edu/documents/1896-democratic-party-platform [accessed 12 June 2019].

Grant, U. (1869) 'Inaugural Address, 4 March', *Avalon Project*. Yale Law School. Available at: https://avalon.law.yale.edu/19th_century/grant1.asp [accessed 28 November 2019].

Johnson, A. (1865) 'First Annual Message, 4 December', *American Presidency Project*. Available at: www.presidency.ucsb.edu/ws/index.php?pid=29506 [accessed 12 June 2019].

Lincoln, A. (1861) 'First Inaugural Address, 4 March', *Miller Center*, University of Virginia. Available at: https://millercenter.org/the-presidency/presidential-speeches/march-4-1861-first-inaugural-address [accessed 28 November 2019].

Plessy v. Ferguson. (1896) *Our Documents*. Available at: www.ourdocuments.gov/doc.php?flash=false&doc=52 [accessed 12 June 2019].

Sierra County Advocate. (1887) 'Editor Grady's Oration', 22 January, p. 1.

Sinclair, U. (1906) 'The Jungle', *E-book from Project Gutenberg*. Available at: www.gutenberg.org/files/140/140-h/140-h.htm#link2HCH0001 [accessed 12 June 2019].

Tama County Republican. (1869) 'No Title', 13 May, p. 2.

Tarbell, I.M. (1904) *The History of the Standard Oil Company*. New York: McClure, Phillips & Co. Available at: https://archive.org/stream/historyofstandar01tarbuoft/historyofstandar01tarbuoft_djvu.txt [accessed 12 June 2019].

Williams, C.R. (1914) *The Life of Rutherford Birchard Hayes: Nineteenth President of the United States*, Vol. 2. Boston, MA: Houghton Mifflin.

Wilson, W. (1914) 'Message to Congress, 4 August', *World War I Document Archive*, Brigham Young University. Available at: https://wwi.lib.byu.edu/index.php/President_Wilson%27s_Declaration_of_Neutrality [accessed 12 June 2019].

Wilson, W. (1918) 'The Fourteen Points, 8 January', *Avalon Project*, Yale Law School. Available at: http://avalon.law.yale.edu/20th_century/wilson14.asp [accessed 12 June 2019].

Secondary sources

Some of the texts listed below are presented with two dates, e.g. (1970/1991). The former date is that of initial publication, and the latter that of the imprint or edition that was consulted in the preparation of this book. Only a few dates are presented this way, but this has been done for key texts to indicate to readers that these works are not necessarily recent scholarship, at least in their original form, but have maintained relevance and resonance across many decades.

Aiken, C.S. (1998) *The Cotton Plantation South since the Civil War*. Baltimore, MY: Johns Hopkins University Press.

Ambrosius, L.E. (1991) *Wilsonian Statecraft: Theory and Practice of Liberal Internationalism during World War I*. Wilmington, DE: Scholarly Resources.

Anbinder, T. (2016) *City of Dreams: The 400-year Epic History of Immigrant New York*. Boston, MA: Houghton Mifflin Harcourt.

Arnold, P.E. (2009) *Remaking the Presidency: Roosevelt, Taft, and Wilson, 1901–1916*. Lawrence, KS: University Press of Kansas.

Axelrod, A. (2009) *Selling the Great War: The Making of American Propaganda*. New York: Palgrave Macmillan.

Ayres, E.L. (1992/2007) *The Promise of the New South: Life after Reconstruction*. Oxford: Oxford University Press.

Bade, K.J. (1997) 'From Emigration to Immigration: The German Experience in the Nineteenth and Twentieth Centuries', in K.J. Bade and M. Weiner (eds), *Migration Past, Migration Future: Germany and the United States*. Oxford: Berghahn Books.

Baggett, J.A. (2004) *The Scalawags: Southern Dissenters in the Civil War and Reconstruction*. Baton Rouge, LA: Louisiana State University Press.

Baker, J.H. (1998) *Affairs of Party: The Political Culture of Northern Democrats in the Mid-Nineteenth Century*. New York: Fordham University Press.

Beatty, J. (2007) *Age of Betrayal: The Triumph of Money in American, 1865–1900*. New York: Alfred J. Knopf.

Bederman, G. (1996) *Manliness and Civilization: A Cultural History of Gender and Race in the United States, 1880–1917*. Chicago, IL: University of Chicago Press.

Beeby, J.M. (2012) 'Introduction: Populism in the American South', in J.M. Beeby (ed.), *Populism in the South Revisited: New Interpretations and New Departures*. Jackson, MS: University Press of Mississippi.

Bensel, R.F. (2000) *The Political Economy of American Industrialization, 1877–1900*. Cambridge: Cambridge University Press.

Benton-Cohen, K. (2018) *Inventing the Immigration Problem: The Dillingham Commission and its Legacy*. Cambridge, MA: Harvard University Press.

Bergernon, P.H. (2011) *Andrew Johnson's Civil War and Reconstruction*. Knoxville, TN: University of Tennessee Press.

Billings, R.D. (2012) 'The Homestead Act, Pacific Railroad Act and Morrill Act', *Northern Kentucky Law Review*, 39, 4, pp. 699–736.

Billington, R.A. and Ridge, M. (2001) *Westward Expansion: A History of the American Frontier*, 6th edition, abridged. Albuquerque, NM: University of New Mexico Press.

Bourdon, J.N. (2014) 'Trains, Canes, and Replica Log Cabins: Benjamin Harrison's 1888 Front-Porch Campaign for the Presidency', *Indiana Magazine of History*, 110, 3, pp. 246–269.

Brands, H.W. (2010) *American Colossus: The Triumph of Capitalism, 1865–1900*. New York: Doubleday.

Brown, D. (1970/1991) *Bury My Heart at Wounded Knee: An Indian History of the American West*. London: Vintage.

Brown, D. (1995) *The American West*. New York: Touchstone.

Burns, A. (2010) 'Without Due Process: Albert E. Pillsbury and the Hoar Anti-Lynching Bill', *American Nineteenth Century History*, 11, 2, pp. 233–252.

Burns, A. (2017) *American Imperialism: The Territorial Expansion of the United States, 1783–2013*. Edinburgh: Edinburgh University Press.

Burns, A. (2018) 'Economic Imperialism in Cuba, 1898–2017: Hegemony and Embargo', in C. Grocott and J. Grady (eds), *The Continuing Imperialism of Free Trade: Developments, Trends and the Role of Supranational Agents*. London: Routledge.

Burns, A. (2019) 'Courting White Southerners: Theodore Roosevelt's Quest for the Heart of the South', *American Nineteenth Century History*, 20, 1, pp. 1–18.

Burns, A. (2020) *William Howard Taft and the Philippines: A Blueprint for Empire*. Knoxville, TN: University of Tennessee Press.

Burton, D.H. (2003) *Taft, Wilson and World Order*. Madison, WI: Fairleigh Dickinson Press.

Calhoun, C.W. (2005) *Benjamin Harrison*. New York: Times Books.

Calhoun, C.W. (2017) *The Presidency of Ulysses S. Grant*. Lawrence, KS: University Press of Kansas.

Calloway, C.G. (2013) *Pen & Ink with: Treaties and Treaty Making in American Indian History*. New York: Oxford University Press.

Cannato, V.J. (2010) *American Passage: The History of Ellis Island*. New York: HarperPerennial.

Carle, S.D. (2013) *Defining the Struggle: National Organizing for Racial Justice, 1880–1915*. New York: Oxford University Press.

Carlson, W.B. (2013) *Tesla: Inventor of the Electrical Age*. Princeton, NJ: Princeton University Press.

Cashman, S.D. (1993) *America in the Gilded Age: From the Death of Lincoln to the Rise of Theodore Roosevelt*, 3rd edition. New York: New York University Press.

Cassidy, T. (2019) *Mr. President, How Long Must We Wait? Alice Paul, Woodrow Wilson and the Fight for the Right to Vote*. New York: 37 INK/Atria.

Chace, J. (2005) *1912: Wilson, Roosevelt, Taft & Debs—The Election that Changed the Country*. New York: Simon & Schuster.

Chernow, R. (1990) *The House of Morgan*. London: Simon & Schuster.

Chernow, R. (1998) *Titan: The Life of John D. Rockefeller, Sr*. New York: Random House.

Chernow, R. (2017) *Grant*. London: Head of Zeus.

Clements, K.A. (1999) *Woodrow Wilson: World Statesman*. Chicago, IL: Ivan R. Dee.

Coates, B.A. (2016) *Legalist Empire: International Law and American Foreign Relations in the Early Twentieth Century*. Oxford: Oxford University Press.

Coletta, P.E. (1973) *The Presidency of William Howard Taft*. Lawrence, KS: University Press of Kansas.

Collins, B. (2010) 'Southern Secession in 1860–1861', in S. Grant and B.H. Reid (eds), *Themes of the American Civil War: The War between the States*. New York: Routledge.

Collins, R.M. (1989) 'The Originality Trap: Richard Hofstadter on Populism', *Journal of American History*, 76, 1, pp. 150–167.

Cooper, J.M. (2001) *Breaking the Heart of the World: Woodrow Wilson and the Fight for the League of Nations*. Cambridge: Cambridge University Press.

Cooper, J.M. (2009) *Woodrow Wilson: A Biography*. New York: Vintage.

Cowdrey, A.E. (1996) *This Land, This South: An Environmental History*, Revised edition. Lexington, KY: University Press of Kentucky.

Crapol, E.P. (2000) *James G. Blaine: Architect of Empire*. Wilmington, DE: Scholarly Resources.

Crockett, D.A. (2012) 'The Historical Presidency the Perils of Restoration Politics: Nineteenth-Century Antecedents', *Presidential Studies Quarterly*, 42, 4, pp. 881–902.

Cronon, W. (1991) *Nature's Metropolis: Chicago and the Great West*. New York: W. W. Norton.

Cross, G. (2012) *The Diplomatic Education of Franklin D. Roosevelt, 1882–1933*. New York: Palgrave Macmillan.

Cullinane, M.P. (2012) *Liberty and American Anti-Imperialism: 1898–1909*. New York: Palgrave Macmillan.

Cullinane, M.P. and Goodall, A. (2017) *The Open Door Era: United States Foreign Policy in the Twentieth Century*. Edinburgh: Edinburgh University Press.

Dalton, K. (2002) *Theodore Roosevelt: A Strenuous Life*. New York: Alfred A. Knopf.

Daniels, R. (1991) *Coming to America: A History of Immigration and Ethnicity in American Life*. New York: HarperPerennial.

Davis, H.E. (1990) *Henry Grady's New South: Atlanta, A Brave and Beautiful City*. Tuscaloosa, AL: University of Alabama Press.

De León, A. (2002) *Racial Frontiers: Africans, Chinese, and Mexicans in Western American, 1848–1890*. Albuquerque, NM: University of New Mexico Press.

De Santis, V.P. (1963) 'The Republican Party Revisited, 1877–1897', in H.W. Morgan (ed.), *The Gilded Age: A Reappraisal*. Syracuse, NY: Syracuse University Press.

DiAngelo, R. (2018) *White Fragility: Why It's So Hard for White People to Talk about Racism*. Boston, MA: Beacon Press.

Doenecke, J.D. (2011) *Nothing Less than War: A New History of America's Entry into World War I*. Lexington, KY: University Press of Kentucky.

Donahue, D.L. (1999) *The Western Range Revisited: Removing Livestock from Public Lands to Conserve Native Biodiversity*. Norman, OK: University of Oklahoma Press.

Downs, G.P. (2011) *Declarations of Dependence: The Long Reconstruction of Popular Politics in the South, 1861–1908*. Chapel Hill, NC: University of North Carolina Press.

Downs, G.P. (2015) *After Appomattox: Military Occupation and the Ends of War*. Cambridge, MA: Harvard University Press.

Du Bois, W.E.B. (1935/1998) *Black Reconstruction in America*. New York: Free Press.

Dubofsky, M. (2000) *Hard Work: The Making of Labor History*. Urbana, IL: University of Illinois Press.

Durham, K.R., Jr. (1980) 'The Longview Race Riot of 1919', *East Texas Historical Journal*, 18, 2, pp. 13–24.

Dyer, T.G. (1980) *Theodore Roosevelt and the Idea of Race*. Baton Rouge, LA: Louisiana State University Press.

Elofson, W.M. (2000) *Cowboys, Gentlemen and Cattle Thieves: Ranching on the Western Frontier*. Montreal: McGill-Queen's University Press.

Etulain, R.W. (2004) 'Meeting Places, Intersections, Crossroads, and Borders: Toward a Complex Western Cultural History', *Historian*, 66, 3, pp. 509–517.

Feldman, G. (2013) *The Irony of the Solid South: Democrats, Republicans, and Race, 1865–1944*. Tuscaloosa, AL: University of Alabama Press.

Fink, L. (1985) *Workingmen's Democracy: The Knights of Labor and American Politics*. Urbana, IL: University of Illinois Press.

Fink, L. (2015) *The Long Gilded Age: American Capitalism and the Lessons of a New World Order*. Philadelphia, PA: University of Pennsylvania Press.

Flanagan, M.A. (2007) *America Reformed: Progressives and Progressivisms, 1890s–1920s*. New York: Oxford University Press.

Flores, D. (1991) 'Bison Ecology and Bison Diplomacy: The Southern Plains from 1800 to 1850', *Journal of American History*, 78, 2, pp. 465–485.

Floyd, M.R. (2013) *Abandoning American Neutrality: Woodrow Wilson and the Beginning of the Great War, August 1914–December 1915*. New York: Springer.

Foner, E. (1988/2002) *Reconstruction: America's Unfinished Revolution, 1863–1877*. New York: Perennial Classics.

Foner, E. (2019) *The Second Founding: How the Civil War and Reconstruction Remade the Constitution*. New York: W. W. Norton.

Foster, G.M. (1987) *Ghosts of the Confederacy: Defeat, the Lost Cause, and the Emergence of the New South, 1865 to 1913*. New York: Oxford University Press.

Franklin, J.H. (1961) *Reconstruction: After the Civil War*. Chicago, IL: University of Chicago Press.

Freeberg, E. (2014) *The Age of Edison: Electric Light and the Invention of Modern America*. New York: Penguin.

Freehling, W.W. (2001) *The South v. The South: How Anti-Confederate Southerners Shaped the Course of the Civil War*. Oxford: Oxford University Press.

Friedheim, R.L. (2018) *The Seattle General Strike: Centennial Edition*. Seattle, WA: University of Washington Press.

Friedlander, R.A. (1961) 'A Reassessment of Roosevelt's Role in the Panamanian Revolution of 1903', *Western Political Quarterly*, 14, 2, pp. 535–543.

Frymer, P. (2017) *Building an American Empire: The Era of Territorial and Political Expansion*. Princeton, NJ: Princeton University Press.

Gates, H.L., Jr. (2019) *Stony the Road: Reconstruction, White Supremacy, and the Rise of Jim Crow*. New York: Penguin.

George, P. (1982) *The Emergence of Industrial America: Strategic Factors in American Economic Growth since 1870*. Albany, NY: State University of New York Press.

Goldfrank, D.M. (2013) *The Origins of the Crimean War*. Abingdon: Routledge.

Goodwin, D.K. (2005) *Team of Rivals: The Political Genius of Abraham Lincoln*. New York: Simon & Schuster.

Goodwin, D.K. (2013) *The Bully Pulpit: Theodore Roosevelt, William Howard Taft, and the Golden Age of Journalism*. New York: Simon & Schuster.

Gordon, R.J. (2017) *The Rise and Fall of American Growth: The U.S. Standard of Living since the Civil War*. Princeton, NJ: Princeton University Press.

Gould, L. (2001/2013) *America in the Progressive Era, 1890–1914*. New York: Routledge.

Gould, L. (2014) *The Republicans: A History of the Grand Old Party*. Oxford: Oxford University Press.

Gram, J.R. (2016) 'Acting Out Assimilation: Playing Indian and Becoming American in the Federal Indian Boarding Schools', *American Indian Quarterly*, 40, 3, pp. 251–273.

Grant, S. and Reid, B.H. (eds) (2010) *Themes of the American Civil War: The War between the States*. New York: Routledge.

Green, E.C. (1997) *Southern Strategies: Southern Women and the Woman Suffrage Question*. Chapel Hill, NC: University of North Carolina Press.

Green, J. (2006) *Death in the Haymarket: A Story of Chicago, the First Labor Movement and the Bombing that Divided Gilded Age America*. New York: Anchor Books.

Greenberger, S.S. (2017) *The Unexpected President: The Life and Times of Chester A. Arthur*. Boston, MA: De Capo Press.

Greene, J. (2004) *Pure and Simple Politics: The American Federation of Labor and Political Activism, 1881–1917*. Cambridge: Cambridge University Press.

Guglielmo, J. (2003) 'Introduction: White Lies, Dark Truths', in J. Guglielmo and S. Salerno (eds), *Are Italians White?: How Race is Made in America*. New York: Routledge.

Hajimu, M. (2009) 'Rumors of War: Immigration Disputes and the Social Construction of American-Japanese Relations, 1905–1913', *Diplomatic History*, 33, 1, pp. 1–37.

Harpine, W.D. (2006) *From the Front Porch to the Front Page: McKinley and Bryan in the 1896 Presidential Campaign*. College Station, TX: Texas A&M University Press.

Harris, W.C. (1997) *With Charity for All: Lincoln and the Restoration of the Union*. Lexington, KY: University Press of Kentucky.

Henretta, J.A. (2006) 'Charles Evans Hughes and the Strange Death of Liberal America', *Law and History Review*, 24, 1, pp. 115–171.

Higham, J. (1955/2002) *Strangers in the Land: Patterns of American Nativism, 1860–1925*. New Brunswick, NJ: Rutgers University Press.

Hinckley, T.C. (1973) 'Alaska as an American Botany Bay', *Pacific Historical Review*, 42, 1, pp. 1–19.

Hoganson, K. (1998) *Fighting for American Manhood: How Gender Politics Provoked the Spanish-American and Philippine-American Wars*. New Haven, CT: Yale University Press.

Holmes, J.R. (2006) *Theodore Roosevelt and World Order: Police Power in International Relations*. Washington, DC: Potomac Books.

Hoogenboom, A. (2003) 'Rutherford B. Hayes', in P. Weeks (ed.), *Buckeye Presidents: Ohioans in the White House*. Kent, OH: Kent State University Press.

Hopkins, A.G. (2018) *American Empire: A Global History*. Princeton, NJ: Princeton University Press.

Hunt, M.H. (1987) *Ideology and U.S. Foreign Policy*. New Haven, CT: Yale University Press.

Jackson, B. (1991) 'Introduction: A Street of Dreams', in A. Harrison (ed.), *Black Exodus: The Great Migration from the American South*. Jackson, MS: University Press of Mississippi.

Jensen, J.M. and Miller, D.A. (2004) 'The Gentle Tamers Revisited: New Approaches to the History of Women in the American West', in M.A. Irwin and J.F. Brooks (eds), *Women and Gender in the American West*. Albuquerque, NM: University of New Mexico Press.

Karabell, Z. (2004) *Chester Alan Arthur*. New York: Times Books.

Kato, D. (2016) *Liberalizing Lynching: Building a New Racialized State*. New York: Oxford University Press.

Kazin, M. (2007) *A Godly Hero: The Life of William Jennings Bryan*. New York: Anchor Books.

Kazin, M. (2017) *War against War: The American Fight for Peace, 1914–1918*. New York: Simon & Schuster.

Keith, J. (2004) *Rich Man's War, Poor Man's Fight: Race, Class, and Power in the Rural South during the First World War*. Chapel Hill, NC: University of North Carolina Press.

Keith, L. (2008) *The Colfax Massacre: The Untold Story of Black Power, White Terror and the Death of Reconstruction*. Oxford: Oxford University Press.

Kennedy, D. (1980/2004) *Over Here: The First World War and American Society*. New York: Oxford University Press.

Kenny, K. (1998) *Making Sense of the Molly Maguires*. New York: Oxford University Press.

Kenny, K. (2000) *The American Irish: A History*. New York: Routledge.

Keohane, R.O. (2002) 'International Commitments and American Political Institutions in the Nineteenth Century', in I. Katznelson and M. Shefter (eds), *Shaped by War and Trade: International Influence on American Political Development*. Princeton, NJ: Princeton University Press.

Knight, L.W. (2005) *Citizen: Jane Addams and the Struggle for Democracy*. Chicago, IL: University of Chicago Press.

Knowlton, C. (2017) *Cattle Kingdom: The Hidden History of the Cowboy West*. New York: Houghton Mifflin Harcourt.

Kramer, P.A. (2006) *The Blood of Government: Race, Empire, the United States, and the Philippines*. Chapel Hill, NC: University of North Carolina Press.

Krause, P. (1992) *The Battle for Homestead, 1880–1892: Politics, Culture, and Steel*. Pittsburgh, PA: University of Pittsburgh Press.

Krenn, M.L. (2006) *The Color of Empire: Race and American Foreign Relations*. Dulles, VA: Potomac Books.

LaFeber, W. (1989) *The American Age: United States Foreign Policy at Home and Abroad since 1750*. New York: W. W. Norton.

Lambert, V. (2016) 'The Big Black Box of Indian Country: The Bureau of Indian Affairs and the Federal-Indian Relationship', *American Indian Quarterly*, 40, 4, pp. 333–363.

Lears, J. (2010) *Rebirth of a Nation: The Making of Modern America, 1877–1920*. New York: Harper Perennial.

Lee, E. and Yung, J. (2010) *Angel Island: Immigrant Gateway to America*. Oxford: Oxford University Press.

Lewis, D.L. (1993) *W. E. B. Du Bois: Biography of a Race, 1868–1919*. New York: Henry Holt.

Link, W.A. and Link, S.J. (eds) (2012) *The Gilded Age and Progressive Era: A Documentary Reader*. West Sussex: Wiley Blackwell.

Linn, B.M. (2000) *The Philippine War 1899–1902*. Lawrence, KS: University Press of Kansas.

Ljungmark, L. (2008) *Swedish Exodus*. Trans. by Kermit B. Westerberg. Carbondale, IL: Southern Illinois University Press.
Luebke, F.C. (ed.) (1998) *European Immigrants in the American West: Community Histories*. Albuquerque, NM: University of New Mexico Press.
Lurie, J. (2012) *William Howard Taft: The Travails of a Progressive Conservative*. New York: Cambridge University Press.
Maass, M. (2009) 'Catalyst for the Roosevelt Corollary: Arbitrating the 1902–1903 Venezuela Crisis and Its Impact on the Development of the Roosevelt Corollary to the Monroe Doctrine', *Diplomacy & Statecraft*, 20, 3, pp. 383–402.
Macmillan, M. (2002) *Peacemakers: The Paris Conference of 1919 and Its Attempt to End War*. London: John Murray.
Manela, E. (2009) *The Wilsonian Moment: Self-Determination and the International Origins of Anticolonial Nationalism*. Oxford: Oxford University Press.
Marinbach, B. (1983) *Galveston: Ellis Island of the West*. Albany, NY: State University of New York Press.
Marks, P.M. (1998) *In a Barren Land: The American Indian Quest for Cultural Survival, 1607 to the Present*. New York: Perennial.
Martin, A. (1992) *Railroads Triumphant: The Growth, Rejection, and Rebirth of a Vital American Force*. New York: Oxford University Press.
McConnaughty, C. (2015) *The Woman Suffrage Movement in America: A Reassessment*. New York: Cambridge University Press.
McCulley, R.T. (2012) *Banks and Politics during the Progressive Era: The Origins of the Federal Reserve System, 1897–1913*. New York: Routledge.
McFarland, G.W. (1975) *Mugwumps, Morals, and Politics, 1884–1920*. Amherst, MA: University of Massachusetts Press.
McGerr, M. (2003) *A Fierce Discontent: The Rise and Fall of the Progressive Movement in America, 1870–1920*. New York: Simon & Schuster.
McGrath, R.D. (1984) *Gunfighters, Highwaymen, and Vigilantes: Violence on the Frontier*. Berkeley, CA: University of California Press.
McKitrick, E.L. (1960/1988) *Andrew Johnson and Reconstruction*. New York: Oxford University Press.
McLaird, J.D. (2005) *Calamity Jane: The Woman and the Legend*. Norman, OK: University of Oklahoma Press.
McPherson, J.M. (1975) *The Abolitionist Legacy: From Reconstruction to the NAACP*. Princeton, NJ: Princeton University Press.
McPherson, J.M. (1988) *Battle Cry of Freedom: The Civil War Era*. New York: Oxford University Press.
Meier, A. and Bracey, J.H., Jr. (1993) 'The NAACP as a Reform Movement, 1909–1965: "To Reach the Conscience of America"', *Journal of Southern History*, 59, 1, pp. 3–30.
Meiser, J.W. (2015) *Power and Restraint: The Rise of the United States, 1898–1941*. Washington, DC: Georgetown University Press.
Merchant, C. (2007) *American Environmental History: An Introduction*. New York: Columbia University Press.
Merry, R.W. (2017) *President McKinley: Architect of the American Century*. New York: Simon & Schuster.
Mitchell, R. (2001/2013) *The American Civil War*. New York: Routledge.
Montgomery, D. (1987) 'William H. Sylvis and the Search for Working-Class Citizenship', in M. Dubofsky and W. Van Tine (eds), *Labor Leaders in America*. Urbana, IL: University of Illinois Press.

Morris, C.R. (2005) *The Tycoons: How Andrew Carnegie, John D. Rockefeller, Jay Gould, and J. P. Morgan Invented the American Supereconomy*. New York: Owl Books.

Morris, E. (1979) *The Rise of Theodore Roosevelt*. New York: Coward, McCann & Geoghegan.

Morris, E. (2001) *Theodore Rex*. New York: Random House.

Morris, E. (2010) *Colonel Roosevelt*. New York: Random House.

Munene, G.M. (1990) 'The United States and the Berlin Conference on the Partition of Africa, 1884–1885', *Transafrican Journal of History*, 19, pp. 73–79.

Nasaw, D. (2007) *Andrew Carnegie*. New York: Penguin.

Nester, W. (2013) *The Age of Lincoln and the Art of American Power, 1848–1876*. Lincoln, NE: University of Nebraska Press.

Norrell, R.J. (2009) *Up from History: The Life of Booker T. Washington*. Cambridge, MA: Harvard University Press.

O'Toole, P. (2018) *The Moralist: Woodrow Wilson and the World He Made*. New York: Simon & Schuster.

Osborne, T.J. (1981) 'Trade or War? America's Annexation of Hawaii Reconsidered', *Pacific Historical Review*, 50, 3, pp. 285–307.

Pafford, J.M. (2013) *The Forgotten Conservative: Rediscovering Grover Cleveland*. Washington, DC: Regnery History.

Pak, S.J. (2013) *Gentlemen Bankers: The World of J. P. Morgan*. Cambridge, MA: Harvard University Press.

Pascal, J.B. (2005) *Jacob Riis: Reporter and Reformer*. Oxford: Oxford University Press.

Pérez, L. (1998) *The War of 1898: The United States and Cuba in History and Historiography*. Chapel Hill, NC: University of North Carolina Press.

Perman, M. (1973) *Reunion without Compromise: The South and Reconstruction, 1865–1868*. London: Cambridge University Press.

Perman, M. (1984) *The Road to Redemption: Southern Politics, 1869–1879*. Chapel Hill, NC: University of North Carolina Press.

Perman, M. (2001) *Struggle for Mastery: Disenfranchisement in the South, 1888–1908*. Chapel Hill, NC: University of North Carolina Press.

Phelan, C. (2000) *Grand Master Workman: Terence Powderly and the Knights of Labor*. Westport, CT: Greenwood Press.

Pierce, M. (2012) 'Agrarian Rebel, Industrial Workers: Tom Watson and the Prospects of a Farmer-Labor Alliance', in J.M. Beeby (ed.), *Populism in the South Revisited: New Interpretations and New Departures*. Jackson, MS: University Press of Mississippi.

Plummer, B.G. (1992) *Haiti and the United States: The Psychological Moment*. Athens, GA: University of Georgia Press.

Poole, K.T. and Rosenthal, H. (1997) *Congress: A Political-Economic History of Roll Call Voting*. New York: Oxford University Press.

Postel, C. (2007) *The Populist Vision*. Oxford: Oxford University Press.

Prucha, F.P. (1994) *American Indian Treaties: The History of a Political Anomaly*. Berkeley, CA: University of California Press.

Rable, G.C. (1984/2017) *But There Was No Peace: The Role of Violence in the Politics of Reconstruction*. Athens, GA: University of Georgia Press.

Rauchway, E. (2003) *Murdering McKinley: The Making of Theodore Roosevelt's America*. New York: Hill and Wang.

Reitano, J. (1994) *The Tariff Question in the Gilded Age: The Great Debate of 1888*. University Park, PA: Pennsylvania State University Press.

Reyhner, J. and Eder, J. (2004) *American Indian Education: A History*. Norman, OK: University of Oklahoma Press.

Richardson, H.C. (2004) *The Death of Reconstruction: Race, Labor, and Politics in the Post-Civil War North, 1865–1901*. Cambridge, MA: Harvard University Press.

Risjord, N.K. (2005) *Representative Americans: Populists and Progressives*. Lanham, MD: Rowman & Littlefield.

Ritter, G. (1999) *Goldbugs and Greenbacks: The Antimonopoly Tradition and the Politics of Finance in America*. Cambridge: Cambridge University Press.

Rockoff, H. (2005) 'Until It's Over, Over There: The US Economy in World War I', in S. Broadberry and M. Harrison (eds), *The Economics of World War I*. Cambridge: Cambridge University Press.

Rohrbough, M.J. (2004) 'Mining and the Nineteenth-Century American West', in W. Deverell (ed.), *A Companion to the American West*. Malden, MA: Blackwell.

Rosen, J. (2016) *Louis D. Brandeis: American Prophet*. New Haven, CT: Yale University Press.

Rosenburg, C.E. (1968) *The Trial of the Assassin Guiteau: Psychiatry and the Law in the Gilded Age*. Chicago, IL: University of Chicago Press.

Rubin, A.S. (2014) *Through the Heart of Dixie: Sherman's March and American Memory*. Chapel Hill, NC: University of North Carolina Press.

Rudwick, E. (1957) 'The Niagara Movement', *Journal of Negro History*, 42, 3, pp. 177–200.

Sater, W.F. (1990) *Chile and the United States: Empires in Conflict*. Athens, GA: University of Georgia Press.

Schneirov, R., Stromquist, S. and Salvatore, N. (1999) 'Introduction', in R. Schneirov, S. Stromquist and N. Salvatore (eds), *The Pullman Strike and the Crisis of the 1890s: Essays on Labor and Politics*. Urbana, IL: University of Illinois Press.

Schrag, P. (2010) *Not Fit for our Society: Nativism and Immigration*. Berkeley, CA: University of California Press.

Shaw, J.B. (2003) 'James A. Garfield', in P. Weeks (ed.), *Buckeye Presidents: Ohioans in the White House*. Kent, OH: Kent State University Press.

Sheffield, G.D. (2002) *Forgotten Victory: The First World War: Myths and Realities*. London: Review.

Silkenat, D. (2016) *Driven from Home: North Carolina's Civil War Refugee Crisis*. Athens, GA: University of Georgia Press.

Sim, D. (2011) 'Filibusters, Fenians, and a Contested Neutrality: The Irish Question and US Diplomacy, 1848–1871', *American Nineteenth Century History*, 12, 3, pp. 265–287.

Simpson, B.D. (1991) *Let Us Have Peace: Ulysses S. Grant and the Politics of War & Reconstruction*. Chapel Hill, NC: University of North Carolina Press.

Smith, J. (1994) *The Spanish-American War, 1895–1902: Conflict in the Caribbean and the Pacific*. New York: Routledge.

Smith, J.E. (2001) *Grant*. New York: Simon & Schuster.

Smith, P. (1984) *The Rise of Industrial America: A People's History of the Post-Reconstruction Era*. New York: McGraw-Hill.

Stevenson, D. (2017) *1917: War, Peace and Revolution*. Oxford: Oxford University Press.

Stewart, D.O. (2010) *Impeached: The Trial of President Andrew Johnson and the Fight for Lincoln's Legacy*. New York: Simon & Schuster.

Stowell, D.O. (2008) 'Introduction', in D.O. Stowell (ed.), *The Great Strikes of 1877*. Urbana, IL: University of Illinois Press.

Sussman, R.W. (2014) *The Myth of Race: The Troubling Persistence of an Unscientific Idea*. Cambridge, MA: Harvard University Press.

Trachtenberg, A. (1982) *The Incorporation of America: Culture and Society in the Gilded Age*. New York: Hill and Wang.

Traxel, D. (2006) *Crusader Nation: The United States in Peace and the Great War, 1898–1920*. New York: Alfred A. Knopf.

Tyrrell, I. (2015) *Crisis of the Wasteful Nation: Empire and Conservation in Theodore Roosevelt's America*. Chicago, IL: University of Chicago Press.

Tyson, T.B. and Cecelski, D.S. (1998) 'Introduction', in D.S. Cecelski and T.B. Tyson (eds), *Democracy Betrayed: The Wilmington Race Riot of 1898 and Its Legacy*. Chapel Hill, NC: University of North Carolina Press.

Unger, N.C. (2000) *Fighting Bob La Follette: The Righteous Reformer*. Chapel Hill, NC: University of North Carolina Press.

Urban, A. (2009) 'Irish Domestic Servants, "Biddy" and Rebellion in the American Home, 1850–1900', *Gender & History*, 21, 2, pp. 263–286.

Utley, R.M. and Washburn, W.E. (1977/1987) *Indian Wars*. Boston, MA: Houghton Mifflin.

Van Atta, J.R. (2018) *Charging up San Juan Hill: Theodore Roosevelt and the Making of Imperial America*. Baltimore, MY: Johns Hopkins University Press.

Van Vugt, W.E. (1999) *Britain to America: Mid-Nineteenth-Century Immigrants to the United States*. Urbana, IL: University of Illinois Press.

Vaughn, W.P. (1974) *Schools for All: The Blacks & Public Education in the South, 1865–1877*. Lexington, KY: University Press of Kentucky.

Vazzano, F.P. (2006) 'Rutherford B. Hayes and the Politics of Discord', *Historian*, 68, 3, pp. 519–540.

Waldrep, C. (2009) *African Americans Confront Lynching: Strategies of Resistance from the Civil War to the Civil Rights Era*. Lanham, MD: Rowman & Littlefield.

Weinberg, S. (2008) *Taking on the Trust: How Ida Tarbell Brought down John D. Rockefeller and Standard Oil*. New York: W. W. Norton.

Weir, R.E. (1996) *Beyond Labor's Veil: The Culture of the Knights of Labor*. University Park, PA: Pennsylvania State University Press.

Welch, R.E. (1988) *The Presidencies of Grover Cleveland*. Lawrence, KS: University Press of Kansas.

White, R. (1991) *It's Your Misfortune and None of My Own: A New History of the American West*. Norman, OK: University of Oklahoma Press.

White, R. (2011) *Railroaded: The Transcontinentals and the Making of Modern America*. New York: W. W. Norton.

White, R. (2017) *The Republic for Which it Stands: The United States during Reconstruction and the Gilded Age, 1865–1896*. Oxford: Oxford University Press.

Williams, P.G. (2007) *Beyond Redemption: Texas Democrats after Reconstruction*. College Station, TX: Texas A&M University Press.

Wilson, K.M. (2014) *The International Impact of the Boer War*. New York: Routledge.

Woodward, C.V. (1971) *Origins of the New South, 1877–1913*. Baton Rouge, LA: Louisiana State University Press.

Woodward, C.V. (1951/1991) *Reunion and Reaction: The Compromise of 1877 and the End of Reconstruction*. Oxford: Oxford University Press.

Woodward, C.V. (1955/2002) *The Strange Career of Jim Crow*. Oxford: Oxford University Press.
Woodward, D.R. (1993) *Trial by Friendship: Anglo-American Relations, 1917–1918*. Lexington, KY: University Press of Kentucky.
Zieger, R. (2001) *America's Great War: World War I and the American Experience*. Lanham, MD: Rowman & Littlefield.

Index

Page numbers in **bold** refer to content in maps and figures.